D0882512

WITHDRAWN

Natural Resources, Uncertainty, and General Equilibrium Systems

Essays in Memory of Rafael Lusky

ECONOMIC THEORY AND MATHEMATICAL ECONOMICS

Consulting Editor: Karl Shell

UNIVERSITY OF PENNSYLVANIA
PHILADELPHIA, PENNSYLVANIA

Franklin M. Fisher and Karl Shell. The Economic Theory of Price Indices: *Two Essays on the Effects of Taste, Quality, and Technological Change*

Luis Eugenio Di Marco (Ed.). International Economics and Development: *Essays in Honor of Raúl Presbisch*

Erwin Klein. Mathematical Methods in Theoretical Economics: *Topological and Vector Space Foundations of Equilibrium Analysis*

Paul Zarembka (Ed.). Frontiers in Econometrics

George Horwich and Paul A. Samuelson (Eds.). Trade, Stability, and Macroeconomics: *Essays in Honor of Lloyd A. Metzler*

W. T. Ziemba and R. G. Vickson (Eds.). Stochastic Optimization Models in Finance

Steven A. Y. Lin (Ed.). Theory and Measurement of Economic Externalities

David Cass and Karl Shell (Eds.). The Hamiltonian Approach to Dynamic Economics

R. Shone. Microeconomics: *A Modern Treatment*

C. W. J. Granger and Paul Newbold. Forecasting Economic Time Series

Michael Szenberg, John W. Lombardi, and Eric Y. Lee. Welfare Effects of Trade Restrictions: *A Case Study of the U.S. Footwear Industry*

Haim Levy and Marshall Sarnat (Eds.). Financial Decision Making under Uncertainty

Yasuo Murata. Mathematics for Stability and Optimization of Economic Systems

Alan S. Blinder and Philip Friedman (Eds.). Natural Resources, Uncertainty, and General Equilibrium Systems: *Essays in Memory of Rafael Lusky*

In preparation

Jerry S. Kelly. Arrow Impossibility Theorems

Natural Resources, Uncertainty, and General Equilibrium Systems

Essays in Memory of Rafael Lusky

Edited by ALAN S. BLINDER

DEPARTMENT OF ECONOMICS
PRINCETON UNIVERSITY
PRINCETON, NEW JERSEY

PHILIP FRIEDMAN

DEPARTMENT OF ECONOMICS AND FINANCE
SCHOOL OF MANAGEMENT
BOSTON UNIVERSITY
BOSTON, MASSACHUSETTS

ACADEMIC PRESS   New York   San Francisco   London   1977
A Subsidiary of Harcourt Brace Jovanovich, Publishers

HB
171
N33

COPYRIGHT © 1977, BY ACADEMIC PRESS, INC.
ALL RIGHTS RESERVED.
NO PART OF THIS PUBLICATION MAY BE REPRODUCED OR
TRANSMITTED IN ANY FORM OR BY ANY MEANS, ELECTRONIC
OR MECHANICAL, INCLUDING PHOTOCOPY, RECORDING, OR ANY
INFORMATION STORAGE AND RETRIEVAL SYSTEM, WITHOUT
PERMISSION IN WRITING FROM THE PUBLISHER.

ACADEMIC PRESS, INC.
111 Fifth Avenue, New York, New York 10003

United Kingdom Edition published by
ACADEMIC PRESS, INC. (LONDON) LTD.
24/28 Oval Road, London NW1

Library of Congress Cataloging in Publication Data

Main entry under title:

Natural resources, uncertainty, and general equilibrium
    systems.

    1.   Economics—Addresses, essays, lectures.   2.   Un-
certainty—Addresses, essays, lectures.   3.   Insurance—
Addresses, essays, lectures.   4.   Equilibrium (Econom-
ics)—Addresses, essays, lectures.   5.   Lusky, Rafael.
I.   Lusky, Rafael.   II.   Blinder, Alan S.   III.   Friedman,
Philip,   Date
HB171.N33   330   77-6587
ISBN 0−12−106150−7

PRINTED IN THE UNITED STATES OF AMERICA

RAFAEL LUSKY (1939–1976)

Rafael Lusky was born on June 11, 1939 in Tel Aviv, Israel. He studied statistics and economics at the Hebrew University of Jerusalem, and was married to Ayala in January 1968. A few months later Rafy, as everyone called him, came to America to continue his graduate studies at MIT, bringing with him a dry wit, a zest for life, and an ability to laugh at the kinds of troubles that every graduate student faces. It is said that "Sabras" are tough on the outside, but sweet on the inside. Rafy Lusky belied that: He was not tough on the outside.

His specialty was economic theory from the start; and his dissertation, "Conservation of Natural Resources and the Theory of Recycling," was finished in the Summer of 1972. It led to several published papers, and an abiding interest in problems connected with resource economics.

With their daughter Ronit, Rafy and Ayala came to the University of Florida in August, 1972. There he taught mathematical economics, price theory, and econometrics, all with great success—no small achievement for a foreign teacher. His rare combination of humor, rigor, and concern for the education of his students made him an exceptional teacher.

After some initial difficulties (writing English was always hard for Rafy), his research on resource economics as well as in other areas began to progress rapidly. His work included four major contributions to theoretical resource economics, three of which appeared in 1975: "Consumers' Preferences and Ecological Consciousness," *International Economic Review*, February 1975; "A Model of Recycling and Pollution Control," *The Canadian Journal of Economics*, November 1975, and "Optimal Taxation Policies for Conservation and Recycling," *Journal of Economic Theory*, December 1975. "On the Choice of Recycling Destinations" is forthcoming in *Journal of Economic Theory*, posthumously. Two other papers, "On

Forests and Paper Recycling," and "Conservation of Natural Resources and the Theory of Recycling" are forthcoming in a collected volume. His future seemed bright.

Rafy was himself a natural resource to those who knew him. He worked on joint projects effectively with his colleagues Roger Blair ("The Influence of Uncertainty on Estimation of Production Function Models," *Journal of Econometrics*, **3**, No. 4 1975 and "A Note on Random Demand and Duality under Competition," *International Economic Review*, October 1976), Israel Luski ("On External Diseconomies in Consumption and Monopoly Pricing," *Econometrica*, March 1975), Michael Connolly ("Optimum Foreign Borrowing"), and Philip Friedman ("The Level of International Trade"). (The latter two will appear in a collected volume.) His easy wit, keen intelligence, and deep concern for others made him a rare colleague and friend. It is not possible to list those works and efforts to which he contributed time, intellect, and energy. Those of us who borrowed from his talents remain in his debt.

Rafy was a resource to many others as well: to the small Israeli community in Gainesville, to his students, and above all to his family, which by then included a second daughter, Sharon, and now includes his third daughter, Ravit.

In November 1975, Rafy and Ayala arrived late to a party for Phillip Musgrove, who was visiting the Florida campus. Rafy, who was always so lively and gregarious, sat in a corner, pale and withdrawn. Later it was learned that a large tumor had been discovered in his leg; it was probably malignant. There was some optimism after an apparently successful operation to remove the tumor in December. However, more tumors appeared and Rafy began to fail. On Sunday, May 9, 1976, he died in Gainesville, about a month before his 37th birthday.

This volume was conceived as a memorial to a friend whose promising career was cut short. The authors—Rafy's former teachers, fellow graduate students at MIT, and colleagues at the University of Florida—hope it will serve as a lasting tribute to him, for he is deeply missed.

CONTENTS

List of Contributors   xiii
Preface   xv

NATURAL RESOURCES

Resource depletion with technological uncertainty and the Rawlsian Fairness Principle

JOHN G. RILEY

1. Introduction   3
2. The Structure of the Model and Other Preliminaries   7
3. The Just Rate of Resource Depletion   10
4. Concluding Remark   15
   References   16

Monopoly, uncertainty, and exploration

ROBERT M. SOLOW

1. Introduction   17
2. Social Optimality in a Two-Period Model   18
3. Social Optimality: An Alternative Formulation   20
4. Monopoly   21
5. The Case of Certainty   23
6. The Case of Certainty (Alternative Formulation)   26

7. The Impact of Uncertainty   28
8. Uncertainty Continued   30
9. General Remarks   31

UNCERTAINTY

Leverage, bankruptcy, and the cost of capital

FRED D. ARDITTI AND YORAM C. PELES

1. Introduction   35
2. Stochastic Dominance Analysis   36
3. Analysis with a Linear Utility Function   43
4. Concluding Remarks   50
    References   51

Price discrimination under uncertainty

ROGER D. BLAIR AND ARNOLD A. HEGGESTAD

1. Introduction   53
2. The Nonstochastic Case   54
3. The Objective of the Firm under Uncertainty   55
4. First-Order Conditions   57
5. Some Results for an Exponential Utility Function   61
6. Implications for Legal Analysis   63
7. Conclusion   64
    References   64

Insurance theoretic aspects of workers' compensation

PETER DIAMOND

1. Introduction   67
2. Accidents and Full Efficiency   68
3. Ideal Insurance   70
4. Less-than-Ideal Insurance   72
5. The Present Workers' Compensation Program   74
6. Voluntary Insurance   75
7. Wage Bargains and Worker Misperceptions   77
8. Choice of Technology   80
9. Variation among Workers   81
10. On-the-Job Safety   83
11. Concluding Remarks   88
    References   89

Multiperiod stochastic dominance with one-period parameters, liquidity preference, and equilibrium in the log-normal case

HAIM LEVY

1. Introduction   91
2. Assumptions and Notations   92
3. Comparison of the Normal and the Log-Normal Efficiency Frontiers   97
4. Equilibrium and Log-Normal Efficiency Analysis with One-Period Parameters   101
5. Concluding Remarks   109
   References   110

Adverse selection and optimum insurance policies

EYTAN SHESHINSKI

1. Introduction   113
2. The General Problem   114
3. The Optimum Linear Policy with a Ceiling   116
4. Comparison with the Socially Optimal Policy   118
5. A Nonlinear Example   120
   References   122

GENERAL EQUILIBRIUM SYSTEMS: STABILITY, OPTIMALITY, AND DISTRIBUTION

A difficulty with Keynesian models of aggregate demand

ALAN S. BLINDER

1. Statement of the Problem   125
2. The Conventional Keynesian Model   126
3. An Alternative Model of Output Adjustment Decisions   128
4. A Model of Output Level Decisions   129
5. Dynamic Properties of the Preferred Model   131
6. Recapitulation   134
   References   135

Continuously dated commodities and nontâtonnement with production and consumption

FRANKLIN M. FISHER

1. Introduction: The Problem of Dated Commodities   137
2. The Hahn Process and Money   139
3. Topological Issues   140

4.	Behavior of Households	143
5.	Behavior of Firms	148
6.	Closure Equations and Walras' Law	151
7.	The Present Action Postulate	151
8.	The Hahn Process and Trading Rules	153
9.	Price Adjustment	154
10.	Decline of Target Profits	155
11.	Decline of Target Utilities	157
12.	Properties of Equilibrium	158
13.	Boundedness	160
14.	Compactness and Quasi-Stability	161
15.	Global Stability	163
	References	166

An exchange model of bilateral trade

PHILIP FRIEDMAN

1.	Introduction	169
2.	A General Model of Bilateralism	170
3.	Conclusion	173
	References	173

When it is ethically optimal to allocate money income in stipulated fractional shares

PAUL A. SAMUELSON

1.	Introduction and Summary	175
2.	Social Welfare Functions	176
3.	Constancy of Relative Risk Aversion	179
4.	Optimality Conditions	183
5.	Symmetry Situations and Generalizations	189
6.	Qualifications	193
	References	193

POLICY AND APPLICATIONS

Optimal taxes on foreign lending

MICHAEL CONNOLLY

1.	Introduction	199
2.	The Optimum Tax: Simple Case	200
3.	The Many-Good, Many-Period Case	202

4. Optimum Taxes on Exchange: General Case   204
5. Related Approaches   205
6. Summary   207
   References   207

Monopoly, regulation, waiting lines, and investment in service capacity

ISRAEL LUSKI AND DAVID LEVHARI

1. Introduction   209
2. The Model   210
3. Comparison between Monopoly and the Social Optimal Case   213
4. Regulation of Monopoly   216
   Reference   218

Identification and estimation problems in limited dependent variable models

G. S. MADDALA

1. Introduction   219
2. The Simple Probit Model   219
3. The Tobit Model   221
4. Simple Extensions of the Tobit Model   223
5. Stochastic Threshold Models   225
6. Simultaneous Equations Models   231
7. Conclusions   237
   References   238

An extended linear permanent expenditure system (ELPES)

PHILIP MUSGROVE

1. Introduction   241
2. Permanent-Income Approaches   244
3. Formulation of the ELPES   246
4. Estimation of Parameters   249
5. Standard Errors   251
6. Concluding Remarks   253
   References   254

LIST OF CONTRIBUTORS

Numbers in parentheses indicate the pages on which the authors' contributions begin.

FRED D. ARDITTI (35), University of Florida, College of Business Administration, Gainesville, Florida

ROGER D. BLAIR (53), Department of Economics, University of Florida, Gainesville, Florida

ALAN S. BLINDER (125), Department of Economics, Princeton University, Princeton, New Jersey

MICHAEL CONNOLLY (199), Department of Economics, University of Florida, Gainesville, Florida

PETER DIAMOND (67), Department of Economics, Massachusetts Institute of Technology, Cambridge, Massachusetts

FRANKLIN M. FISHER (137), Department of Economics, Massachusetts Institute of Technology, Cambridge, Massachusetts

PHILIP FRIEDMAN (169), Department of Economics and Finance, School of Management, Boston University, Boston, Massachusetts

ARNOLD A. HEGGESTAD (53), Department of Economics, University of Florida, Gainesville, Florida

DAVID LEVHARI (209), Department of Economics, The Hebrew University, Jerusalem, Israel

HAIM LEVY (91), College of Business Administration, University of Florida, Gainesville, Florida and School of Business Administration, The Hebrew University, Jerusalem, Israel

ISRAEL LUSKI (209), Department of Economics, Ben Gurion University, Beer Sheba, Israel

G. S. MADDALA (219), Department of Economics, University of Florida, Gainesville, Florida

PHILIP MUSGROVE (241), The Brookings Institution, Washington, D. C.

YORAM C. PELES (35), School of Business Administration, The Hebrew University, Jerusalem, Israel

JOHN G. RILEY (3), Department of Economics, University of California, Los Angeles, Los Angeles, California

PAUL A. SAMUELSON (175), Department of Economics, Massachusetts Institute of Technology, Cambridge, Massachusetts

EYTAN SHESHINSKI (113), Department of Economics, The Hebrew University, Jerusalem, Israel

ROBERT M. SOLOW (17), Department of Economics, Massachusetts Institute of Technology, Cambridge, Massachusetts

PREFACE

This volume owes its existence to the cooperation and contributions of its contributors. Our choice of prospective contributors was extremely difficult. A collection of works by all those economists who had been friends and colleagues of Rafy would have been of unmanageable proportions. We chose to seek papers of a theoretical nature spanning the areas in which Rafy had taught and done research.

The collection is divided into four sections: natural resources, uncertainty, the dynamics and optimality of general equilibrium systems, and policy and applications. Even these divisions are arbitrary; several of the articles could be classified in several sections.

The works in this volume represent more than a tribute to Rafael Lusky. They are an indication of the direction of his life's work, and of the kinds of research which he might have done himself, had he been given more time.

Jerusalem, Israel
Gainesville, Florida

ALAN S. BLINDER
PHILIP FRIEDMAN

NATURAL RESOURCES

Resource depletion with technological uncertainty and the Rawlsian Fairness Principle

JOHN G. RILEY

UNIVERSITY OF CALIFORNIA
LOS ANGELES

1. INTRODUCTION

It is hardly surprising that one of the sharpest controversies arising from *A Theory of Justice* by Rawls (1971) is linked to his discussion of the intergenerational distribution of wealth. Despite its continual usage, the standard modified utilitarian approach is really no more than a bastardized version of classical utilitarianism. To quote from Arrow (1973b, p. 260):

> The most straightforward utilitarian answer is that the utilities of future generations enter equally with those of the present. But since the present generation is a very small part of the total number of individuals over a horizon easily measurable in thousands of years, the policy conclusion would be that virtually everything should be saved and very little consumed, a conclusion which seems offensive to common sense. The most usual formulation has been to assert a criterion of maximizing a sum of *discounted* utilities, in which the utilities of future generations are given successively smaller weights. The implications of such policies seem to be more in accordance with common sense and practice, but the foundations of such a criterion seem arbitrary.

3

An alternative approach, which avoids the asymmetry associated with discounting, is to introduce a social welfare function of the form

$$W = \sum_{t=1}^{\infty} w(U_t), \qquad w' > 0, \quad w'' < 0.$$

By increasing the curvature of $w(\cdot)$, it is possible to weight more heavily those generations with lower utility and thereby reduce the degree of inequality. For example, if $w(U) = (1 - r)^{-1}(U)^{1-r}$, the parameter $r = -Uw''(U)/w'(U)$ is naturally interpreted as the social relative aversion to intergenerational inequality. At least for the standard, neoclassical, one-sector growth model, if $\{U_t^*\}$ maximizes social welfare, the ratio $\inf_t\{U_t^*\}/\sup_t\{U_t^*\}$ is increasing in r and approaches unity as $r \to \infty$. However, in the absence of a principle upon which to select the parameter r, this approach is no less arbitrary.

In this unsatisfactory state it was natural that economic theorists would focus upon the application of the Rawlsian principle of justice as "fairness" to the question of intergenerational transfers.

In this context, a natural interpretation is that it would not be fair for the present generation to exploit its position in time, to the relative disadvantage of any of those following. Putting this slightly differently, generation τ's plan is unjust if the generation would be willing to pay to avoid having to change places with any future generation. Then a plan at time τ is just only if the associated stream of utilities $\{U_t\}$ satisfies the constraint

$$\inf_{t>\tau} \{U_t\} \geq U_\tau.$$

Generation τ, maximizing its own utility subject to the constraint of intergenerational justice, must therefore seek the solution of

$$\max \left\{ U_\tau \middle| \inf_{t>\tau} \{U_t\} \geq U_\tau \right\}. \tag{1}$$

In the simplest of neoclassical models, discussed by Arrow (1973a) and Solow (1974), each generation is assumed to live in one period enjoying consumption available in that period. Then, to satisfy the fairness principle, it is obvious that the consumption plan $\{C_t\}$ must be nondecreasing over time. The solution to (1) therefore involves choosing a consumption plan which equalizes consumption levels over time. It is a trivial matter to show that the optimal investment plan is simply to maintain the capital stock at its initial level. Both Arrow and Solow concluded that a welfare criterion which tied an economy so rigidly to the initial capital stock seemed highly unsatisfactory.[1]

In apparent response, Rawls (1974) withdrew any claim that the fairness principle could be applied to the question of *inter*generational justice. However, to this author at least, such a retreat was premature. Elsewhere with Phelps (1977), I have argued that the conclusion that Rawlsian justice freezes society essentially into its initial state is based on oversimplified analysis. Only in the absence of an overlap between generations is it impossible for different cohorts to make mutually beneficial trades. Utilizing standard assumptions, it can be shown that such trades lead to a monotonic increase in the capital stock while the utility levels of all generations are equalized.

These results hold even though each generation is egoistic, with tastes only for its own consumption of commodities and leisure. The "just" economy is further freed from its initial position if it is assumed that generation τ cares also about the preferences of its immediate descendants, who in turn care about generation $\tau + 2, \ldots$, and so on. Following Koopmans (1960), this is very naturally expressed as

$$U_\tau = U(u_\tau, U_{\tau+1}), \qquad \tau = 1, 2, \ldots. \tag{2}$$

For simplicity, the additive form of (2) is used throughout, that is,

$$U_\tau = u_\tau + \left(\frac{1}{1+\rho}\right) U_{\tau+1}, \qquad \tau = 1, 2, \ldots.$$

$$= \sum_{t=\tau}^{\infty} \left(\frac{1}{1+\rho}\right)^{t-\tau} u_t. \tag{2'}$$

Applying the fairness principle to generations interconnected by these "intergenerational ties of sentiment," the following principle emerges for the standard neoclassical model.

If the initial state is such that it is not possible to maintain indefinitely a level of $u_\tau = u(C_\tau)$ greater than the "Golden Rule" level,[2] the justice

---

[1] Independently, Arrow and also Dasgupta (1974) extended the analysis to allow for individuals who also care about the consumption of the following generation. Both argued that the economy would not move permanently away from the initial capital stock. However, as Riley (1976) has indicated, even in such a model a higher long run capital stock may satisfy the constraints of Rawlsian justice.

[2] That is, the efficient stationary level of u associated with a capital stock K_ρ, such that the net marginal product of capital is equal to ρ, the private rate of pure time preference. For a more complete discussion see Phelps and Riley (1977).

constraint is not binding. In contrast, if the Golden Rule level of u_τ is sustainable, the justice constraint is binding. Each generation is obliged to plan a savings policy in such a way as to equalize the level of u_τ, and hence U_τ, at the highest feasible level.

The reasoning is relatively straightforward. In the former case, maximization of

$$U_1 = \sum_{t=1}^{\infty} \left(\frac{1}{1+\rho}\right)^{t-1} u(C_t)$$

requires following a plan which involves a steady increase in consumption levels and hence in the sequence $\{u(C_t)\}$. This in turn implies that the sequence of utility levels

$$\{U_\tau\} = \left\{\sum_{t=\tau}^{\infty} \left(\frac{1}{1+\rho}\right)^{t-\tau} u(C_t)\right\}$$

is strictly increasing. Then maximizing U_1 yields an allocation satisfying the fairness principle. If, however, the initial state is such that a level of u_t higher than the Golden Rule level is sustainable, maximizing U_1 yields a strictly decreasing sequence $\{C_t\}$ and hence a strictly decreasing sequence $\{u(C_t)\}$. Since the asymptotic level of u_t is the Golden Rule level, such a policy cannot be just.

All the above of course depends upon the standard neoclassical assumptions that nonlabor inputs are themselves produced goods, and that the economy is "productive." Moreover, the discussion lies within the analytically convenient world of certainty. In the following pages the goal is to examine the implications of Rawlsian justice in a world of social risk. The model analyzed is a simplification of that suggested by Dasgupta and Heal (1974) in their discussion of natural resource depletion. In contrast with the standard neoclassical model, it is assumed that initially there exists only a finite quantity of some resource essential to survival. Social risk is introduced by supposing that at some unknown future date there will be a technological advance which renders the natural resource inessential.

Despite the contrasts between the model to be discussed and previously analyzed models, it will be seen that the conclusions are similar. For initial states which are poorly endowed with resources relative to postinnovation states, a generation with intergenerational ties to its immediate descendants has no further obligations toward the future. However, for all initial states which are sufficiently well-endowed with resources, the fairness principle calls for a slower utilization of the natural resource over some initial phase than what would result from maximization of the first generation's utility.

2. THE STRUCTURE OF THE MODEL
AND OTHER PRELIMINARIES

In order to focus upon the essentials without bogging down in what may be analytically impenetrable concessions to reality, we consider the simplest possible model. The discussion in this section follows very closely that of Dasgupta and Heal. At time zero there exists a stock S_0 of the only consumable good. There is no production. Writing consumption at time t as $C(t)$, we then have

$$\dot{S} = -C; \qquad S(t) \geq 0. \tag{3}$$

At some time T there will be a technological discovery. All remaining natural stock $S(T)$ is destroyed in the chain reaction resulting from the discovery. In its place is a new process which yields a perfect substitute at a rate of M units per period.[3]

The date of discovery is uncertain. However, it is believed that the probability that the discovery will take place *after* any given time T is a differentiable function $\Omega(T)$, where $\Omega'(T) < 0$ and $\lim_{T \to \infty} \Omega(T) = 0$. Unless $\Omega(0) = 1$, there is some finite probability, $1 - \Omega(0)$, that the discovery will never take place.

Each generation cares about its own consumption and the utility level of its immediate descendants according to (2)'. On introducing the expectation operator E, the welfare of generation τ can then be expressed as

$$V_\tau = E \sum_{t=\tau}^{\infty} (1/1 + \rho)^{t-\tau-1} u(C_t). \tag{4}$$

It turns out to be more convenient to work in continuous time. On taking the appropriate limit, the utility level of generation τ becomes

$$V(\tau) = E \int_{t=\tau}^{\infty} e^{-\rho(t-\tau)} u(C(t)) \, dt. \tag{4'}$$

Consider first the utility level of generation T, that is, the generation immediately following the technological breakthrough. Since there is no longer any uncertainty, $V(T)$ is simply a discounted sum of future levels of $u(C(t))$. Given that after the breakthrough the single commodity, produced at a rate M, can only be consumed or stored, it is a straightforward matter to show that maximization of $V(T)$ requires a consumption at a rate of M.[4]

---

[3] The destruction of the remaining natural stock greatly simplifies the analysis since all postinnovation decisions are then independent of the time of discovery.

[4] Since generation T discounts future consumption it would prefer to borrow from the future, that is, plan a declining consumption profile $C(t)$. However, this is impossible since the consumption good is produced at a fixed rate M. Then the best generation T can do is to consume all that is produced and plan for all future generations to do likewise.

Then

$$V^*(T) = \max_{C(t)} V(T) = \int_T^\infty e^{-\rho t} u(M)\, dt = \rho^{-1} u(M).$$

Of course, exactly the same argument can be applied for all generations following the Tth, that is,

$$V^*(\tau) = \rho^{-1} u(M), \qquad \tau \geq T. \tag{5}$$

Thus the policy chosen by generation T, and all generations thereafter, *is* the solution to (1), that is, it is the just plan. Summarizing we have:

PROPOSITION 1   For all postdiscovery generations, the consumption plan yielding greatest utility, $C^*(t) = M$, is the just plan.

Next consider the expected utility maximizing plan for the present generation. Only by solving for this plan will it be possible to see whether it is consistent with the overriding obligations resulting from adoption of the fairness principle.

Let $C(t)$ be the consumption rate at a time t conditional upon no prior technological breakthrough, as planned by the present generation. If the discovery were to take place at time T, the utility of the latter would be

$$\int_0^T e^{-\rho t} u(C(t))\, dt + e^{-\rho T} \rho^{-1} u(M).$$

Since $\Omega(T)$ is the probability of discovery later than time T, $-\Omega'(T)\,dT$ is the probability of discovery in the interval $[T, T + dT]$. Expected utility at time zero is therefore

$$V(0) = \int_0^\infty -\Omega'(T) \left[\int_0^T e^{-\rho t} u(C(t))\, dt + e^{-\rho T} \rho^{-1} u(M) \right] dT$$
$$+ (1 - \Omega(0)) \int_0^\infty e^{-\rho T} u(C(t))\, dt. \tag{6}$$

Integrating by parts, this can be rewritten as

$$V(0) = \int_0^\infty (1 - \Omega(0) + \Omega(T)) e^{-\rho T} [u(C(T)) - u(M)]\, dT + \rho^{-1} u(M).$$
$$\tag{6'}$$

It is assumed that

$$u(0) = 0, \qquad \lim_{C \to 0} u'(C) = \infty, \qquad u'(C) > 0, \quad u''(C) < 0. \tag{7}$$

Note that if $C(t)$ maximizes $V(0)$, it must also maximize

$$\int_0^\infty w(t) u(C(t))\, dt \qquad \text{where} \quad w(t) = (1 - \Omega(0) - \Omega(t)) e^{-\rho t}. \tag{8}$$

But it is well known that these assumptions ensure that there exists a unique interior solution to the maximization of (8) subject to the "equation of motion" (3). Moreover, the necessary conditions for maximizing (8) are easily seen to be

$$w(t)u'(C(t)) = \text{constant}, \qquad \int_0^\infty C(t)\,dt = S_0. \qquad (9)$$

These two conditions completely characterize $C(t)$.

Then $V(0)$ is maximized by choosing a prediscovery consumption plan $C(t)$, satisfying (9). Since $w(t)$ is strictly decreasing in t and $u(\cdot)$ is concave, it follows that the optimal plan $C(t)$ is decreasing in t.

To summarize we have:

PROPOSITION 2   The expected utility of the present generation is maximized by following a declining prediscovery consumption path which is the solution of

$$\max \int_0^\infty w(t)u(C(t))\,dt \qquad \text{s.t.} \qquad \int_0^\infty C(t)\,dt = S_0,$$

where $w(t) = (1 - \Omega(0) + \Omega(t))e^{-\rho t}$.

Before turning to a discussion of the just rate of extraction, it should be noted that in general the Strotz–Pollak time inconsistency problem arises. Let $\Omega(\tau + T | \tau)$ be the probability that discovery takes place after time $\tau + T$, conditional upon its not having occurred prior to time τ. The expected utility of generation τ, conditional upon no discovery prior to τ, is then

$$V(\tau) = \int_0^\infty (1 - \Omega(\tau|\tau) + \Omega(\tau + T|\tau))e^{-\rho T}[u(C(\tau + T)) - u(M)]\,dT$$
$$+ \rho^{-1}u(M). \qquad (10)$$

From (9) it follows that the first-order conditions for the maximization of $V(\tau)$ can be written as

$$e^{-\rho T}\frac{u'(C(\tau + T))}{u'(C(\tau))} = \frac{1}{1 - \Omega(\tau|\tau) + \Omega(\tau + T|\tau)}. \qquad (11)$$

But (9) must hold at every point in time, and in particular at $t = \tau$ and $t = \tau + T$. Moreover, for consistency between the plans of generation τ and the present generation, both (9) and (11) must be satisfied. Eliminating the intertemporal marginal rate of substitution, we thus require

$$1 - \Omega(\tau|\tau) + \Omega(\tau + T|\tau) = \frac{1 - \Omega(0) + \Omega(\tau + T)}{1 - \Omega(0) + \Omega(\tau)}. \qquad (12)$$

There are two rather natural ways in which these conditional probabilities may be defined. The first alternative is to assume that the probability of discovery after calendar time T is unaffected by failure to make the discovery in some intervening subinterval, that is,

$$\Omega(\tau + T|\tau) = \Omega(T + \tau). \tag{13}$$

The second alternative is to assume independence with respect to calendar rather than lapsed time. By this it is meant that the probability of discovery over the time interval $[\tau, \tau + T]$ is dependent only upon whether or not discovery was made prior to this interval and not on calendar time t. We must then have

$$\Omega(\tau + T|\tau) = \Omega(T). \tag{14}$$

It is a relatively straightforward matter to check that for the first alternative (13), there is no distribution function satisfying (12). Furthermore, the only family of distribution functions satisfying (12) and (14) are given by

$$\Omega(T) = \Omega(0)e^{-\pi T}. \tag{15}$$

Since the exponential distribution both avoids time-inconsistency problems and is especially amenable to analysis, it is adopted throughout the following discussion. For such a class of distributions allowing for the possibility that the discovery will be made with probability less than one adds little. It is therefore assumed that $\Omega(0) = 1$.

3. THE JUST RATE OF RESOURCE DEPLETION

To see whether the Rawlsian fairness principle obligates the initial generation to consume less of the natural resource requires an examination of the expected utility of future generations. Consider some arbitrary feasible consumption profile $C(t)$. If at time τ, the discovery has not taken place ($\tau < T$), the expected utility of generation τ is given by (10). Moreover, the probability that τ is less than T is $\Omega(\tau) = e^{-\pi\tau}$. Therefore, writing the expected utility of generation τ from the vantage point of time zero as $EU(\tau)$, we have

$$EU(\tau) = \Omega(\tau)V(\tau) + (1 - \Omega(\tau))\rho^{-1}u(M)$$
$$= \rho^{-1}u(M) + e^{-\pi\tau}\int_0^\infty e^{-(\rho+\pi)t}[u(C(\tau + t)) - u(M)]\,dt. \tag{16}$$

From the previous section, the consumption plan $C_0(t)$ that maximizes the expected utility of the present generation must satisfy (9), that is

$$e^{-(\rho+\pi)t}u'(C(t)) = u'(C(0)). \tag{17}$$

Consider the slope of the expected utility profile, given the consumption plan $C_0(t)$. Differentiating (16) yields

$$\frac{d}{d\tau}(EU(\tau)) = -\pi e^{-\pi\tau} \int_0^\infty e^{-(\rho+\pi)t}[u(C_0(\tau+t)) - u(M)]\,dt$$

$$+ e^{-\pi\tau} \int_0^\infty e^{-(\rho+\pi)t}u'(C_0(\tau+t))\frac{d}{d\tau}C_0(\tau+t)\,dt.$$

On rearranging terms and utilizing (17), this derivative can be rewritten as

$$\frac{d}{d\tau}(EU(\tau))$$

$$= -e^{-\pi\tau}\left\{\pi\int_0^\infty e^{-(\rho+\pi)t}[u(C_0(\tau+t)) - u(M)]\,dt + u'(C_0(\tau))C_0(\tau)\right\}.$$

$$(18)$$

Since $u(C)$ is concave, and $C_0(t)$ must satisfy (17), $C_0(\tau+t)$ is decreasing in τ. Then the integral in (18) is decreasing in τ. As $\tau \to \infty$, $C_0(\tau+t) \to 0$, hence, the integral approaches $-u(M)/(\rho+\pi)$. Moreover, as $\tau \to \infty$, the second term within the braces must approach zero, since for small C, $u(0) \approx u(C) + u'(C)C$, and by assumption $u(0) = 0$. Therefore, for sufficiently large τ, the brace of (18) is negative, implying that the expected utility profile is essentially upward sloping.

We now introduce the additional restriction that the elasticity of $u(c)$ is less than unity,[5] that is,

$$- Cu''(C)/u'(C) < 1. \qquad (19)$$

In all the discussion that follows it will be assumed that (19) is satisfied. Given this restriction on preferences,

$$\frac{\partial}{\partial C}(Cu'(C)) = u'\left(1 + \frac{Cu''}{u'}\right) > 0,$$

and it follows that the second term in the brace of (18) is also strictly decreasing in τ. We have therefore proved:

PROPOSITION 3   The expected utility profile $EV(\tau)$, resulting from maximizing $EV(0)$, the expected utility of the present generation, is upward sloping for all sufficiently large τ. Moreover, if the elasticity of $u(C)$ is less

---

[5] Without this technical assumption it is not possible to derive the strong implications of the following pages. Note that of the class of constant elasticity functions, the assumption that $u(0) = 0$ is satisfied only if (19) is satisfied.

than unity, the profile is *either* upward sloping for all generations or has a unique turning point.

Intuitively, the pure time preference of the present generation leads to a declining consumption profile and, in the absence of a prior discovery, a declining expected utility. For generations sufficiently far into the future, this decline is outweighed by the rising probability of previous discovery.

We next consider the impact of increasing the initial stock S_0. Given (17), the consumption profile maximal for the initial generation is strictly increasing in S_0. Therefore an increase in S_0 increases the two terms within the braces of (18). As $S_0 \to 0$, the first term approaches its lower bound $[-\pi/(\rho + \pi)]u(M)$ and the second term approaches zero. Therefore $(d/d\tau)(EU(\tau))|_{\tau=0}$ is positive for sufficiently small S_0. Moreover, for sufficiently large S_0, both terms within the braces of (18) are positive, hence $(d/d\tau)EU(\tau)$ is negative. These results can be summarized as:

PROPOSITION 4   The profile of expected utilities associated with the optimal plan for the present generation is upward sloping at $\tau = 0$, if and only if the initial stock of resources is less than some $S_0 = \hat{S}(M, \rho, \pi)$.

Together Propositions 3 and 4 imply:

PROPOSITION 5   Under Rawlsian justice, the present generation have obligations to future generations over and above their own direct concern for their descendants, if and only if the initial resource level is sufficiently large.

Expected utility profiles associated with different initial levels of S_0 are depicted in Figure 1. As $\tau \to \infty$, $\Omega(\tau) \to 0$; therefore from (16), all such profiles approach asymptotically $\rho^{-1}u(M)$.

We next examine the shape of the "just" depletion and expected utility profiles. From (16), for all τ less than some arbitrary $\bar{\tau}$:

$$EU(\tau) - \rho^{-1}u(M) = e^{-\pi\tau}\left\{ \int_0^{\bar{\tau}-\tau} e^{-(\rho+\pi)t}[u(C(\tau + t)) - u(M)]\,dt \right.$$

$$\left. + e^{-\rho(\bar{\tau}-\tau)}[EU(\bar{\tau}) - \rho^{-1}u(M)] \right\}. \tag{20}$$

Suppose two consumption plans are identical for all $t < \bar{\tau}$. Then for all generations prior to $\bar{\tau}$, the plan yielding higher expected utility is that which yields the larger expected utility at time $\bar{\tau}$.

At some time $\hat{\tau}$ the "just" planned stock of the resource must equal $\hat{S}$. From Proposition 4, if the expected utility of generation $\hat{\tau}$, $EV(\hat{\tau})$ is maximized, the resulting expected utility profile is upward sloping for all $\tau > \hat{\tau}$.

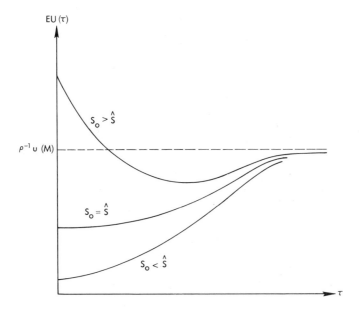

FIGURE 1   Expected utility of future generations as a result of a depletion policy which maximizes the utility of the initial generation.

Then any other consumption profile lowers $\inf_{\tau \geq 0} EV(\tau)$, since it lowers the expected utility of all generations $\tau < \hat{\tau}$.

Therefore from $\hat{\tau}$, when the "just" resource stock $S_*(\hat{\tau}) = \hat{S}$, it is optimal to follow the unconstrained depletion policy satisfying (17).

We now show that for $\tau < \hat{\tau}$ the "just" consumption/depletion plan, $C_*(t)$, must be such as to equalize expected utilities.

Suppose not. Since $EU(0) = \inf_{\tau \geq 0} EU(\tau)$, either the profile is upward sloping for all τ, or there is some interval over which $EU(\tau) > EU(0)$ and $EU(\tau)$ is decreasing with τ.

Consider the former possibility, depicted in Figure 2. $EU_0(\tau)$ is the expected utility profile resulting from following a depletion policy $C_0(t)$ which maximizes $EU(0)$. $EU_*(t)$ is the expected utility profile resulting from following the just policy $C_*(t)$. Both $C_0(t)$ and $C_*(t)$ must satisfy the feasibility constraint $\int_0^\infty C(t)\, dt \leq S_0$. Therefore so must all convex combinations $C_\lambda(t) = \lambda C_0(t) + (1 - \lambda)C_*(t)$. Since $u(C)$ is strictly concave, $EU(\tau)$ is strictly concave. Hence,

$$EU_\lambda(\tau) > \lambda EU_0(\tau) + (1 - \lambda)EU_*(\tau), \qquad 0 < \lambda < 1,$$
$$\geq \inf_{\tau \geq 0} \{\lambda EU_0(\tau) + (1 - \lambda)EU_*(\tau)\}.$$

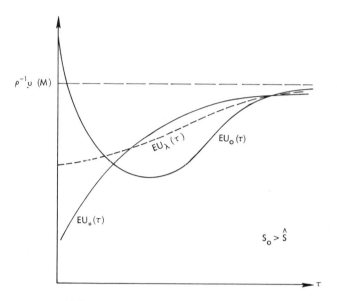

FIGURE 2   Unjust expected utility profiles.

From Figure 2 it can be seen that the latter exceeds $\inf_{\tau \geq 0} EU_*(\tau)$ for all λ sufficiently close to zero. But this contradicts our assumption that $C_*(t)$ is the "just" policy. A similar argument which considers changes in the consumption path for an interval over which $EU_*(\tau)$ is negatively sloped, rules out this possibility as well. Hence:

PROPOSITION 6   The "just" depletion policy equalizes expected utility until some time $\hat{\tau}$ when $S_*(\hat{\tau}) = \hat{S}(M, \rho, \pi)$. Beyond this time the constraints of intergenerational justice are no longer binding and expected utility rises to its asymptote $\rho^{-1} u(M)$.

We have therefore shown that if the initial stock S_0 is sufficiently large, the difference principle imposes an obligation on early generations to reduce their expected utility. However, these obligations are binding only until the stock reaches $\hat{S}(M, \rho, \pi)$.

We now consider the effect of parameter changes on this switching level of the resource stock. Recall from (18) that

$$\frac{d}{d\tau}(EU_0(\tau))$$

$$= -e^{-\pi\tau}\left\{\pi \int_0^\infty e^{-(\rho+\pi)t}[u(C_0(\tau + t)) - u(M)]\,dt - u'(C_0(\tau))C_0(\tau)\right\}.$$

An increase in M has no effect on the depletion plan $C_0(t)$ which maximizes $EU(0)$. Therefore if M increases, $(d/d\tau)(EU_0(\tau))$ increases owing to the increase in $u(M)$. From Proposition 4, $(d/d\tau)(EU_0(0)) = 0$ if $S_0 = \hat{S}$ and $(d/d\tau)(EU_0(0))$ is decreasing in S. Then with the postdiscovery flow equal to $M + \Delta M$ and $S_0 = \hat{S}(M, \rho, \pi)$, $(d/d\tau)(EU_0(0))$ is strictly positive. It follows that $\partial \hat{S}/\partial M > 0$.

While there seems to be no simple way to sign the impact of a ceteris paribus increase in ρ or π, suppose π is increased, and ρ is simultaneously decreased so that $\rho + \pi$ is unchanged. Once again there is no effect on the depletion policy $C_0(t)$. Moreover, if $S_0 = \hat{S}$, $(d/d\tau)EU_0(0) = 0$. Then since the second term within the braces is negative, the first must be positive. The latter is therefore an increasing function of π. Thus the compensated increase in π results in an increase in $(d/d\tau)EU_0(0)$. Applying exactly the same argument as above, we then have $(\partial \hat{S}/\partial \pi)|_{\rho + \pi = \text{constant}} > 0$.

To summarize we have:

PROPOSITION 7   The level of resources, $\hat{S} = \hat{S}(M, \pi, \rho + \pi)$, below which Rawlsian justice imposes no obligations, is increasing in both M and π.

While attempts at providing an intuitive explanation of the latter result seem unconvincing, the former is certainly reasonable. An increase in M raises the expected return to later generations more than to earlier generations, since for the former, the probability of prior discovery is higher. This increases the slope of the expected utility profile, $EU_0(\tau)$, and thereby reduces the domain of initial resource levels for which $EU_0(\tau)$ is initially downward sloping.

4.   CONCLUDING REMARK

In the previous section it was shown that when there is the prospect of rendering a finite nonrenewable resource inessential, the Rawlsian fairness principle operates to reduce expected utility levels of early generations below the maximum that each could potentially attain, if and only if the initial resource stock is sufficiently large.

The discussion would be incomplete without asking what role competitive markets might play in achieving the "just" depletion policy. Specifically, once society has agreed to accept the fairness principle, is it possible for the government to intervene in competitive markets in such a way that if each generation were to maximize its own expected utility, the resulting depletion rate would be the "just" rate?

Suppose at time zero, individuals can trade in contingent futures markets. Let $p(\tau)$ be the price per unit of the exhaustible resource, to be delivered at time τ, conditional upon no discovery prior to this time. Owners of the resource will only be willing to sell the resource at the higher price. Then for positive supply in all periods we require $p(\tau) = p(0)$.

It is easy to check that, given such a price schedule, the initial generation if it ignores the difference principle, will choose a depletion policy which maximizes its expected utility, $EU(0)$.

Then if $S_0 > \hat{S}(M, \pi, \rho + \pi)$, some intervention is clearly necessary in order to maximize $EU(0)$ subject to the constraints of intergenerational justice. Recently, Barro (1974) has pointed out that it is not enough, in a regime of complete markets, for the government to float public debt over an initial interval. Individuals, if they anticipate correctly the profile of government transactions, will simply offset the latter by adjusting private saving.

However, it does not follow that government is powerless to affect intergenerational transfers. By introducing an appropriate profile of sales taxes, it is able to drive a wedge between producer and consumer prices and thereby achieve any technologically feasible depletion policy.

REFERENCES

Arrow, K. J. (1973a). Rawls's Principle of Just Saving, *Swedish Journal of Economics* **75**, 323–335.

Arrow, K. J. (1973b). Some Ordinalist–Utilitarian Notes on Rawls's Theory of Justice, *Journal of Philosophy* **70**, 245–263, 422.

Barro, R. J. (1974). Are Government Bonds Net Wealth? *Journal of Political Economy* **82**, 1095–1118.

Dasgupta, P. (1974). On Some Alternative Criteria for Justice between Generations, *Journal of Public Economics* **3**, 405–423.

Dasgupta, P., and Heal, G. M. (1974). The Optimal Depletion of Exhaustible Resources, *The Review of Economic Studies* (Symposium), 3–28.

Koopmans, T. C. (1960). Stationary Ordinal Utility and Impatience, *Econometrica* **28**, 287–309.

Phelps, E. S., and Riley, J. G. (1977). Rawlsian Growth: Dynamic Programming of Capital and Wealth for Intergeneration "Maximin Justice," *The Review of Economic Studies* (to be published).

Rawls, J. (1971). *A Theory of Justice.* Cambridge, Massachusetts: Harvard Univ. Press.

Rawls, J. (1974). Some Reasons for the Maximin Criterion, *American Economic Review* **64**, 141–146.

Riley, J. G. (1976). Further Remarks on the Rawlsian Principle of Just Saving, *Scandinavian Journal of Economics* **78**, 16–26.

Solow, R. M. (1974). Intergenerational Equity and Exhaustible Resources, *The Review of Economic Studies* (Symposium), 29–46.

Monopoly, uncertainty, and exploration

ROBERT M. SOLOW

MASSACHUSETTS INSTITUTE OF TECHNOLOGY

1. INTRODUCTION

What are the consequences of monopoly in extractive industries for the allocation of exhaustible resources over time? The economic theory of exhaustible resources suggests a presumption that the monopoly overconserves—uses up the resource too slowly—as compared with the ideal path. For any given remaining stock, the monopolist tends to set too high a price, for the standard reasons, and thus consumption is too low early in the story. By virtue of this very fact, the monopolist's remaining stock will be higher than that of the ideal path at each time. Eventually the monopolist's price must fall below the ideal price, and therefore consumption exceed the ideal consumption, if the monopolist is to use up the entire stock in due course. This presumption is reinforced by the possibility that the monopolist may find it profitable not to exhaust the whole stock, although the ideal path would do so. This is only a presumption, not a theorem, because it is not true for all demand functions. It is true in what one might call a central case—that of a constant-elasticity demand curve and positive constant marginal cost of extraction.

The theory that leads to this presumption assumes that the initial stock of the resource is known with certainty from the very beginning. It is natural to wonder if the same presumption holds under uncertainty about reserves.

I am grateful to the National Science Foundation for financial assistance, and to Michael Hoel of Oslo for interesting ideas on this subject.

There are many reasonable ways to introduce uncertainty into this picture, as one would expect from the fact that uncertainty about the future pervades the whole practical problem of resource-management. This paper tests the standard presumption in one simple context: there is a costly exploration activity, and the question to be answered is whether the monopolist over-conserves and underexplores as compared with the ideal pattern of activity. The answer seems to be that the standard presumption hangs on by the skin of its teeth, with an extra assumption or two. But it should be emphasized that the context is indeed simple. For instance, the whole story takes place in two periods. (The reason for this restriction is that if there were more than two periods, the story would have to include a learning process, with successive updating of prior distributions of the extent of reserves. This would in turn involve an inordinate amount of complication on an issue that has nothing intrinsically to do with monopoly.) It is worth mentioning at the start that the context is partial equilibrium. Other gross simplifications will be noted *en passant*.

2. SOCIAL OPTIMALITY IN A TWO-PERIOD MODEL

The first period begins with "proved reserves" R of a homogeneous non-renewable resource. During the first period, an amount X is (costlessly) extracted, and there is exploration activity at a level of E units of effort. Suppose that the cost of a unit of exploration is k units of the resource. Then consumption of the resource in the first period is $C_1 = X - kE$, yielding $U(X - kE)$ in social utility, where U is the usual increasing concave function. The decision variables X and E must naturally satisfy the inequalities $0 \leq E \leq X/k$ and $0 \leq X \leq R$. Thus the feasible set is the triangle in the (X, E) plane with vertices at the origin, $(R, 0)$, and $(R, R/k)$ (see Figure 1). Optima on the boundary are possible, but I think they are a distraction from the main issue, so I shall ignore them.

Exploration in the first period leads to a discovery of new reserves for the second and last period. The amount discovered, D, is a nonnegative random variable with a density function $f(D; E)$ conditional on the amount of exploration undertaken. One could allow more general probability distributions than those admitting densities, but that does not seem to be useful. More important, one would want to make f conditional on the amount of reserves previously discovered; since R is not a decision variable in the two-period case, this does not matter, but an extension to three or more periods would have to take this learning effect into account.

Take the usual additive social welfare function, and let the discount factor applied to second-period utility be A. Then the socially optimal strategy is

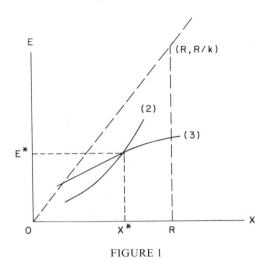

FIGURE 1

to choose X and E in the feasible set to maximize

$$U(X - kE) + A \int_0^\infty U(R - X + D)f(D; E)\,dD. \tag{1}$$

The second term is the discounted expected utility in period 2. $R - X + D = C_2$ is consumption in period 2 because it represents the whole available supply—unextracted reserve plus new discovery—which will surely be consumed in the second and last period except in the uninteresting case of complete saturation in both periods. Obviously one could get a little cheap generality by insisting on a fixed bequest at the end of period 2, or by adding a utility-of-bequest function.

The routine first-order conditions for an interior optimum are

$$U'(X - kE) - A \int_0^\infty U'(R - X + D)f(D; E)\,dD = 0, \tag{2}$$

$$-kU'(X - kE) + A \int_0^\infty U(R - X + D)f_E(D; E)\,dD = 0. \tag{3'}$$

The first condition, which must clearly hold except at boundaries, requires the equalization of first-period marginal utility and expected discounted second-period marginal utility. The second condition equalizes the marginal cost and expected marginal yield of exploration, in utility (or shadow-price) units. After an integration by parts, (3′) becomes

$$-kU'(X - kE) - A \int_0^\infty U'(R - X + D)F_E(D; E)\,dD = 0. \tag{3}$$

Here $F(D; E)$ is the cumulative distribution corresponding to f. To get (3) from (3′) one assumes that $U(R - X + D)F_E(D; E)$ vanishes both at $D = 0$

and $D = \infty$. That is not an unreasonable assumption given that $F(\infty; E) = 1$ and $F(0; E) = 0$, for all E.

I shall also be assuming that $F_E \leqq 0$ and $F_{EE} > 0$ always. The first inequality says that the marginal product of exploration is nonnegative; if you explore more, the probability falls that D will be less than Y for any given Y. The second inequality is a form of diminishing stochastic returns to exploration; it says that as E rises, the amount by which it diminishes that probability gets progressively smaller. These are natural assumptions.

The Hessian matrix for this problem is, in compressed notation,

$$
\begin{pmatrix}
U''(C_1) + A \int U''(C_2)f \, dD & -kU''(C_1) - A \int U'(C_2)f_E \, dD \\
-kU''(C_1) + A \int U''(C_2)F_E \, dD & k^2 U''(C_1) - A \int U'(C_2)F_{EE} \, dD
\end{pmatrix}
$$

$$
= \begin{pmatrix} H_{XX} & H_{XE} \\ H_{EX} & H_{EE} \end{pmatrix}.
$$

It is, of course, symmetric; the off-diagonal elements are equal by virtue of integration by parts. The second-order condition for this problem is that the diagonal elements be negative and the determinant positive. The first part is clearly satisfied; I have to assume that the determinant is positive. The off-diagonal elements are positive.

It follows directly that (2) and (3) represent upward-sloping curves in the (X, E) plane. From the assumed positivity of the determinant of the Hessian, (2) defines a steeper curve than (3); i.e., dE/dX along (2) exceeds dE/dX along (3), at least in the neighborhood of their intersection. The picture is thus as drawn in Figure 1. X^* and E^* are the socially optimal amounts of first-period extraction and exploration. The object of the exercise is to compare them with the solution to the profit-maximization problem of a monopoly. Before proceeding to the monopolist, however, I want to consider a slight variant on the formulation used so far.

3. SOCIAL OPTIMALITY:
   AN ALTERNATIVE FORMULATION

At the very beginning, I assumed without comment that the cost of a unit of exploration was k units of the resource. One could tell the story differently. Imagine that the resource is not consumed directly, but used as an input in the production of generalized "output." If all other productive inputs are given exogenously, $U(\cdot)$ can be interpreted as the production function giving output as a function of the resource input. In this interpretation, $U(\cdot)$ would still be an increasing concave function of its argument. But now it is rather more natural to suppose that a unit of exploration has a constant cost k in terms of output. (In the direct-consumption story, with U a utility function, the equivalent assumption is that k is the constant cost of exploration in terms of a background good with constant marginal utility.)

In that case, the social optimum calls for maximization of

$$U(X) - kE + A \int_0^\infty U(R - X + D)f(D; E)\,dD. \tag{1a}$$

The first-order conditions corresponding to (2) and (3) are

$$U'(X) - A \int_0^\infty U'(R - X + D)f(D; E)\,dD = 0, \tag{2a}$$

$$-k - A \int_0^\infty U'(R - X + D)F_E(D; E)\,dD = 0; \tag{3a}$$

(3a) involves an integration by parts, analogous to (3). The interpretation is similar.

The Hessian matrix is slightly simpler in this version, namely

$$\begin{pmatrix} U''(C_1) + A \int U''(C_2)f\,dD & -A \int U'(C_2)f_E\,dD \\ A \int U''(C_2)F_E\,dD & -A \int U'(C_2)F_{EE}\,dD \end{pmatrix}.$$

The diagonal elements are negative and the off-diagonal positive. For a true interior maximum, one has to assume the determinant to be positive, and then the qualitative picture is exactly as in Figure 1, with the curves defined by (2a) and (3a) both positively sloped, and (2a) steeper.

The point of introducing this alternative formulation will appear later.

4. MONOPOLY

How will the outcomes differ from X^* and E^* if extraction and exploration decisions were controlled by a monopoly mine? Obviously, to get any systematic results, one has to assume that the demand curve perceived by the monopolist is the one implicit in the social utility function. The monopolist's inverse demand curve is thus $p = U'(q)$ and the associated total revenue function is $V(q) = qU'(q)$. If the monopolist chooses X and E to maximize the expected present value of profit, then the monopolist's objective function is

$$V(X - kE) + A \int_0^\infty V(R - X + D)f(D; E)\,dD.$$

This is exactly like the initial formulation of the social-optimum problem, except that V has replaced U. The nature of the monopolistic bias thus turns on the change in X^* and E^* when $U(q)$ is replaced by $V(q) = qU'(q)$.

This way of looking at the monopolist's problem involves some tacit assumptions that ought to be made explicit.

(a) This monopolist is risk-neutral, except as *social* risk aversion is embodied in the curvature of the social utility function U. But that observation only raises the question as to why the monopolist should perceive *that* demand curve.

(b) This monopolist is assumed to discount future profit at the same rate at which society discounts future utility. The common presumption is that the monopolist has a higher discount rate (smaller A). One would like to be able to say that the bias from assuming equal discount factors is predictable: common sense seems to suggest that a higher discount rate would tend to push the monopolist toward less exploration and more net extraction $(X - kE)$ in the first period, though the effect on X itself seems less clear. In fact, (2) and (3) or (2a) and (3a) do not assign unambiguous signs to dX^*/dA or dE^*/dA. The underlying reason must be that the higher discount rate might lead to very much higher initial extraction to such an extent that it pays to provide for the future by increased exploration. Or exploration might be reduced so drastically that the first period is sufficiently favored even with less gross extraction. The only outcome definitely excluded by the first-order conditions is higher exploration *and* smaller extraction in response to a higher discount rate. The equal-discount-factor assumption has to be accepted for want of anything better.

(c) The absence of extraction costs may bias the comparison between the monopolistic and socially optimal outcomes. For instance, in the already-mentioned "central" case with constant-elasticity demand and positive constant marginal costs of extraction from known reserves, the monopoly overconserves; but if extraction costs are zero, the monopolistic and socially optimal outcomes coincide. This oddity arises because marginal revenue is proportional to price in the constant elasticity case; but marginal profit is not proportional to average profit unless marginal cost in zero. The assumption of zero extraction costs may thus mask a tendency for the monopolist to overconserve, but one can hardly be sure on such skimpy evidence. Eventually extraction costs will have to be included in the analysis.

(d) A monopolist would under no circumstances sell an output at which marginal revenue were negative. If the random discovery turns out to be very large, therefore, the monopolist might simply refrain from selling all the remaining reserve in the second period. Thus the monopolist's expected-profit integral is not after all exactly like society's expected-utility integral with U replaced by V. The correct formula is easy to write. Let Q be the sales volume at which the (concave) total-revenue function reaches its maximum, so the marginal revenue turns negative. Then $D(R, X) = Q - R + X$ is the largest useful discovery, given the inherited reserves. The monopolist maximizes

$$V(X - kE) + A \int_0^{D(R,X)} V(R - X + D)f(D; E)\, dD + AV(Q) \int_{D(R,X)}^{\infty} f(D; E)\, dD.$$

This is awkward to use, so I shall simply assume that $D(R, X)$ is so large that the tail effect is negligible. The important consequence of this observation is presumably an argument for underexploration and overconservation by the monopolist, even to the extent of failure to exhaust the resource. In principle, however, it might lead to excessive first-period consumption, because a large chance discovery might render carry-over stocks valueless.

Finally, the case of the monopolist reveals clearly the difference between the two alternative formulations proposed earlier. In the original version, as written in this section, the relative price of exploration is fixed in terms of the monopolist's own product. Moreover, the quantity of the resource paid out to the exploration activity disappears from the market and does not return to compete with the monopolist's own sales. Hence the first-period revenue is, as stated, $V(X - kE)$.

To see what the alternative story says, it is clearer to revert to the interpretation in which the monopolist sells the resource to an industry producing "output" with the production function $U(\cdot)$. That industry's inverse demand curve for the resource is given by the marginal-product function $U'(\cdot)$. Now the price of exploration is fixed in terms of output; the monopolist must decide an amount X to sell to the output industry, in exchange for a total revenue $V(X)$ in terms of output, from which kE units of output get paid to the exploration activity. In this formulation, the monopolist maximizes

$$V(X) - kE + A \int_0^\infty V(R - X + D)f(D; E)\,dD,$$

which is, of course, exactly like the alternative version of the social-optimum problem, with U replaced by V. The economic difference between the two situations is this: in the second version, when the monopolist restricts output and thus raises the price of the resource in terms of output, this act also raises the price of the resource in terms of exploration, i.e., lowers the price of exploration effort in terms of the resource. Thus in a sense the monopolist can exploit the exploration industry exactly as it exploits the market. In the first version, the exploration activity shares the monopolist's power to exploit the market.

There is no reason to write explicitly the conditions for maximization of expected discounted profit by the monopolist. Under the assumption that V is an increasing concave (i.e., falling marginal revenue) function of its argument, they are exactly (2) and (3) or (2a) and (3a) and the associated second-order conditions, with U replaced by V.

5. THE CASE OF CERTAINTY

One way to see into this problem is to consider first the extreme case in which the outcome of exploration is known in advance with certainty, so that exploration is just a sure investment. If the density $f(D; E)$ degenerates into a spike at $D = D(E)$,[1] then the original problem (1) becomes the maximization of

$$U(X - kE) + AU(R - X + D(E))$$ (4)

with obvious first-order conditions

$$U'(C_1) - AU'(C_2) = 0$$ (5)

$$-kU'(C_1) + AU'(C_2)D'(E) = 0$$ (6)

which imply, by (5),

$$k = D'(E).$$ (7)

The monopolist's decision is defined by (5) with V instead of U and by (7). Since (7) does not depend on U or V, the monopolist explores exactly the socially optimal amount. (This happens precisely because the monopolist cannot exploit the exploration activity in this model. It clearly pays the monopolist to explore until the marginal yield in resource equals the marginal cost in resource, and this is obviously also socially optimal.)

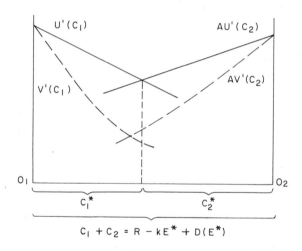

FIGURE 2

This simple determination of E^* permits the use of a standard diagram, which in turn will lead to the "empirical" heart of the problem. Remember that $p = U'(q)$ is the inverse demand curve embedded in the problem. So (7) determines E^* and (5) equates the discounted (shadow-) price in the two periods. In Figure 2 the horizontal axis has length $R - kE^* + D(E^*)$, which is the total amount to be consumed in the two periods. Measure C_1 from the

---

[1] The natural assumption is that $D' \geq 0$, $D'' < 0$.

left-hand origin and C_2 from the right-hand origin, and plot the curves $U'(C_1)$ and $AU'(C_2)$ respectively. The abscissa of their intersection determines $C_1{}^*$ and $C_2{}^*$, and therefore X^*. Notice that the curves must intersect so long as the marginal utility of the resource is always positive. Notice also that $U'(C_1{}^*) = AU'(C_2{}^*) < U'(C_2{}^*)$ because $A < 1$, so, by diminishing marginal utility, $C_1{}^* > C_2{}^*$.

For the monopolist, just replace U' by V', or price by marginal revenue. The monopoly outcome is given the intersection of the marginal revenue curves in Figure 2 also, because the amount of exploration is the same in the two cases. Since total revenue is assumed to be increasing and concave, the marginal revenue curves are falling and do not reach the horizontal axis. (If they did reach the axis before crossing, the message would be that the monopolist does not exhaust the resource; but of course then a more exact statement of the problem would show that the monopolist explores less than E^*.)

Do marginal revenue curves intersect to the right or the left of the intersection of the demand curves? If the demand curves had constant elasticity (exceeding unity for the usual reason), marginal revenue would be proportional to average revenue and the two intersections would lie on the same vertical. The monopoly outcome would be identical with the social optimum. (Reminder: positive extraction costs would change this conclusion, but not the main point up to which I am leading.) Since the constant-elasticity case is not extreme in any significant way, it is plain that in general the marginal revenue curves can intersect on either side of the intersection of the demand curves. Without more specific assumptions, one cannot evaluate the monopoly bias.

It is obvious from Figure 2 that the marginal revenue curves intersect to the left (right) of the social optimum according as the right-hand (left-hand) marginal revenue curve is higher at the social optimum; that is to say, the monopoly underconsumes (overconsumes) in the first period according as $AV'(C_2{}^*)$ is greater than (less than) $V'(C_1{}^*)$. Remembering that V' is the marginal revenue curve corresponding to U' taken as an inverse demand curve, a moment's calculation shows that $AV'(C_2{}^*) \gtreqless V'(C_1{}^*)$ as $\eta(C_2{}^*) \gtreqless \eta(C_1{}^*)$, where η is the ordinary elasticity of demand (taken as positive). Since it is known that $C_1{}^* > C_2{}^*$, we can state that: monopoly leads to underconsumption in the first period if and only if the elasticity of demand is bigger at smaller quantities, i.e., at higher prices. (Obviously I am here tacitly assuming that the elasticity moves monotonically one way or the other along the demand curve.)

I do not want to pretend that intuition or casual empiricism or, for that matter, econometrics is entitled to speak with any confidence on this matter. But it will make the exposition of the rest of the analysis easier if I choose a "likely" case in terms of which to present it. My own inclination would be to choose as the central case the one in which the elasticity of demand is higher at higher prices. The whole framework of this paper is partial equilibrium; the "resource" in question should be interpreted as a single mineral, such as copper or aluminum. Most such minerals, one would imagine, have very good substitutes at very high prices. They would, therefore, have demand curves that intersect the price axis—in other words, there is a price high enough to choke off the demand completely. For such demand curves, the presumption I have stated would be the plausible one.

There are some considerations that go the other way. Consider the interpretation in which $U(\cdot)$ is a production function with the nonresource inputs fixed exogenously. Then $U'(\cdot)$ is the marginal-product curve or demand curve for the resource. Suppose $U(\cdot)$ is taken as CES. Then, as it turns out, the elasticity of demand for the resource is higher at higher prices if the elasticity of substitution is less than one, and higher at lower prices if the elasticity of substitution exceeds unity. It still seems mildly counterintuitive to me that the case of a high elasticity of substitution should be the one in which a positive demand for the resource should persist at any price, although production can actually take place without any resource input; while, with small elasticity of substitution, when the resource input is indispensable for production, the demand for the resource can be choked off by a finite price. Probably it is the fixity of the other inputs that creates this result.

In any case, if one accepts that the elasticity of substitution between natural resources and other inputs is fairly large, then what I have called the plausible case is, on the contrary, exceptional. But that is hardly conclusive either. A persuasive case could be made that the elasticity of substitution between natural resources and other inputs is quite large in some aggregate sense, while partial-equilibrium single-product substitutability is quite small. The two statements are made compatible by relatively free substitution on the demand side between resource-intensive products and others. In that view of the world, the appropriate elasticity of substitution for $U(\cdot)$ may be less than one, and it then remains plausible that the monopoly tends to overconserve the resources.

6. THE CASE OF CERTAINTY
(ALTERNATIVE FORMULATION)

If the appropriate planning problem is the maximization of

$$U(X) - kE + AU(R - X + D(E)), \tag{4a}$$

then the first-order conditions corresponding to (5)–(7) are

$$U'(X) - AU'(C_2) = 0, \tag{5a}$$

$$-k + AU'(C_2)D'(E) = 0, \tag{6a}$$

which together imply

$$-k + U'(X)D'(E) = 0. \tag{7a}$$

Now—compare (7) and (7a)—E^* and X^* have to be determined simultaneously, not sequentially. A plot of (5a) and (6a) in the (X, E) plane gives a configuration exactly like Figure 1, with both curves sloping upward and (6a) steeper than (5a) by virtue of the second-order conditions for maximization of (4a). For analytical purposes, it turns out to be more useful to plot (5a) and (7a) in Figure 3. The negative slope of (7a) makes the picture look different, but of course the intersection at (E^*, X^*) is unchanged.

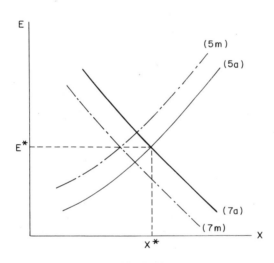

FIGURE 3

To work out the relation between the monopoly outcome and the social optimum, we need to reckon how the two curves shift when U is replaced by V in (5a) and (7a). I do not need to rewrite the equations, but I shall refer to them as (5m) and (7m) for ease of notation. The strategy is to evaluate (5m) and (7m) at the social optimum and then calculate the direction in which the curve has to be shifted to restore the equality disturbed by the substitution of V for U. Since $V(C) = CU'(C)$ by definition, $V'(C) = U'(C) + CU''(C) < U'(C)$ by the concavity of U. Moreover, I have assumed that marginal revenue is positive and falling, so $V''(C) < 0$.

Take (7m) first. Since $0 < V'(X^*) < U'(X^*)$ and $D' > 0$, clearly $-k + V'(X^*)D'(E^*) < 0$. Hold E^*; to restore equality, X^* must fall. Hence (7m) lies to the left of (7a), and this is recorded in Figure 3.

As for (5m), observe first that (5a) implies that $X^* > C_2^*$. Then, a little calculation shows that $V'(X^*) - AV'(C_2^*) < 0$ in the "central" case in which the elasticity of demand is an increasing function of price (decreasing function of quantity). Now hold $X = X^*$; to restore equality, $V'(C_2)$ must decrease, hence C_2 increase, hence E increase. Therefore (5m) lies above (5a) in Figure 3. The intersection of (5m) and (7m) yields the monopoly outcome.

There are now some conclusions to be drawn. Let the monopoly outcome (the coordinates of the point where (5m) and (7m) intersect) be designated X^m and E^m. Then Figure 3 makes it obvious that $X_m < X^*$ in the so-called "central" case. The monopolist extracts less than the socially optimal point in the first period. So the standard presumption is confirmed in this case (and would be confirmed with constant-elasticity demand and positive extraction cost).

Furthermore, from the fact that $X^m < X^*$ it follows that $E^m < E^*$. This is not obvious from Figure 3, but it is a consequence of the following chain of equalities and inequalities:

$$\frac{U'(X^*)D'(E^*)}{D'(E^m)} = \frac{k}{D'(E^m)} \qquad \text{by} \quad (7a),$$

$$= V'(X^m) \qquad \text{by} \quad (7m),$$
$$= AV'(R - X^m + D(E^m)) \qquad \text{by} \quad (5m),$$
$$< AV'(R - X^* + D(E^m)) \qquad \text{because} \quad X^m < X^*$$
$$\text{and} \quad V'' < 0,$$
$$< AU'(R - X^* + D(E^m)) \qquad \text{because} \quad V'(C) < U'(C).$$

Remember that $D'(E) > 0$ and $D''(E) \leqq 0$. Now suppose $E^m \geqq E^*$. Then the first term in this chain is not less than $U'(X^*)$. Also the last term is not greater than $AU'(R - X^* + D(E^*))$, by diminishing marginal utility. Thus $U'(X^*) < AU'(R - X^* + D(E^*))$, which contradicts (5a). Hence indeed $E^m < E^*$; the monopolist underexplores. (I owe this line of argument to Michael Hoel.) In this formulation, the monopolist explores only until the marginal revenue yield of exploration is equal to its marginal cost.

7. THE IMPACT OF UNCERTAINTY

It remains to go back and see how uncertainty about the yield of exploration affects the general picture. For that we can use (2)–(3) and (2a)–(3a) as we have just used (5)–(6) and (5a)–(6a). I am going to take up (2a) and (3a) first, because they lead to slightly more straightforward results. The qualitative determination of the social optimum is described in Figure 1.

Exactly as before, we replace U by V in (2a) and (3a) and call the resulting equations (2m) and (3m), whose solution gives the monopoly outcome. (I am tacitly assuming that the marginal revenue function never falls below zero, or does so for so implausibly large a sales volume as to have negligible impact on the solution.) The strategy, as before, is to evaluate (2m) and (3m) at (X^*, E^*). The shift from (3a) to (3m) is easy:

$$-k - A \int V'F_E \, dD = -k - A \int U'F_E \, dD + A \int (U' - V')F_E \, dD$$

$$= A \int (U' - V')F_E \, dD < 0$$

using (3a) at the social optimum, and because $V' < U'$ and $F_E < 0$. To restore equality, the LHS of (3m) has to be increased: for $E = E^*$, given that $F_E < 0$, one wants to make $V'(C_2)$ bigger, hence C_2 smaller, hence X larger. So (3m) lies to the right of (3a), at least near (X^*, E^*). The configuration is drawn in Figure 4.

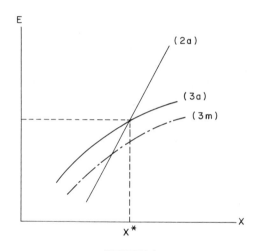

FIGURE 4

As always, the relation between (2a) and (2m) is more problematical. If the inverse demand curve $p = U'(q)$ has constant elasticity, then V' is a constant multiple of U' and (2a) and (2m) obviously coincide. In that case, Figure 4 confirms that the monopoly underextracts and underexplores in the first period.

If the inverse demand curve is linear (the case of a quadratic utility function), a little direct calculation shows that (2m) lies to the left of (2a). That case, too, leads to the conclusion that the monopolist underextracts and underexplores in the first period.

Accounting for uncertainty makes it harder to come to any definite conclusions without much stronger assumptions. For example, from (5a) for the certainty case we were able to conclude that $X^* > C_2^*$, given only $A < 1$

and diminishing marginal utility. The analogous conclusion from (2a) would be that $X^* > \mathscr{E}(C_2^*)$, where the expectation operator is with respect to the probability distribution of D given E^*. But (2a) only tells us that $U'(X^*) < \mathscr{E}(U'(C_2^*))$ and to take the next step we would need to assume that $U'(\cdot)$ (the demand curve) is not only decreasing but concave. In turn, concavity of the demand curve is a stronger property than (implies but is not implied by) the property of diminishing elasticity of demand as quantity increases, discussed earlier.

Returning to the relation between (2a) and (2m), one can substitute $qU'(q)$ for $V(q)$ in (2m) and evaluate at (X^*, E^*). It then follows that (2m) lies to the left (right) of (2a) near (X^*, E^*) according as

$$X^*U''(X^*) - A \int_0^\infty (R - X^* + D)U''(R - X^* + D)f(D; E^*)\,dD < (>)0. \quad (8)$$

Thus one would like to know the sign of $X^*U''(X^*) - A\mathscr{E}(C_2^*U''(C_2^*))$; but this is wanting to know a lot. Concavity of the demand curve tells us that $X^* > \mathscr{E}(C_2^*)$ and also that $qU''(q)$, which one could write as $qp'(q)$, is a decreasing function of q. But that is not enough for (8); and the curvature of $qU''(q)$ depends on the *third* derivative of the demand curve.

One last transformation may add a little insight. The inequality (8) is equivalent to

$$\frac{U'(X^*)}{\eta(X^*)} - A\mathscr{E}\left(\frac{U'(C_2^*)}{\eta(C_2^*)}\right) > (<) 0 \qquad (9)$$

or

$$\mathscr{E}\left(U'(C_2^*)\left(\frac{1}{\eta(X^*)} - \frac{1}{\eta(C_2^*)}\right)\right) > (<) 0. \qquad (10)$$

The formulation (10) shows at once that the constant-elasticity demand curve is the borderline case. Moreover, by loose and heuristic reasoning, concavity of the demand curve suggests that X^* is large relative to the distribution of C_2^*; the implied property of decreasing elasticity of demand suggests that $\eta(X^*)$ is small relative to the distribution of $\eta(C_2^*)$, so that ">" is likely to hold in (10), (2m) is to the left of (2a), and the monopolist underextracts and underexplores in the first period. The uncertainty case is rather like the certainty case, only a little more uncertain.

8.   UNCERTAINTY CONTINUED

At the end, I return briefly to the very first formulation that leads to the conditions (2) and (3) for the social optimum and correspondingly (2n) and (3n) for the monopoly outcome. When the yield of exploration is certain, this formulation leads to the sharp conclusion—see (7)—that the monopolist does the socially optimal amount of exploration; and then the comparison of extraction policies is simply described in Figure 2. Perhaps just because the certainty case is so precisely balanced, the introduction of uncertainty makes it hard to find any interpretable general results at all. The shift from (2) to (2n) is as before, and depends on the same demand-side factors. The added complication is that the relation between (3) and (3n) also becomes problematical. In particular, the direction of the shift seems to depend on the interaction between the slope of the demand curve and the marginal effect of changes in exploration effort on the shape of the probability distribution of discoveries. One would hardly know how to begin to speculate about that.

I will quote only one specific result, to show that the added complication is just complication, and not a symptom of some fundamental instability. Suppose the demand curve is linear. Then, as usual, the curve representing (2n) lies to the left of (2) in Figure 1. The curve (3n) lies to the right of (3) if

$$k < A \frac{\partial}{\partial E} \mathscr{E}(D|E^*), \tag{11}$$

and to the right if the inequality is reversed. This is as close to (7) as one could hope to get, depending as it does on the relation between the marginal cost of exploration and the marginal expected yield. The important difference is that (7) determines the monopolist's level of exploration independently of demand conditions, whereas (3n)—the analogous condition under uncertainty—does not. In other words, the E^* at which (11) has to be evaluated depends on the shape of the demand curve and the shape and behavior of the discovery distribution as E changes.

9. GENERAL REMARKS

What are the consequences of monopoly in extractive industries for the allocation of exhaustible resources over time?

The routine tendency for monopoly to produce less than the "ideal output" and to price it too high operates here as elsewhere. In the extreme case, this tendency could lead the industry to go to bed with unextracted resource at the end of the final period. The profit-maximizing program could call for ultimate extraction of less than the available reserves. I have mentioned this possibility but deliberately excluded it from detailed analysis, in order to isolate those factors peculiar to exhaustible resources.

When exploration is possible, the same tendency would push a monopolist in the direction of underexploration. If the formal argument of the paper had allowed for the possibility that marginal revenue (or marginal profit, if there are extraction costs) might fall to zero in the range of outputs considered, that would certainly have served to reduce the profit-maximizing level of exploration effort in the first period (i.e., in the penultimate stages of the extraction process).

In the detailed analysis, these relatively unsubtle forces have been excluded. It has been assumed that the monopoly always finds itself operating on the rising part of its total-revenue curve, and always expects to do so. Thus, for example, whatever discoveries are made in the first period are fully exploited in the second. Another less definite but perhaps more important source of bias is revealed.

Generally speaking, the higher the elasticity of demand, the less the monopoly output differs from the competitive—"ideal"—output. More precisely, the higher the elasticity of demand, the less marginal revenue differs from average revenue, and the higher the monopoly output will be. The essential property of an exhuastible resource is that its price—net of extraction costs—must rise over time for asset-equilibrium reasons. This is the Hotelling Rule so much elaborated in the recent literature. Other things equal, then, one expects higher prices later than earlier. Unless the demand curve is very special—constant elasticity in terms of net price—the elasticity of demand will differ systematically between the early and late stages of the extraction history. If, for instance, the elasticity of demand tends to be higher at higher prices, as I have tended to assume, more for definiteness than from conviction, it will tend to be systematically higher late in the history than at the beginning. Hence monopoly tends to shift production to later times as compared with the ideal path. This is the origin of the monopolistic bias toward overconservation. If total reserves are known, and if the monopoly will eventually use them all, it must be the case that the monopoly underproduces early in the game and overproduces later. The possibility of exploration changes the context, because aggregate extraction over time is not invariant. But the analysis shows that the same assumptions that lead to the overconservation bias in the absence of exploration tend to preserve that bias, and to combine it with a probable bias toward underexploration as well.

UNCERTAINTY

Leverage, bankruptcy, and the cost of capital

FRED D. ARDITTI

UNIVERSITY OF FLORIDA
GAINESVILLE

YORAM C. PELES

THE HEBREW UNIVERSITY
JERUSALEM

1. INTRODUCTION

In a world where firms face corporate taxes and zero default risk, Modigliani and Miller (hereafter M&M) proved (1963) that if a firm wishes to maximize its market value, then it should seek as much debt as commercially possible, hereafter termed a corner solution. They call this theorem Proposition I. Only recently has the possibility of bankruptcy and its effects on the capital structure of a firm been considered in the economic literature.[1] Bankruptcy, the result of the firm being unable to meet its cash obligations as they come due, entails extra costs from liquidation or reorganization. Liquidation necessarily curtails the time the firm has to search for the "best"

The authors are indebted to Haim Levy for helpful comments.

[1] Considering default risk with incomplete security markets, Smith (1972, Theorem 2) finds that an investor will prefer an increase or decrease in the firm's debt–equity ratio according to whether the ratio is greater or less than the proportion of debt to equity in the investor's security portfolio.

price for its assets and the costs of transferring property rights in a reorganization may be substantial. The purpose of this paper is to demonstrate that if one considers these extraordinary losses when bankruptcy is followed by liquidation or reorganization in a framework that acknowledges the existence of a corporate tax t, then, a noncorner optimal debt–equity ratio may exist for the firm.

In Section 2, the capital structure problem of the firm is analyzed by application of the stochastic dominance technique to the investment decisions of expected utility maximizers, assuming only that these individuals prefer more wealth to less. While this approach provides general results, it is bought at the cost of only being able to indicate the possibility of an interior capital structure. To identify a specific case in which a unique, noncorner debt–equity ratio obtains, Section 3 provides a model in which the firm issues debt so as to maximize the market value of its assets and where potential debtholders are characterized by von Neumann–Morgenstern utility functions that are linear in wealth. We also find that the value maximizing debt–equity ratio of the firm is identical to that which solves the problem of firm and bondholders banding together to maximize the tax benefits of interest payments less the expected losses arising from the failure of the firm to meet its interest obligation.

2. STOCHASTIC DOMINANCE ANALYSIS[2]

The analysis will proceed in a stepwise fashion by considering two identical firms in varying market environments:

(1)   no taxes, but the certainty of extraordinary bankruptcy losses if bankruptcy occurs;

---

[2] The two main theorems of stochastic dominance are:

FIRST DEGREE STOCHASTIC DOMINANCE   Given two cumulative probability distributions $G_1(Y)$ and $G_2(Y)$ with Y symbolizing the investment dollar return variable, $G_1(Y)$ will be preferred to $G_2(Y)$ by every expected utility maximizer whose utility is an increasing function of wealth, if $G_1(Y) \leq G_2(Y)$ for all possible Y and $G_1(Y) < G_2(Y)$ for at least one value of Y.

SECOND DEGREE STOCHASTIC DOMINANCE   Distribution $G_1(Y)$ will be preferred to $G_2(Y)$, again in the sense that the expected utility associated with investment 1 is greater than that associated with investment 2, by all individuals with nondecreasing–concave utility functions, if the area between $G_1(Y)$ and $G_2(Y)$ up to any Y is never positive, that is $\int_{-\infty}^{Y} [G_1(Y) - G_2(Y)] \, dY \leq 0$, and for at least one Y value this area is negative.

For the reader who wishes to explore the subject of stochastic dominance in depth, see Hadar and Russell (1969) and Hanoch and Levy (1969).

(2) no extraordinary losses due to bankruptcy, but the existence of a corporate tax; and

(3) both corporate taxes and extraordinary losses in bankruptcy are brought together to demonstrate why the optimal structure of a firm may not be at a corner.

Firm 1 has no debt, and its end-of-period total aftertax earnings, or more appropriately the end-of-period value of the firm as a going concern—that is, if it could continue to operate into the subsequent period—is symbolized by X, a random variable associated with cumulative distribution function $F(X)$. This X variable may assume negative values if, for example, business losses are so large that the firm cannot cover the wages owed its employees. Firm 2 is identical to firm 1 except that it has debt. This levered firm attaches to each bond a dollar coupon payment of C such that the bond is issued at a market price equal to its face or par value of \$1000. C may vary with the amount of debt in the capital structure of the firm as measured by its debt–equity ratio. Because we assume that the firm can deduct these coupon payments prior to computing its tax bill, the aftertax earnings of firm 2 amounts to $X + tnC$, where t and n respectively denote the corporate tax rate and the number of bonds the firm has outstanding.

Since these bonds comprise a senior lien on the earnings of the firm, failure to pay the promised amount $[n(C + 10^3)]$ to these senior security holders can force liquidation of the assets of the firm. This statement translates into the mathematical condition that if

$$X + tnC < nC + n10^3 \tag{1}$$

or

$$X < n[(1 - t)C + 10^3], \tag{1a}$$

then bankruptcy occurs and the creditors of the firm force liquidation.

We assume that liquidation entails extraordinary costs to the firm, e.g. the loss of its going-concern value or losses due to having to sell its assets "too quickly." Given that the state of the firm is characterized by (1a), bankruptcy, and furthermore given that $X > 0$, then the firm suffers liquidation kX, where $0 < k \leq 1$, and receives a net amount of $(1 - k)X$—plus tnC if the firm is levered. Since the firm cannot assess its shareholders if $X < 0$, then $X \leq 0$ implies $(1 - k)X = 0$.

A. Extraordinary Bankruptcy Losses—No Taxes

In a world of no taxes and extraordinary bankruptcy losses, it is easy to show that the unlevered firm commands a premium in total market value over the levered firm, i.e. V_1 must exceed V_2. We do so by demonstrating that if $V_1 = V_2$, then purchasing fraction α of firm 1 results in dollar return

$$Y_1 = \begin{cases} 0 & \text{if } X \leq 0, \\ \alpha X & \text{if } X > 0, \end{cases}$$

with cumulative probability distribution

$$G_1(Y) = \begin{cases} F(0) & \text{if } Y = 0, \\ F(Y/\alpha) & \text{if } Y > 0, \end{cases}$$

that stochastically dominates on a first-degree basis an equal dollar investment in firm 2, resulting in the ownership of fraction α of the equity of firm 2 and the same fraction α of its debt, yielding dollar return,

$$Y_2 = \begin{cases} 0 & \text{if } X \leq 0, \\ \alpha(1-k)X & \text{if } 0 < X < n(C + 10^3), \\ \alpha X & \text{if } X \geq n(C + 10^3), \end{cases}$$

with cumulative distribution

$$G_2(Y) = \begin{cases} F(0) & \text{if } Y = 0, \\ F[Y/\alpha(1-k)] & \text{if } 0 < Y < \alpha n(C + 10^3), \\ F(Y/\alpha) & \text{if } Y \geq \alpha n(C + 10^3). \end{cases}$$

This is obvious once $G_1(Y)$ and $G_2(Y)$ are plotted on the same diagram (see Figure 1).

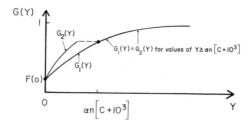

FIGURE 1   Extraordinary bankruptcy losses—no taxes.

B.   Taxes—No Extraordinary Bankruptcy Losses

In this case, it is simple to show that the levered firm must command a premium in total market value over the unlevered firm, i.e. $V_1 < V_2$, the M&M Proposition I when a corporate tax rate enters their perfect capital market framework (see Hadar and Russell, 1969). The proof follows the mode of Section A by demonstrating that if $V_1 = V_2$, then purchasing α of the total value of firm 1 results in a dollar return to the investor of

$$Y_1 = \begin{cases} 0 & \text{if } X \le 0, \\ \alpha X & \text{if } X > 0, \end{cases}$$

with corresponding cumulative distribution

$$G_1(Y) = \begin{cases} F(0) & \text{if } Y = 0, \\ F(Y/\alpha) & \text{if } Y > 0, \end{cases}$$

that in this case is first-degree stochastically dominated by an equivalent dollar investment in the levered firm resulting in dollar return—given that interest expense of nC can be sold for tnC, but that such proceeds must first be used to pay priority obligations such as wages before they can be distributed to bondholders—of

$$Y_2 = \begin{cases} 0 & \text{if } X \le -tnC \\ \alpha(X + tnC) & \text{if } -tnC < X \le 0, \\ \alpha(X + tnC) & \text{if } 0 < X, \end{cases}$$

with corresponding probability distribution of

$$G_2(Y) = \begin{cases} F(-tnC) & \text{if } Y = 0, \\ F[(Y/\alpha) - tnC] & \text{for } Y > 0. \end{cases}$$

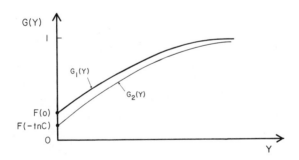

FIGURE 2   Taxes—no extraordinary bankruptcy losses.

Again a graph of $G_1(Y)$ and $G_2(Y)$ makes the result apparent (see Figure 2). Note there is a limit on the amount of debt the firm may issue. Obviously it cannot raise more debt than it has capital, but more likely it cannot issue so much debt that the expected value of its income stream is less than interest plus principal owed.

C. Taxes and Extraordinary Bankruptcy Losses

Let n_m be any maximum number of bonds, that is, n_m represents a *corner capital structure point*; we will then demonstrate that when both t and k are simultaneously considered, the cumulative return distribution $G_m(Y)$ associated with n_m does not dominate on a first-degree basis, nor does it not necessarily dominate on a second-degree basis the distribution $G_L(Y)$ associated with a lower amount of debt n_L, which represents an interior capital structure point. The implication of this result is that there may exist groups of investors with von Neumann–Morgenstern utility functions that prefer the smaller amount of debt n_L to the maximum n_m, that is an interior capital structure point may be optimal. To prove this, we will show that $G_m(Y)$ and $G_L(Y)$ cross at least twice.

The general expression for $G(Y)$, taking into account both k and t, is

$$G(Y) = \begin{cases} F(-tnC) & \text{for} \quad X \le -tnC \quad \text{and} \quad Y = 0, \\[6pt] F[(Y/\alpha) - tnC] & \text{for} \quad -tnC < X \le 0 \\ & \qquad \text{and} \quad 0 < Y \le \alpha tnC, \\[6pt] F([(Y/\alpha) - tnC](1-k)^{-1}) & \text{for} \quad 0 < X < n[(1-t)C + 10^3] \\ & \qquad \text{and} \quad \alpha tnC < Y \\ & \qquad < \alpha(1-k)n[(1-t)C + 10^3] \\ & \qquad + \alpha tnC, \\[6pt] F[(Y/\alpha) - tnC] & \text{for} \quad X \ge n[(1-t)C + 10^3] \\ & \qquad \text{and} \quad Y \ge \alpha n[C + 10^3], \end{cases}$$

(2)

where C, as usual, denotes the coupon payment necessary to sell an amount of n bonds at their par value, $1000.

Given (2), we now can turn to a comparison of cumulative distribution $G_m(Y)$ associated with n_m bonds and corresponding coupon C_m and cumulative distribution $G_L(Y)$ associated with n_L bonds and corresponding coupon C_L. Since by assumption $n_m > n_L$, then $C_m \ge C_L$. This follows because the maximum amount that bondholders can obtain is the coupon plus $1000, while the probability of losing all or part of that amount increases with n.[3] Normally one would assume that bondholders would expect extra compensation for the increased chance of loss, i.e. $C_m > C_L$ (this would hold even if the bondholder were risk neutral simply to keep the expected payment of each bond at the old level); however, we need make only the weaker assumption of $C_m \ge C_L$.

---

[3] Recall that the X distribution is given; therefore, raising n increases the probability of $X < n[C(1-t) + 10^3]$.

The above reasoning implies that

$$n_L C_L < n_m C_m \tag{3}$$

and there is some $\delta > 0$ such that

$$n_L C_L (1 + \delta) = n_m C_m, \tag{3a}$$

where the size of δ is determined as a function of the difference between n_m and n_L, and of course the difference between C_m and C_L which in turn is a direct function of the difference $n_m - n_L$. Since we assume that $n_m - n_L$ can be made arbitrarily small, so can δ.

We now *consider three distinct levels of* $G(Y)$ and compare at each level the Y value, label it Y_m, that satisfies $G_m(Y) = G(Y)$ with the Y value, label it Y_L, that satisfies $G_L(Y) = G(Y)$.

(1) Consider $G(Y) = F(-tn_L C_L)$. For the firm with n_L bonds,

$$G_L(Y) = F(-tn_L C_L) \qquad \text{at} \quad Y_L = 0,$$

while for the firm with n_m bonds,

$$G_m(Y) = F(-tn_L C_L) \qquad \text{at } Y_m > 0,$$

since at $Y_m = 0$, $G_m(Y) = F(-tn_m C_m) < F(-tn_L C_L)$ by (3). Therefore at $G(Y) = F(-tn_L C_L)$, $Y_m > Y_L = 0$ and the $G_m(Y)$ function lies to the right of the $G_L(Y)$ at this given probability value.

(2) Consider $G(Y) = F(n_L[(1 - t)C_L + 10^3])$. Then for the firm with n_L bonds,

$$G_L(Y) = F(n_L[(1 - t)C_L + 10^3])$$

at

$$Y_L = \alpha n_L[(1 - t)C_L + 10^3] + \alpha t n_L C_L.$$

However, given that $X = n_L[(1 - t)C_L + 10^3]$ means bankruptcy for the firm with n_m bonds, we obtain

$$G_m(Y) = F(n_L[(1 - t)C_L + 10^3])$$

at

$$Y_m = \alpha(1 - k)n_L[(1 - t)C_L + 10^3] + \alpha t n_m C_m,$$

or using (3a),

$$Y_m = \alpha(1 - k)n_L[(1 - t)C_L + 10^3] + \alpha t(1 + \delta)n_L C_L.$$

Then at this selected $G(Y)$ level $Y_m - Y_L = -\alpha n_L[k(1 - t)C_L + 10^3] + \alpha t \delta n_L C_L$. Given $t < 1$, there exists a $\delta > 0$ small enough such that $Y_m - Y_L < 0$, or equivalently at $G(Y) = F(n_L[(1 - t)C_L + 10^3])$ the $G_L(Y)$ function now

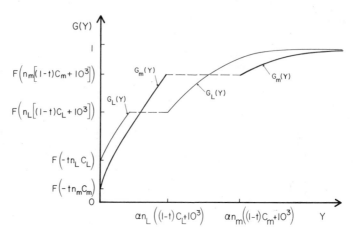

FIGURE 3　The possibility of a noncorner optimal capital structure.

lies to the right of the $G_m(Y)$ function; therefore we have proved that these two functions have crossed between $Y = 0$ and $Y = \alpha n_L[C_L + 10^3]$.

(3)　Consider $G(Y) = F(n_m[(1 - t)C_m + 10^3])$. Then

$$G_L(Y) = F(n_m[(1 - t)C_m + 10^3])$$

at

$$Y_L = \alpha n_m[(1 - t)C_m + 10^3] + \alpha t n_L C_L,$$

while

$$G_m(Y) = F(n_m[(1 - t)C_m + 10^3]) \quad \text{at} \quad Y_m = \alpha n_m[C_m + 10^3].$$

But at this specific $G(Y)$ value, $Y_m - Y_L = \alpha t[n_m C_m - n_L C_L] > 0$ by (3), which means that at $G(Y) = F(n_m[(1 - t)C_m + 10^3])$, the $G_m(Y)$ function now lies to the right of the $G_L(Y)$ function; therefore we have proved that these two functions have crossed between $Y = \alpha n_L[C_L + 10^3]$ and $Y = \alpha n_m[C_m + 10^3]$. The above analysis is summarized graphically in Figure 3.

Before concluding the analysis we should consider the question of optimal structure when interest losses cannot be sold for their tax value when bankruptcy occurs. Using the notation of (2) we see that

$$G(Y) = \begin{cases} F(0) & \text{for } X \leq 0 \text{ and } Y = 0, \\ F[Y/\alpha(1 - k)] & \text{for } 0 \leq X < n(C + 10^3) \\ & \text{and } 0 < Y < \alpha(1 - k)n[C + 10^3], \\ F[(Y/\alpha) - tnC] & \text{for } n(C + 10^3) \leq X \\ & \text{and } \alpha n[C + 10^3] \leq Y. \end{cases}$$

$$(4)$$

The $G(Y)$ distribution given in (4) again applies to the general firm, with $k = 0$ and $n = 0$ for an unlevered firm.

To make this closing point as simply as possible, let us consider two firms: one levered, L, and one unlevered, u. Then from (4) we see that at $Y = 0$, $G_L(Y) = G_u(Y) = F(0)$, but as Y increases above zero, $G_L(Y) > G_u(Y)$ since $k > 0$ for the levered firm. At $Y > \alpha n(C + 10^3)$, the critical income level for bankruptcy, $G_L(Y)$ shifts below $G_u(Y)$ since the levered firm that remains solvent receives an added amount of tnC. Figure 4 portrays the relation between $G_L(Y)$ and $G_u(Y)$. We can see that in this case, where interest losses cannot be sold during bankruptcy, the levered firm cannot dominate the unlevered firm on a first- or second-degree stochastic dominance basis. Similarly, the unlevered firm cannot dominate the levered firm because the expected return of the levered firm is higher than that of the unlevered (otherwise why lever?), and because the $G_L(Y)$ and $G_u(Y)$ curves intersect only once (see Hanoch and Levy (1969), Theorem 3).

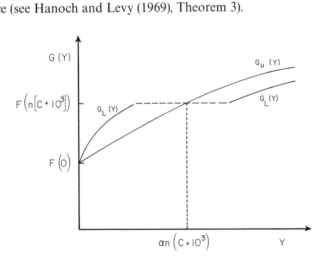

FIGURE 4 The possibility of a noncorner optimal capital structure—no sale of interest losses during bankruptcy.

Therefore a general statement cannot be made with respect to the value of debt or the amount of debt that a firm should issue. Firms that find leverage optimal have security holders whose particular utility functions and *subjective probability distributions* indicate that leverage is beneficial.

3. ANALYSIS WITH A LINEAR UTILITY FUNCTION

To demonstrate that there are probability distributions of earnings for which an interior capital structure is optimal for the firm, consider the following scenario. A new corporation is to be formed which promises an end-of-period dollar return before interest and taxes of X with cumulative distribution function $F(X)$ and is to be financed by some combination of common stock and bonds. The objective of the firm is to offer for sale that combination of debt and equity that will maximize the value of this new firm. Assume that all market participants are risk neutral, and that the risk-free rate of return is r; then the market value of the issued shares is the expected value of X, less what is expected to be paid to bondholders and in taxes, discounted at the risk-free rate of r. The decision variables of the firm are the number of risky bonds n that it chooses to issue and the coupon payment $C > r(1000)$ that we assume, without loss of generality, it attaches to each bond in order for it to sell at its face value of $\$1000$.

We state the problem in terms of the end-of-period *aftertax cash flow* X_e *of an all-equity firm*, where the relation that X_e bears to X for the all-equity firm is

$$X_e = X + \text{depreciation} - \text{taxes} + \left(\begin{array}{c}\text{receipts from end-of-period}\\ \text{dissolution of the firm}\end{array}\right),$$

where X_e has cumulative distribution function $G(X_e)$ and density function $g(X_e)$. For the levered firm, aftertax cash flows are equal to the unlevered receipts X_e plus the savings arising from the tax deductibility of interest tnC.

The objective of the firm, maximization of its market value V, is given by

$$V^* = \text{maximum } V$$

$$= \max_{n,C} \frac{1}{(1+r)} \left[\int_{n(10^3 + C(1-t))}^{\infty} (X_e - n(10^3 + C(1-t)))\, dG(X_e) \right] + n \cdot 10^3,$$

$$(5)$$

where V^* denotes the maximum V value. The first term within the brackets represents the present value of funds expected to accrue to shareholders. The cash flow to shareholders of $[X_e - n(10^3 + C(1-t))]$ is obtained by reducing the firm's total aftertax cash flow of $X_e + tnC$ by payments to bondholders of $n(10^3 + C)$. The lower limit of the integral is explained by the fact that when X_e equals $n(10^3 + C(1-t))$, the cash flow of the levered firm is $n(10^3 + C(1-t)) + tnC = n(10^3 + C)$. Thus this lower limit is that value that X_e must attain before bondholders receive the interest and principal promised to them and stockholders begin to realize a positive return on their investment.[4] The second term of (5) gives the present market value of the

---

[4] Limited liability means that this term accounts for all possible shareholder returns, since they cannot be assesed for payments if the firm earns less than that required to meet its debt obligations.

debt of the firm. Therefore the sum of terms in (5) equals the total market value of the firm V.

Equation (5), however, represents only part of the model, that part which details the aspirations of the firm if it is to act in the best interests of its stockholders. But bondholders' interests must be explicitly represented in this model, for when there is a positive probability of default, bondholders can no longer be considered as passive participants in the decision model of the firm. The prospective, risk-neutral bondholder judges the attractiveness of the bonds of this firm in light of the returns that he could obtain in an alternative investment, the purchase of a riskless bond for $1000 that is certain to pay $(1 + r) \cdot 10^3$ dollars at the end of the period. Consequently, bondholders act to satisfy the constraint

$$n(1 + r)10^3 = \int_{n(10^3 + C(1-t))}^{\infty} [n(C + 10^3)] \, dG(X_e)$$
$$+ \int_0^{n(10^3 + C(1-t))} [X_e(1 - k) + tnC] \, dG(X_e). \tag{6}$$

The first term on the right hand side of (6) is the contribution to expected dollar return if the firm generates a high enough X_e value to avoid bankruptcy; the second term represents the contribution to expected dollar return if the firm defaults on its bond payments, i.e., if $X_e + tnC < n(C + 10^3)$, where $-kX_e$, with $0 \le k \le 1$, is deducted from the cash flows of the firm to account for the fact that bakruptcy involves the extraordinary costs previously outlined.

If we add the constraint that ex ante the firm is expected to meet its promise to debt holders, then the constraint

$$n[C(1 - t) + 10^3] \le \int_0^{\infty} X_e \, dG(X_e) \tag{7}$$

must be added to (5) and (6). We complete the mathematical formulation of the financial decision problem of the firm by noting that for a solution to be feasible it must also satisfy

$$n \ge 0 \quad \text{and} \quad C \ge 0. \tag{8}$$

The importance of constraint (7) to our model cannot be overemphasized. Consider the objective function (5). Its first term is a nonnegative decreasing function of n, while its second term is unbounded from above with respect to n. Note equation (6) imposes no restriction on the size of n, because it can always be satisfied by raising C. Because tC, the receipts in bankruptcy essentially provided by the government, increases with C, as C rises to higher and higher levels management is essentially dooming the firm to a bankrupt state yet promising an expected rate of return r that the government is committed to paying. Since the tax authorities would not be so naive as to allow such behavior, we must place an upper limit on the number of bonds to be issued, and the most reasonable upper bond is that determined by the ability of the firm to meet its debt obligations from expected returns. Thus the rationale for (7).

An alternative to constraint (7) is to assume that the government allows the tax deductibility of bond interest only for the going concern and prohibits the bankrupt firm from this right. Instead of (6) we then have

$$n(1 + r)10^3 = \int_{n(10^3 + C)}^{\infty} [n(C + 10^3)] \, dG(X_e)$$

$$+ \int_0^{n(10^3 + C)} (1 - k)X_e \, dG(X_e). \tag{6a}$$

(The lower limit on the integral in (5) is accordingly altered to $n[C + 10^3]$.) Constraint (6a) eliminates the need for constraint (7). We find in our numerical analysis that using (6a) leads to the same general conclusions as (6) and (7), although slightly different numerical results are obtained (see footnote b of Table I). Therefore only the results that correspond to (6) and (7) are presented.

Before we set about obtaining a solution for the capital structure problem given in (5)–(8), we wish to point out an alternative and rather interesting way to view the question of an optimal debt–equity ratio. Suppose the firm (stockholders) and bondholders form a coalition whose goal is to select a capital structure that will maximize the expected receipts of the coalition from the outside world, Z, in excess of what is provided by income stream X_e. In our framework there are two sources of such receipts:

(1)   the government's tax subsidy on the coupon payment, and
(2)   the cost of reorganization or loss from liquidation.

Consequently, the objective function of the coalition is given by

$$Z^* = \text{maximum } Z = \max_{n,C} \left[ntC - k \cdot \int_0^{n(10^3 + C(1 - t))} X_e \, dG(X_e) \right], \tag{9}$$

subject to the market forces expressed in constraint (6) and the feasibility conditions (7) and (8).

The equations for our two problems appear intractable to a mathematical solution. Nevertheless we can simulate the problem by assuming a specific distribution for $g(X_e)$ and varying the values of the k and t parameters to obtain numerical solutions. These provide an understanding of the forms that the general solutions to our problems take and the importance of roles played by k and t in the solutions. We assume that X_e obeys the binomial

TABLE I

Variable Values at Optimal Point

Column:	I	II	III	IV	V	VI	VII[a] Maximum n	VIII Corresponding V values
	k	t	n^*	V^*	Z^*	C^*	n	V
	1.00	0.5	51	$67,846.	$1179.	$51.5	58	$66,055.
	0.50[b]	0.5	53	67,879.	1211	52.0	60	66,370.
	0.50	0.0	0	66,667.	0	50.0	—	—
	0.25	0.5	55	67,915.	1246	53.0	63	66,388.
	0.00	0.5	67	69,398.	2495	73.0	67	—
	0.00	0.0	No significant differences between V values at various n					

[a] The reader is reminded that each number in column VII must be the maximum number of bonds that the firm may issue when faced with a specific (k, t) pair, i.e., satisfy constraint (7), yet produce a C value that together with this maximum n value satisfy market constraint (6). The C values that satisfy constraint (6) for the corresponding maximum n values of column VII are not shown in this table, but it is important to understand that these C values are not equal to those given in column VI which are labeled C^*, i.e., the optimal values.

[b] We solved equation (5) subject to constraint (6a) rather than (6) and (7) with $k = .5$, $t = .5$, and the same probability distribution used to construct Table I. The optimal n^*, V^*, and Z^* values were somewhat less than the corresponding values given in the second line of Table I.

distribution; that is,

$$g(X_e) = \binom{m}{l} p^l q^{m-l},$$

where m denotes the maximum value that X_e can take and l assumes integer values such that $0 \le l \le m$. The probability p may be interpreted as the probability that the unlevered income of the firm will increase from l to $l + 1$.

Assume the specific values $m = 140{,}000$, $p = q = .5$, and $r = .05$; then

$$E(X_e) = 70{,}000$$

and its present value is

$$\frac{1}{(1.05)}(70{,}000) = 66{,}667.$$

For various combinations of k and t values, the corresponding V^* and Z^* values are presented in Table I.

Roughly speaking we can say, ceteris paribus, that the optimal value n^* varies directly with t and inversely with k. In addition, it appears that the n^* value varies inversely with the variance of X_e.[5] These conclusions are quite reasonable. The desirability of adding an additional dollar of debt is dependent on the benefit derived from the tax subsidy on interest payments compared to the increase in the probability of bankruptcy and its attendant costs—the probability and costs depending on the size of k, the form of $g(X_e)$, and of course n. The optimal number of bonds n^* is determined by the equality at the margin of these two forces. For several pairs of (k, t) values, the variation of V versus n^* is depicted in Figure 5.

Other characteristics of the problems' solutions can be deduced from Table I:

(a)   When $k, t > 0$, the optimal solution reveals that n assumes an interior value, i.e., a noncorner optimal debt–equity ratio. On the other hand, if either k or t equals zero, a corner solution becomes optimal. Specifically, if

---

[5] A verbal proof suffices. Consider equation (6). If the variance of X_e increases, then the probability of incurring the extraordinary losses associated with bankruptcy increases; but then to satisfy the wealth constraint (6) the firm may either lower n^* or raise C^*. If it chooses to lower n^*, then that is consistent with the statement in the text. Suppose instead it elects to raise C^* in order to keep constraint (6) satisfied, but then equation (5) explicitly shows that raising C^* will lower V; to mitigate the deleterious effects on V of raising C^*, the firm lowers n^*. Consequently, either course of action dictates a reduction of n^* in response to an increase in the variance of X_e.

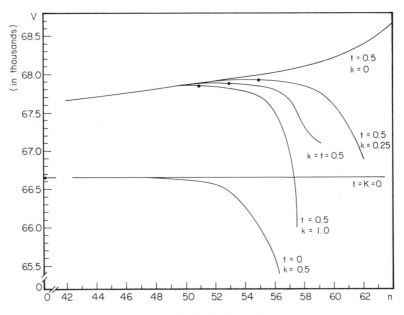

FIGURE 5 Simulation results.

$k > 0$ and $t = 0$, then $n^* = 0$; if $k = 0$ and $t > 0$, then n^* equals the maximum allowable under constraint (7).[6]

(b) The two objective functions (5) and (9) subject to the same constraint set (6)–(8) yield identical n^* values. Moreover, the Z^* value, the expected gain of stockholders and bondholders colluding against the outside world, is nothing but V^* less the V value at $n = 0$, the difference being the increase in the market value of the firm resulting from leverage.[7] Consequently, for $k = .5$ and $t = .5$, the difference between V^* and V at $n = 0$ is \$67,879 − \$66,667 = \$1212 while maximum Z value is \$1211.

Solving our two problems for values k and t other than those listed in Table I gives results that conform to the general pattern depicted in Table I

---

[6] The optimality of the corner solutions under such conditions is quite evident in the collusion problem, equations (9), (6), (7), and (8). First with $t > 0$ and $k = 0$, the objective function of the coalition reduces to tnC. Clearly, since by (6) higher n implies higher C, maximum feasible n gives maximum tnC. Second, with $t = 0$ and $k > 0$, equation (9) reduces to

$$-k \int_0^{n(10^3 + C_d(1 - t))} X_e \, dG(X_e);$$

its maximum is achieved by setting $n^* = 0$.

[7] The numbers of $k = 0$ and $t = .5$ do not fit this conclusion as well because of rounding errors in the computations.

and already discussed. Similar results are obtained for a nonsymmetric binomial. With $t = .5$, $k = .5$, and a nonsymmetric binomial distribution ($p \neq .5$), a pair of solutions is presented in Table II.

Other distributions alter the results and corresponding conclusions. If X_e is assumed to obey a triangular distribution with mean and range identical to the binomial used to generate Table I, that is,

$$g(X_e) = \begin{cases} \dfrac{1}{70,000} X_e & \text{for} \quad 0 \leq X_e < 70,000, \\[3mm] \dfrac{2}{70,000}\left(1 - \dfrac{X_e}{140,000}\right) & \text{for} \quad 70,000 \leq X_e \leq 140,000, \\[3mm] 0 & \text{for} \quad \text{all other } X_e \text{ values,} \end{cases}$$

and $t = .5$, $k = .5$, then $n^* = 59$ and $V^* = 68,300$. However, V^* does not vary significantly in the interval $n = [51, 60]$. Considering the information provided by constraint (7) which tells us that $n \leq 52$, the optimal solution is essentially a corner solution.

The important difference between the solutions for the binomial and triangular distributions is that for the binomial after a given capital structure is reached a sharp rise in the probability of bankruptcy occurs, forcing the firm to curtail its use of debt just prior to reaching this point, i.e., an interior point is selected. On the other hand, for the triangular distribution the probability of bankruptcy becomes significant at low n values with no dramatic rise in the probability of bankruptcy as debt is increased, thus the tendency to select a corner point. Finally, if a rectangular distribution is used, corner solutions are invariably attained for all k,t combinations.

TABLE II

Variable Values at Optimal Point for a Nonsymmetric Binomial Distribution

$(k = .5$ and $t = .5)$

P	$[\int_0^\infty X_e dG(X_e)]/(1 + r)$	n^*	V^*	C^*	Maximum n
.75	$100,000	87	$102,000	$50.9	95
.25	$33,333	23	$33,800	$55.3	28

4. CONCLUDING REMARKS

Some market observations are consistent with the preceding model. In line with the conclusions of our model, firms with low income variability, such as utilities, carry high debt–equity ratios. Firms that have highly marketable assets and therefore low liquidation costs—low k, such as shipping lines, seem to rely heavily on debt financing relative to equity. On the other hand, a loan to finance an investment in human capital, an asset whose resale value in case of loan default is nil, is hard to come by.

REFERENCES

Baron, D. (1974). Default Risk, Homemade Leverage, and the Modigliani–Miller Theorem, *American Economic Review* **64** (March), 176–182.

Coase, R. (1952). The Nature of the Firm, in *AER Readings in Price Theory* (G. Stigler and K. Boulding, eds.), Homewood, Illinois: Irwin.

Diamond, P. (1967). The Role of a Stock Market in a General Equilibrium Model with Technological Uncertainty, *American Economic Review* **57** (September), 759–776.

Hadar, J., and Russell, W. (1969). Rule for Ordering Uncertain Prospects, *American Economic Review* **59** (March), 25–34.

Hanoch, G., and Levy, H. (1969). The Efficiency Analysis of Choices Involving Risk, *Review of Economic Studies* **36** (July), 335–346.

Modigliani, F., and Miller, M. (1958). The Cost of Capital, Corporate Finance and the Theory of Investment, *American Economic Review* **48** (June), 261–297.

Modigliani, F., and Miller, M. (1963). Corporate Income Taxes and the Cost of Capital: A Correction, *American Economic Review* **53** (June), 433–442.

Mossin, J. (1966). Equilibrium in a Capital Asset Market, *Econometrica* **34** (October), 768–783.

Smith, V. (1972). Default Risk, Scale and the Homemade Leverage Theorem, *American Economic Review* **62** (March), 66–76.

Stiglitz, J. (1969). A Re-examination of the Modigliani–Miller Theorem, *American Economic Review* **59** (December), 784–793.

Stiglitz, J. (1972). Some Aspects of the Pure Theory of Corporate Finance; Bankruptcies and Takeovers, *Bell Journal of Economics and Management Science* **3** (Autumn), 458–482.

Price discrimination under uncertainty

ROGER D. BLAIR

ARNOLD A. HEGGESTAD

UNIVERSITY OF FLORIDA
GAINESVILLE

1. INTRODUCTION

The effects of price discrimination have been extensively analyzed in the economics literature. Primarily theoretical, these analyses have investigated the influence of price discrimination upon output and upon profitability when demand and cost functions are known with certainty.[1] It would be of interest to extend this prior work by examining the consequences of uncertainty for the price discriminating firm.[2] In this essay, we initially analyze the case of a monopolist facing random demand functions in separable markets for its product. Confronted with uncertainty, we assume that the goal of the firm is the maximization of expected utility. It is well known that this objective allows the treatment of differing attitudes toward risk by management. Under these assumptions, we show that the traditional price discrimination solution

Financial support from the Center for Public Policy Research at the University of Florida is gratefully acknowledged. Certainly without implicating them for any shortcomings in this paper, we must acknowledge the benefits derived from our discussions with Fred Arditti and Haim Levy.

[1] See e.g. Robinson (1933), Clemens (1951), and Simkin (1947).

[2] Since writing this essay, Meyer (1976) has been published. This article deals, in part, with price discrimination under stochastic conditions, but specifies a different objective function for the firm. The qualitative conclusions of Meyer (1976) and the present essay, however, are similar.

is a special case. More specifically, price differences between markets result from the differential riskiness of markets and the degree of risk aversion of the firm, as well as from differences in the price elasticity of demand.

Subsequently, we examine our results for exponential utility functions. This analysis demonstrates the direct effect of risk exposure in determining relative prices across separable markets. Moreover, it allows us to examine the standard result of the effect of price discrimination on output when demand curves are linear. Finally, we consider the implications of these results for antitrust analysis. Under the Robinson–Patman Act, firms are allowed to discriminate if price differences are cost justified. We briefly examine the problem of interpretation of this law under uncertainty when some costs are real, but subjective, to the firm.

2. THE NONSTOCHASTIC CASE

We shall consider a firm that is able to identify n distinct markets for its output. In such circumstances, one should suspect that the firm may find that price discrimination is a profitable course of action. Generally, the major obstacle to successful price discrimination is the necessity of keeping at least two of the n markets separated. In other words, arbitrage must be prevented. If this requirement is fulfilled, the firm may determine (in principle) the optimal quantity that should be allocated to each of the n markets in order to maximize profit.

Assume that the firm faces the following inverse demand functions:

$$P_i = P_i(Q_i) \qquad (i = 1, 2, \ldots, n), \tag{1}$$

where P_i and Q_i denote the price and quantity in the ith market. We shall assume that $P_i(Q_i) \neq P_j(Q_j)$, in general.[3] We envision that the total output is generated by a single production process, which is nonstochastic. For simplicity, we shall ignore the costs associated with keeping the n markets separated.[4] Thus, we shall define the total cost function of the firm as

$$C(Q) = c(Q_1 + \cdots + Q_n). \tag{2}$$

The objective function of the firm can then be expressed as

$$\pi = \sum_{i=1}^{n} P_i(Q_i)Q_i - C(Q), \tag{3}$$

---

[3] It is quite possible that identicality may hold for some markets. At a minimum, however, the firm must be able to distinguish two markets.

[4] The firm, of course, will expend resources on preventing arbitrage between markets until the marginal return from this activity is equal to its marginal cost.

where π denotes profit. For an interior maximum of profit, the first-order conditions require

$$\frac{\partial \pi}{\partial Q_i} = P_i(Q_i) + Q_i \frac{\partial P_i(Q_i)}{\partial Q_i} - \frac{\partial C(Q)}{\partial Q} = 0 \tag{4}$$

for $i = 1, \ldots, n$ since $\partial Q / \partial Q_i = 1$. This, of course, yields the optimality rule that the firm should allocate its output such that the marginal cost of producing the total output is equal to the marginal revenue in each of the n separate markets.

The economic definition of price discrimination (as opposed to the legal definition) requires different price–cost ratios. Since we have suppressed all costs other than production costs, marginal cost is the same for each of the n markets. Thus, price differences alone will constitute price discrimination. In fact, such price differences will exist whenever demand elasticities vary across the n markets and the firm allocates output to maximize profit. From (4), we can write the first-order conditions as

$$P_i(1 + 1/\eta_i) - \partial C(Q)/\partial Q = 0 \qquad (i = 1, \ldots, n), \tag{5}$$

where η_i denotes the demand elasticity in the ith market. For every two markets i and j, the ratios of prices will depend solely on differences in the elasticity of demand:

$$P_i/P_k = (1 + 1/\eta_k)/(1 + 1/\eta_i). \tag{6}$$

This follows as a consequence of equating marginal revenue to a common marginal cost in each market.

3. THE OBJECTIVE OF THE FIRM UNDER UNCERTAINTY

There are a variety of ways one can introduce uncertainty into the price discrimination model. For example, one could assume that input prices[5] are random. This, in turn, would make the cost function random. Alternatively, one could permit some randomness in the production function of the firm.[6] This, of course, would mean that the quantity of the various inputs needed to generate a particular level of output is a random variable. Production function uncertainty, therefore, leads inexorably to randomness in the cost

---

[5] For some developments regarding random input prices, see Blair (1974a,b).

[6] This form of uncertainty has been discussed by Feldstein (1971) and Horowitz (1970). The influence of uncertainty on econometric methodology is touched upon by Blair (1974b), Blair and Lusky (1975), and Feldstein (1971).

function. Although such sources of randomness are significant, we shall abstract from these issues and focus on the influence of random demand. More specifically, we shall denote the random inverse demand functions by

$$P_i = P_i(Q_i, u_i) \qquad (i = 1, 2, \ldots, n), \tag{7}$$

where P_i and Q_i again represent the price and quantity in the ith market. The random variable u_i may enter the demand function additively with an expected value of zero, multiplicatively with an expected value of one, or in some more general manner. Since u_i is a random variable, P_i is also a random variable. It is assumed that each output price is distributed according to its own (subjective) density function $f_i(P_i)$ with mean $\bar{P}_i$. Finally, we assume that the P_i are independently, but not necessarily identically, distributed. This assumption is not wholly innocent, for without it the analysis would be far less tractable and the very possibility of price discrimination may be called into question. Nevertheless, this assumption is relaxed in our discussion of the exponential utility function. In any event, we find that the total revenue of the firm is a random variable. More precisely, total revenue R is the sum of n random variables:

$$R(Q) = \sum_{i=1}^{n} P_i(Q_i, u_i)Q_i. \tag{8}$$

We have assumed that the inputs of the firm are employed at deterministic prices and that the constraints imposed by the production function are nonstochastic. Thus, the cost function in (2) will suffice for the present analysis. The combination of (8) and (2) define the *random* profit π as

$$\pi = \sum_{i=1}^{n} P_i(Q_i, u_i)Q_i - C(Q). \tag{9}$$

We shall assume that production is not instantaneous. Thus, the firm must decide upon a production plan prior to observing the actual prices that will prevail in each market.[7] This assumption is not innocuous. If production were instantaneous, the firm could wait until the actual demand was observed in each market before producing the optimal total output. The influence of the random demands would then be to simply shift the demand functions. As Oi (1961) has shown, the output decision in each period would be the rather uninteresting one of selecting the output and

[7] It should be emphasized that we are considering quantity-setting behavior on the part of the firm. In the absence of uncertainty, there is clearly no distinction between price setters and quantity setters. Uncertainty, however, causes some difficulties in analyzing the behavior of a price setter. Moreover, the type of behavior requires instantaneous production. See Leland (1972) for a thorough analysis of the differences.

market allocation that maximizes short-run *nonstochastic* profit.[8] In any event, we shall proceed under the assumption that the firm will specify its output prior to observing the market prices. We also assume that output is highly perishable, i.e., output must be sold in the period in which it is produced. Thus, we view the firm as making an output and market allocation decision and subsequently selling that output for whatever price clears the market. This assumption, too, is not without some significance: we avoid a real world problem by assuming away inventory considerations.[9]

In principle, a firm need not behave in any fashion other than as an expected value maximizer. Since the owners of the firm can diversify their personal portfolios to obtain the preferred risk–return configuration, the management of the firm should strive to maximize the expected present value of the firm. This, in fact, is the model adopted by Meyer (1976). In this context, the managers would then attempt to maximize expected profit. Firm decision makers, however, may well be concerned with avoiding poor performance since control of the firm may lie with management rather than the owners. Moreover, the standard portfolio argument loses some of its force when one considers capital market imperfections and the possibility of bankruptcy. In this vein, we shall assume that the objective of the firm is to maximize the expected utility of profit. This formulation will accommodate nonneutral risk preferences:

$$E[U(\pi)] = E\left[U\left(\sum_{i=1}^{n} P_i(Q_i, u_i)Q_i - C(Q) \right) \right], \tag{10}$$

where E is the expectations operator and U denotes a von Neumann–Morgenstern utility function.

4. FIRST-ORDER CONDITIONS

To obtain the first-order conditions for the maximization of expected utility, differentiate (10) with respect to the Q_i:

$$\frac{\partial E[U(\pi)]}{\partial Q_i} = E\left[U'(\pi)\left(P_i + Q_i \frac{\partial P_i}{\partial Q_i} - \frac{\partial C(Q)}{\partial Q} \right) \right] = 0 \qquad (i = 1, 2, \ldots, n). \tag{11}$$

---

[8] The force of Oi's analysis was to show that random prices are desirable under the assumptions he made. That these assumptions are a bit extreme did not go unnoticed by Tisdell (1963).

[9] Turnovsky (1973) recognizes the polar nature of the most common models. He introduces production flexibility, which imposes added costs upon the firm. Unfortunately, the comparative static analysis becomes even more unwieldy in this context and many results become indeterminate.

The first-order conditions (11) can be rearranged as

$$E[U'(\pi)(P_i + Q_i \partial P_i/\partial Q_i)] - E[U'(\pi) \partial C(Q)/\partial Q] = 0, \qquad (12)$$

or written as

$$E[P_i + Q_i \partial P_i/\partial Q_i] - \partial C(Q)/\partial Q = \frac{-\text{cov}[U'(\pi), P_i + Q_i \partial P_i/\partial Q_i]}{E[U'(\pi)]}, \qquad (13)$$

where the numerator on the right-hand side of (13) represents the covariance between the marginal utility of profit and marginal revenue in the ith market.[10]

We should compare conditions (13) and the deterministic first-order conditions (4) to determine the influence of uncertainty. First, if the firm is risk neutral, the von Neumann–Morgenstern utility index is linear and $U'(\pi)$ is constant. Since the covariance between the marginal utility of profit $U'(\pi)$ and a random variable $P_i + Q_i \partial P_i/\partial Q_i$ is zero, the right-hand side of (13) will be zero for the risk-neutral firm. This yields the stochastic analog of the deterministic result in (4). The risk neutral firm should allocate its output among the n markets such that the marginal cost of production is equal to the expected marginal revenue in each market.

The stochastic analog of conditions (5) can readily be given. For the risk-neutral firm, we have

$$E[P_i](1 + 1/E[\eta_i]) - \partial C(Q)/\partial Q = 0. \qquad (14)$$

In this case, we must refer to *expected* price discrimination.[11] When markets are separated and demand is random within each market, one should expect ex post price differences to be the rule rather than the exception. For a risk-neutral firm, then, expected prices will be different when there are differences in expected elasticities. Since marginal production costs are the same for all markets, the expected price differences lead to ex ante expected price discrimination.

For the firm with nonneutral risk preferences, the right-hand side of (13) is not necessarily zero. The denominator of the term on the right is the expected marginal utility of profit, which is positive irrespective of risk preferences because the von Neumann–Morgenstern utility function is mono-

---

[10] Conditions (13) follow from (12) by a direct application of the definition of covariance: $\text{cov}[X, Y] = E[XY] - E[X]E[Y]$. It appears that Penner (1967) was the first to use this definition to obtain qualitative results.

[11] We assume that the demand function shifts up and down in some random, but parallel fashion. Thus, the slope of the demand function is not random, which makes the computation of expected elasticity possible.

tonically increasing. Thus, the sign of the right-hand side of (13) will be opposite that of the covariance term in the numerator. Since the firm we have been analyzing is a quantity setter, the price in each market remains random. We can determine the sign of the covariance by examining the effect of a change in the random variable P_i upon the marginal utility of profits and upon marginal revenue. Differentiating $U'(\pi)$ with respect to P_i yields $U''(\pi)\, \partial\pi/\partial P_i$. It is clear that $\partial\pi/\partial P_i$ is positive, i.e., a random increase in the ith market will have a favorable impact upon profit. The sign of $U''(\pi)$, however, depends upon attitudes toward risk. Firms that are risk averse are characterized by concave utility functions, i.e., $U''(\pi)$ is negative for the risk-averse firm. In contrast, $U''(\pi)$ is positive for the risk preferring firm. Thus, $\partial U'(\pi)/\partial P_i$ is negative for the risk averse firm and positive for the risk-preferring firm. Since the derivative of marginal revenue with respect to P_i is positive, the covariance on the right-hand side of (13) is positive for the risk-preferring firm and negative for the risk-averse firm. This, of course, means that the right-hand side of (13) is positive for the risk-averse firm and negative for the risk-preferring firm.

In fact, we ought to expect these qualitative results. For the risk-averse firm, expected marginal revenue in each market will exceed marginal production costs at the optimum. As a matter of intuition, this clearly makes sense. The risk-averse quantity setter guards against overproduction by selecting a smaller output than that which equates expected marginal revenue to marginal production cost. The opposite qualitative conclusion holds for the risk-preferring firm: optimal output is greater than that which equates expected marginal revenue to marginal production cost. We see in the first-order conditions that these differences are due to the covariance term. A better understanding of these results can be obtained from a utility interpretation of the preceding model because it provides an economic interpretation of the covariance term.[12]

Consider the risk premium defined by Pratt (1964). In the context of our model, the risk premium Z is defined by

$$U(E[\pi] - Z) = E[U(\pi)], \tag{15}$$

i.e., the risk premium Z is the amount by which expected profit can be reduced and still leave the decision maker indifferent between that certain amount and the uncertain profit. For a risk-averse decision maker, Z must be positive. The larger the value of the risk premium, the greater the compensation must

---

[12] Baron (1970) did this for a single product firm operating in one market with random demand. Blair (1974a) did the same thing for a single product, multi-input firm facing random input prices.

be to offset the utility loss of accepting the uncertain prospect. We can differentiate the left-hand side of (15) with respect to the Q_i and evaluate at the optimum:

$$U'(E[\pi] - Z)(E[P_i + Q_i \, \partial P_i/\partial Q_i]$$
$$- \partial C/\partial Q - \partial Z/\partial Q_i) = 0 \qquad (i = 1, 2, \ldots, n). \qquad (16)$$

Since the marginal utility is always positive by hypothesis, at the optimum it must be true that

$$E[P_i + Q_i \, \partial P_i/\partial Q_i] - \partial C/\partial Q - \partial Z/\partial Q_i = 0 \qquad (i = 1, 2, \ldots, n). \qquad (17)$$

Moreover, from the first-order conditions (13), we can infer that (17) implies

$$\frac{\partial Z}{\partial Q_i} = \frac{-\text{cov}[U'(\pi), P_i + Q_i \, \partial P_i/\partial Q_i]}{E[U'(\pi)]} \qquad (i = 1, 2, \ldots, n). \qquad (18)$$

In other words, the rate of change in the risk premium for each market equals the covariance term. Since we know from our preceding discussion that the sign of the right-hand side of (18) is determined by the attitude of the firm toward risk, we can ascertain that the changes in the risk premium also depend upon attitudes toward risk. Specifically, for the risk-averse firm, the risk premium is an increasing function of output in the ith market. For the risk taker, the risk premium is a decreasing function of output.

The risk premium can be viewed as the payment necessary for a decision maker to accept a given risk. Thus, the first-order conditions (13) require that expected marginal revenue in each market *exceed* marginal production cost by the marginal impact on the firm's risk premium of dealing in that market. This latter "cost" is subjective and observable only by inference as a residual. Nonetheless, the marginal (utility) cost of bearing risk must be recognized in the discussion of price discrimination.

At the optimum, the marginal cost of production, $\partial C(Q)/\partial Q$, is constant across all markets. The marginal (utility) cost of bearing risk, however, can vary across markets. Thus, the first-order conditions (13) for a risk-averse firm can be written as

$$E[P_i](1 + 1/E[\eta_i]) - \partial C(Q)/\partial Q = \partial Z/\partial Q_i \qquad (i = 1, 2, \ldots, n), \qquad (19)$$

and *expected* price discrimination depends upon more than differences in *expected* elasticities. In fact, identical demand functions can lead to different expected prices even with equal marginal production costs and expected demand elasticities due to differences in marginal impacts upon the risk premium.

5. SOME RESULTS FOR AN EXPONENTIAL UTILITY FUNCTION

The exponential utility function provides a vehicle for obtaining some more concrete results for the price discriminating firm. Moreover, it allows a relatively convenient relaxation of the assumption that the various markets are stochastically independent. Thus, in this section, assume that the von Neumann–Morgenstern utility function of the firm is given by

$$U(\pi) = -e^{-\alpha\pi} \qquad (\alpha > 0). \tag{20}$$

It is well-known that α is the Pratt–Arrow index of absolute risk aversion,[13] which is constant for the exponential utility function. Constant absolute risk aversion implies that the *scale* of profit does not influence the willingness of the firm to bear risk. Although decreasing absolute risk aversion is much more appealing intuitively, constant absolute risk aversion may be a reasonable approximation for intermediate and small output decisions of the firm.[14]

It can be shown that normal probability distributions for the prices coupled with an exponential utility function leads to the following simplification: maximizing the expected utility of profit is equivalent to maximizing[15]

$$\sum_{j=1}^{n} \bar{P}_i Q_i - C(Q) - \alpha/2 \sum_{i=1}^{n} \sum_{j=1}^{n} Q_i Q_j \rho_{ij} \sigma_i \sigma_j, \tag{21}$$

where $\bar{P}_i$ denotes the expected price in the ith market, σ_i^2 is the variance of the price in the ith market, and ρ_{ij} is the correlation coefficient between P_i and P_j. This formulation explicitly relaxes the earlier assumption that the markets are independent in a statistical sense. The consequent first-order conditions are

$$E[MR_i] - \partial C/\partial Q - \alpha\sigma_i \sum_{j=1}^{n} Q_j \rho_{ij} \sigma_j = 0 \tag{22}$$

which can be expressed as

$$E[P_i](1 + 1/E[\eta_i]) - \partial C/\partial Q - \alpha\sigma_i \sum_{j=1}^{n} Q_j \rho_{ij} \sigma_j = 0. \tag{23}$$

---

[13] Specifically, the Pratt–Arrow index of absolute risk aversion is given by $-U''(\pi)/U'(\pi)$. For the exponential utility function, this index is the constant α.

[14] For a further discussion of this point, cf. Lintner (1970).

[15] We may observe that $E(U(\cdot)) = -\int_{-\infty}^{+\infty} \exp(-\alpha\bar{\pi})\exp[-\alpha(\pi - \bar{\pi})]N(\cdot)\,d\pi$, where $\bar{\pi}$ is the mean of profit. Since the moment generating function for a normal distribution is given by $M_{(\pi-\pi)}^2 = e^{\alpha^2\sigma^2/2}$, we can express $E(U(\cdot)) = -\exp(-\alpha\bar{\pi})\exp(\alpha^2\sigma^2/2) = \exp[-\alpha(\bar{\pi} - \alpha\sigma^2/2)]$. To maximize expected utility, one must minimize $-\alpha(\bar{\pi} - \alpha\sigma^2/2)$, or maximize $(\bar{\pi} - \alpha\sigma^2/2)$. This result is given in (20).

If the firm were risk neutral, then α would be identically zero and we would have the same expression as found in (14). We can examine the first-order conditions in (12) or (23) more carefully. It is straightforward to show that the marginal rate of substitution between the mean and variance of profits is given by $\alpha/2$.[16] Of course, the variance of total profit is

$$V(\pi) = \sum_i \sum_j Q_i Q_j \rho_{ij} \sigma_i \sigma_j. \tag{24}$$

It is natural to consider the risk of one more unit of output in the ith market as its contribution to the risk of the total profit of the firm. The marginal contribution to total risk is given by

$$\partial V/\partial Q_i = 2\sigma_i \sum_j Q_j \rho_{ij} \sigma_j. \tag{25}$$

Thus, the first-order condition (22) denotes the marginal contribution to expected profit of an increment of output minus the marginal contribution to total variance after converting to units of required profit by multiplying by $\alpha/2$. In other words, the first-order conditions show the certainty equivalent marginal expected profit conditions. Production, therefore, will change if any of the marginal revenue functions change or if the contribution of the respective markets to the variance of profit changes. It is clear that the degree of absolute risk aversion determines the relative impact of changes in the variance vis-a-vis changes in revenue.

This result may be better demonstrated by comparing prices in two markets. As shown in (6), under certainty, price differences result solely from differences in demand elasticity. This no longer holds when demand is uncertain. For any two markets i and k,

$$\frac{E[P_i]}{E[P_k]} = \frac{(1 + E[\eta_j])^{-1}[\partial C/\partial Q - \alpha/2\, \partial V(\pi)/\partial Q_j]}{(1 + E[\eta_k])^{-1}[\partial C/\partial Q - \alpha/2\, \partial V(\pi)/\partial Q_k]}. \tag{26}$$

Thus, even markets with common expected demand elasticities, $E[\eta_i] = E[\eta_k]$, will exhibit different expected prices if one market is riskier than the other. For risk-averse firms, output will be restricted more and expected price will be higher in the market with the highest contribution to the variance of profits. The relative effects of differences in expected demand elasticity and contribution to the variance of profits will depend on the degree of risk aversion.

It is well known that if demand curves are linear, price discrimination will have no effect on total output of the monopolist. If the demand curves are not linear, the effect of discrimination on output depends on their con-

---

[16] If $E(U(\cdot)) = -\exp[-\alpha(\bar{\pi} - \alpha\sigma^2/2)]$, $dE(U(\cdot)) = 0 = \alpha\exp[-\alpha(\bar{\pi} - \alpha\sigma^2/2)]\,d\bar{\pi} - (\alpha^2/2)$. $\exp[-\alpha(\bar{\pi} - \alpha\sigma^2/2)]\,d\sigma^2$. Solving for $d\bar{\pi}/d\sigma^2$ yields the result sought.

cavity properties.[17] If demand functions are random, however, price discrimination even with linear expected demand curves will result in a total output which is different from that of a monopolist (price discriminating or otherwise) facing deterministic demand.

Assume two simple demand curves

$$P_1 = a_1 - b_1 Q_1 + u_1, \tag{27}$$

$$P_2 = a_2 - b_2 Q_2 + u_2, \tag{28}$$

with additive error terms such that u_1 has mean 0 and variance σ_1^2 and u_2 has mean 0 and variance σ_2^2. Quantity will be set in each market following (23) to reflect differences in expected demand elasticities and the contributions of each market to total profit variance.

A new demand curve can be derived under the assumption that the monopolist cannot discriminate. This demand function will be

$$P = m_1 - m_2 Q + u, \tag{29}$$

where m_1, m_2, and u are derived from (27) and (28). In this formation, the variance of u is

$$(b_1 b_2)^{-2}[b_2 \sigma_1^2 + b_1 \sigma_2^2 + 2 b_1 b_2 \rho_{12} \sigma_1 \sigma_2]. \tag{30}$$

Thus, since the variance of profit depends on the slopes of the demand curves as well as their variance, the optimal quantity will differ.

6.   IMPLICATIONS FOR LEGAL ANALYSIS

Under the Robinson–Patman Act, price discrimination is illegal if its effect is to reduce competition. Two absolute defenses are permitted. First, there may be differences in costs between markets. Thus, the price discrimination may be cost justified. Second, the price discrimination may have been necessary to meet competition in good faith.

The introduction of uncertainty raises an interesting issue with respect to the cost justification defense. In the nonstochastic case, all costs are objective. Marginal cost represents the addition to total cost of producing one more unit of output for sale in the market. Society accepts the necessity that the firm be compensated for this cost.

For a risk-averse firm operating under uncertainty, however, the production of one more unit implies an additional cost—an increase in profit risk. To the firm, profit risk reduces utility just as production costs reduce utility. The cost to the firm, however, depends on its aversion to risk. One firm may

[17] See Robinson (1933), pp. 184–195 in particular.

require a small premium for increased risk; another a large premium. If society should rule out these subjective costs as admissible in the cost justification defense, it is clearly making a value judgment about socially optimal behavior under uncertainty that differs from the behavior of most individuals.

7. CONCLUSION

In summary, this study has analyzed the impact of demand uncertainty on the price discriminating monopolist. We have shown that the standard results no longer hold. Price differences may occur because of risk aversion and differences in the riskiness of markets, as well as due to differences in demand elasticities. Further work should be done to introduce different utility functions and different forms of uncertainty to the analysis of the price discriminating firm. By this procedure, we may grope toward a generalization that has significant public policy implications. While the goals of antitrust policy are roundly applauded by most economists, when deleterious consequences can result we should be well aware of their possibility.

REFERENCES

Arrow, K. J. (1971). *Essays in the Theory of Risk-Bearing.* Chicago: Markham.

Baron, D. (1970). Price Uncertainty, Utility, and Industry Equilibrium in Pure Competition, *International Economic Review* 11, No. 3 (October), 463–480.

Blair, R. D. (1974a). Random Input Prices and the Theory of the Firm, *Economic Inquiry* 12, No. 2 (June), 214–226.

Blair, R. D. (1974b). Estimation of the Elasticity of Substitution When Input Prices Are Random, *Southern Economics Journal* 41, No. 1 (July), 141–144.

Blair, R. D., and Lusky, R. (1975). A Note on the Influence of Uncertainty on Estimation of Production Function Models, *Journal of Econometrics* 3, No. 4 (November), 391–394.

Clemens, E. W. (1951). Price Discrimination and the Multiple-Product Firm, *Review of Economic Studies* 19, (1951), 1–11.

Feldstein, M. S. (1971). Production with Uncertain Technology: Some Economic and Econometric Implications, *International Economic Review* 12, No. 1 (February), 27–38.

Horowitz, I. (1970). *Decision Making and the Theory of the Firm.* New York: Holt.

Leland, H. (1972). Theory of the Firm Facing Uncertain Demand, *American Economic Review* 62, No. 3, (June), 278–291.

Lintner, J. (1970). The Impact of Uncertainty on the "Traditional" Theory of the Firm: Price-Setting and Tax Shifting, in *Industrial Organization and Economic Development* (J. Markham and G. Papanek, eds.), pp. 238–265. Boston: Houghton Mifflin.

McCall, J. (1971). Probabilistic Microeconomics, *Bell Journal of Economics and Management Science* 2, No. 2 (Autumn), 403–433.

Meyer, R. A. (1976). Risk-Efficient Monopoly Pricing for the Multiproduct Firm, *Quarterly Journal of Economics* 90, No. 3 (August), 461–474.

Oi, W. Y. (1961). The Desirability of Price Instability under Perfect Competition, *Econometrica* 29, No. 1 (January), 58–64.

Penner, R. G. (1967). Uncertainty and the Short Run Shifting of the Corporation Tax, *Oxford Economics Papers* **19**, No. 1 (March), 99–110.

Pratt, J. W. (1964). Risk Aversion in the Small and in the Large, *Econometrica* **32**, No. 1 (January/April), 122–136.

Robinson, J. (1933). *The Economics of Imperfect Competition.* New York: Macmillan.

Sandmo, A. (1971). On the Theory of the Competitive Firm under Price Uncertainty, *American Economic Review* **61**, No. 1 (March), 65–73.

Simkin, C. G. F. (1947). Some Aspects and Generalizations of the Theory of Discrimination, *Review of Economic Studies* **15**, 1–13.

Tisdell, C. A. (1963). Uncertainty, Instability, Expected Profit, *Econometrica* **31**, No. 1 (January), 243–247.

Turnovsky, S. J. (1973). Production Flexibility, Price Uncertainty and the Behavior of the Competitive Firm, *International Economic Review* **14**, No. 2 (June), 392–413.

Insurance theoretic aspects of workers' compensation

PETER DIAMOND

MASSACHUSETTS INSTITUTE OF TECHNOLOGY

1. INTRODUCTION

There has been a considerable amount of theoretical research recently on the effects of liability for accidents. This paper draws on this literature to consider the effects of workers' compensation on the efficiency of production.

The paper starts with a presentation of the conditions necessary for production to be fully efficient in the presence of the possibility of job-related accidents. This ideal provides a benchmark against which to appraise the various types of failure of the economy to achieve full efficiency. Then ideal insurance against accidents is discussed, along with the shortcomings actual insurance tends to have. After a brief discussion of possible market equilibrium in the absence of workers' compensation, the paper focuses on three issues of efficiency as a function of the size of the workers' compensation program—implications of failure of workers to correctly perceive job risks for product prices and choice of technology (Sections 7 and 8), difficulties for firms in distinguishing careful workers and the allocation of workers to jobs (Section 9), and incentives for safety on the job (Section 10). Under plausible assumptions, workers' compensation appears to be more likely to improve efficiency in the economy than to worsen it.

Paper prepared for the Department of Labor. The author wishes to thank Alan Blinder for many helpful suggestions.

2. ACCIDENTS AND FULL EFFICIENCY

Economic theorists typically study efficiency in a model with a fixed number of commodities and types of labor, and without work-related accidents. For present purposes it is necessary to consider efficiency in a setting where job-related accidents can occur and where the differences among firms and workers are recognized in the model, although not necessarily by the firms and workers themselves. We will see that satisfying all the conditions for full efficiency is a hopeless task in a world with limitations or costs on the availability and use of information. Nevertheless, such a description will serve two purposes. First, it will alert readers to the issues that might be omitted in particular simplified models which show the full efficiency of particular allocation schemes. Second, it will serve as a benchmark so that the relative efficiencies of two practical allocative mechanisms could be compared by examining the divergences of each of them from the ideal of full efficiency.

Efficiency requires consideration both of the costs of accident occurrence and of accident avoidance.[1] For shorthand I will refer to the sum of both of these costs as the costs of accidents. The expected value of the disutility of the costs of accidents will be taken as the appropriate social measure to be considered.[2] Since individuals are averse to the sizeable risks associated with job-related injuries, this is not equivalent to simply taking the expected value of accident costs. Now let us list seven conditions which are necessary for full efficiency.

(1)   Given the allocation of workers to particular firms which are producing outputs, full efficiency calls for each worker to take that level of care on the job (use safety equipment, be alert, follow correct procedures) which equates the marginal cost of care and the expected marginal *social* costs of an accident. Similarly, firms must select the appropriate level of care (choose production processes, select intermediate good and capital supplies, create an atmosphere of alertness) which equates the marginal costs of care and the expected marginal *social* costs of accidents that might occur. Since accidents frequently increase production costs,[3] and injure both the worker causing the accident and other workers, the relevant social costs of accidents exceed those borne by any agent in the absence of cost shifting.

---

[1] For an elaboration of these two costs and their interaction, see Calabresi (1970).

[2] Objections to this measure arise where one rejects the additivity in utility across states of nature which is implied by the axioms for expected utility. For example, the fear from being in a dangerous situation does not fit in the expected utility framework.

[3] For example, production delays, equipment damage, damage to output, and costs of replacing workers.

This condition takes the volume of output of different goods by different firms as given. The next two conditions refer to the optimal aggregate output of goods and the optimal division of the aggregate among supplying firms.

(2)   Demanders (whether of final or intermediate goods) must equate the marginal value of the commodity demanded to the marginal social cost of production, including costs of accidents. This will give the correct aggregate demand.

(3)   Aggregate supply of each commodity must be divided among firms to reflect the varying accident records, and so varying social costs of production of different firms.

Just as firms differ, so do workers. The ability to work well with different types of risk varies considerably among workers.

(4)   The allocation of different workers to different firms must correctly reflect the comparative advantages of workers in dealing with different kinds and levels of risks.

With full efficiency in production, some accidents will still occur. Thus, efficiency requires appropriate responses to the accidents which do occur.

(5)   Medical care, rehabilitation of workers, and repair of damage to property that take place after accidents must correctly reflect social benefits and costs.

This condition covers the direct use of real resources after an accident. There are also financial repercussions which must be attended to, since they, in turn, affect resource allocation.

(6)   Since individuals are risk averse, and since accidents may well alter the marginal utility of income, the appropriate financial insurance must ensure that the marginal utility of income is the same with or without an accident. Similarly, owners of firms would want adequate risk sharing on profit fluctuations of a firm caused by accidents. Liquidity crises which might affect bankruptcy must be avoided.

All the above conditions for efficient resource allocation have ignored administrative costs. Once we introduce administrative costs which themselves depend on the attempts to satisfy the above conditions, the conditions are no longer necessarily desirable; that is, we move from a first-best to a second-best world. For the sake of completeness, let us list administrative costs too.

(7)   The cost of administering the allocative/compensatory system should not be higher than necessary.

This list is meant to serve as a check list, so that all the allocative implications of any workers' compensation plan are explored. Obviously no scheme will satisfy all these conditions.

3. IDEAL INSURANCE

Before examining the effects of workers' compensation on allocation decisions, it is useful to examine the risks coming from accidents and the mitigation that insurance can provide. Let us assume that before an accident a worker had an income (or wealth) level y and a utility function $u(y)$. Immediately after an accident he may have the same wealth level, but a different utility function, which we will call $v(y)$. One possibility is that the only change in circumstances is an injury requiring an expenditure on medical care to restore him to his previous position. Another example with a simplified structure is that the only cost of accident is a loss in earnings ability. If the cost of the damage is d, then the postaccident utility function is the same as the preaccident utility function, once one adjusts for the income loss to pay medical expenses

$$v(y) = u(y - d). \tag{1}$$

For this case the optimal insurance benefit simply pays the expense of lost income d. Before proceeding, let us stop to define ideal insurance.

We are considering a case where we have no moral hazard or adverse selection problems. (Thus, the adjective ideal.) In the absence of insurance and with no change in wealth level, the expected utility of an individual is

$$EU = (1 - p)u(y) + pv(y), \tag{2}$$

where p is the probability of an accident. The purpose of insurance is to transfer funds from the contingency of no-accident to the contingency where the accident occurs.[4] If a is the premium paid in advance of the possible occurrence of an accident to receive the benefit b in the event of an accident, the expected benefit payment must equal the receipt of funds for the compensation system to break even (ignoring administrative costs which are zero in an ideal system). Thus, we have the breakeven condition

$$a = pb. \tag{3}$$

---

[4] This discussion ignores self-insurance as might occur with a worker who has recurring financial losses, saving when not suffering accident consequences and dissaving otherwise. For a further discussion of insurance and types of accidents (and issues in workers' compensation generally) see Oi (1973b).

With these payments and benefits, expected utility becomes

$$EU = (1 - p)u(y - a) + pv(y - a + b). \tag{4}$$

The design of ideal insurance is to select a and b to maximize expected utility (4) subject to the resource constraint (3). We assume that the individual is risk averse in the sense that both u and v show diminishing marginal utility of income.

Substituting from the resource constraint (3) into the definition of expected utility (4), we can express the choice of benefit as an unconstrained maximization

$$EU = (1 - p)u(y - pb) + pv(y + (1 - p)b). \tag{5}$$

Differentiating with respect to b, we obtain the first-order condition for the ideal insurance

$$u'(y - pb) = v'(y + (1 - p)b). \tag{6}$$

As expected, the first-order condition is the equality of the marginal utilities of income in the two events of accident and no-accident. For the case where the only damage is financial [i.e., (1) holds], the optimal plan is to have the same income net of damage, whether or not the accident occurs; that is, to set the benefit equal to the level of damage. It is important to note, however, that, in general, the ideal insurance does not equate utility levels in the two states of nature, but equates marginal utility levels. This condition could result in a higher level of utility with an accident than without one. Such a situation would create a serious moral hazard problem.

By contrast, we can ask how much income the worker is willing to forego to be free of the risk of having an accident. Let us denote this amount by c. The cash equivalent of the accident risk is the amount which would equate the certain utility without accident risk to the expected utility with the accident and ideal insurance. (Of course, the amount would be greater if less-than-ideal insurance were the only available alternative.) That is, c is defined by

$$u(y - c) = \max_b \left[(1 - p)u(y - pb) + pv(y + (1 - p)b) \right]. \tag{7}$$

Given that the accident lowers utility [$u(y) \geq v(y)$ for all y], it is clear that c is positive and increasing in p.[5] The ideal insurance premium a or pb, however, may be larger or smaller than c depending on the accident-induced

---

[5] Differentiating (7) with respect to p, we have $-u'(y - c) dc/dp = v(y + (1 - p)b) - u(y - pb) - u'(y - pb)b$ [using the first-order condition $u'(y - pb) = v'(y + (1 - p)b)$], since $v(y + (1 - p)b) < u(y + (1 - p)b)$ and (by concavity of u) $u(y - pb + b) \leq u(y - pb) + bu'(y - pb)$. We obtain the conclusion that c increases in p. Since at $p = 0$, c is zero, c is positive with positive accident risk.

change in both utility and the marginal utility of income. When the worker is not so well compensated that he prefers an accident, the value of being free of the risk of accident, c, exceeds the insurance premium.[6] Thus, the insurance premium does not precisely measure the gains from accident avoidance, even with ideal insurance.

4. LESS-THAN-IDEAL INSURANCE

The discussion of ideal insurance serves as a framework for the goals of insurance, not directly as a guide to policy since there are practical limitations on the ability to design insurance to deal with the risks present in the economy. Unavoidably, any insurance scheme will involve administrative costs.[7] There are general overhead costs to having insurance which do not vary significantly with the size of the program. These are relevant for the decision whether to have insurance, but not for the design of an insurance program which is worth having. Other administrative costs vary with the number of policies written. These will make it socially undesirable to insure very small risks or those with probabilities sufficiently close to zero or one.[8] Still other administrative costs depend on the number of claims made. These also make risks with probabilities sufficiently close to one not worth insuring.[9] Some administrative costs depend on the dollar volume of claims paid. These costs make insurance of sufficiently small risks not worthwhile.[10] Thus, administrative costs make it preferable for individuals to self-insure some risks. Since the optimal level of self-insurance depends on the level of administrative costs, a change in the design of workers' compensation which lowered administrative costs would increase the risks worth insuring.[11]

---

[6] In the case of a purely financial risk ($v(y) = u(y - d)$), accident cost c is equal to the insurance amount a. In general, this equality will not hold, and $c \gtreqless a$ as $u(y - pb) \gtreqless v(y + (1 - p)b)$.

[7] For a discussion of administrative costs, see Lees and Rice (1965) and Boland (1965).

[8] For a risk-averse expected utility maximizer with the same utility function with and without an accident, facing a financial loss of d with probability p, we can consider insurance provided at expected cost including a fixed administrative cost. Then, there exist functions $d^*(p)$, $p^*(d)$, and $p^{**}(d)$ such that insurance is worth buying for $d > d^*(p)$ and p satisfying $p^*(d) < p < p^{**}(d)$.

[9] Given the circumstances in footnote 8, with administrative costs now being a constant per claim paid, there exists a function $p^{***}(d)$ such that insurance is worthwhile for $p < p^{***}(d)$.

[10] Given the circumstances in footnote 9, with administrative costs now proportional to the value of claims paid, there exists a function $d^{**}(V)$ such that if $V = pd$ is the expected risk, then insurance is worthwhile for $d > d^{**}(V)$.

[11] From the individual perspective the price paid for insurance is a key variable in the demand for insurance. The preceding discussion considered prices set at expected payments plus administrative costs. Insofar as pricing varies from this standard the preceding analysis would not reflect a relationship between insurance purchases and social cost.

Once an accident has occurred, insurance may have substitution effects on individual behavior. This is part of the familiar problem of moral hazard.[12] Insurance for medical expenses makes the cost of medical expenses to the individual less than social cost. Depending on patient behavior, and that of the medical profession, this can be expected to lead to some overconsumption of medical services and/or very high administrative costs.[13] Some form of coinsurance is frequently selected to lessen this difficulty. Insofar as this need is present and met in this way, insurance will deviate from the ideal described in the previous section.

A similar problem arises from payments to replace lost wages—there is an incentive to slow down actual recovery or to give the appearance of slow recovery. This leads to further administrative costs to police benefit recipients and to payments below the level of actual lost wages to lessen the incentives of staying away from the job. Assuming that ideal insurance would require benefits at least as large as financial losses (i.e., that injury does not reduce the marginal utility of income), this reduction in insurance payments is again a deviation from ideal insurance.

A second moral hazard problem is that some workers may feign injuries to collect insurance in the absence of any injury-causing accident. Again, reduced benefits decrease the incentive for this behavior.

A third moral hazard problem arises from behavior before an accident which affects the probability or severity of an accident. Again, the presence of insurance lessens the incentive to take care unless the premium paid varies appropriately with the underlying risk. The importance of this lessening of incentives depends upon the extent to which insurance covers all the costs of accidents (leaves workers at the same utility level). With limited financial compensation and no compensation for pain and suffering, workers will still have substantial incentives to take care even if neither insurance premia that they might pay nor wages vary with the care they take. The incentives for firms to take care will depend on the relation of premia and wages to accident possibilities. We will return to this issue later.

Another conventional insurance problem is adverse selection—that those who are bad risks tend to insure (or insure more) while those who are good risks tend not to insure (or insure less). This is probably not a serious problem for workers' compensation because of compulsion and near universality of coverage. In addition, the problem does not arise insofar as premiums for the individual decision maker vary correctly with risks. This is accomplished in the long run by an accurate experience-related premium. Conceivably,

---

[12] For a discussion of moral hazard, see Arrow (1968) and Pauly (1968, 1974).

[13] For example, if firms monitor the medical care of their workers, this involves an additional layer of administrative apparatus.

very careful workers have some slight incentive to seek work in uncovered employment. Insofar as workers' compensation programs differ by state and premiums do not reflect individual firm risks, firms have incentives to choose location which may differ from socially desirable incentives.

In concluding this section, it is useful to point out that a governmental system of workers' compensation must apply uniformly (or uniformly within recognized categories). Insofar as different systems would be desirable for different firms or workers, we have the problem of compromising among the systems that would be appropriate for different individuals.

5. THE PRESENT WORKERS' COMPENSATION PROGRAM

Having examined how insurance should ease the effects of risks and listed the practical difficulties arising with insurance from administrative and information problems, let us turn to what workers' compensation does. For some classes of injuries[14] and diseases,[15] workers' compensation provides medical expenses (with limits) and cash (again, with limits) related to the length and severity of disability (or death) and the workers' wage. Thus, workers' compensation provides some degree of insurance for workers in covered employment for some of the risks they face. This compensation system is financed by compulsory insurance (or self-insurance) by firms, with premiums depending on occupational classifications, industrial activities, or accident experiences of the individual firms. The obvious economic issues are the general size of the compensation system, the distribution of benefits by wage or injury of recipients, and the distribution of costs among firms.

To evaluate possible changes in workers' compensation, one would like to know the effects of the changes on voluntary insurance arrangements and then the effects of the change in the complete (compulsory and voluntary) insurance system on wages, profits, and the aspects of efficiency described in Section 2. This is more than we shall do. In Section 6, we will discuss reasons why a voluntary insurance market may underinsure. In Sections 7 and 8 we will examine the implications for efficiency in technology and level of output of increased accident benefits when workers underestimate the risks they face. In Section 9 we will discuss the implications of benefits for the allocation of workers to different jobs. In Section 10 we will consider on-the-job safety given the allocation of workers to jobs. No attempt is made to consider all these issues in a single model.

---

[14] Injuries arising from accidents which arose out of and in the course of employment.
[15] Some occupational diseases are included, with the set varying across states.

6. VOLUNTARY INSURANCE

It is natural to start by asking how a market equilibrium can have short-comings which might make compulsory insurance desirable. This will give us a framework for examining the response of the market to the parameters of workers' compensation. We shall examine the insurance market assuming no compulsion, no provision of insurance by employers, and no group insurance organized by unions.[16]

An individual worker might well consider insuring his life (for the benefit of his dependents), his need for medical expenses, or his earnings level. Before considering the demand side of this market, let us briefly consider supply. Because of the large number of small policies involved (in contrast to group insurance), high administrative costs imply a ratio of benefits paid to premiums collected that is relatively low. A primary element of this is the selling cost which appears to be necessary to bring insurance to large sectors of the American public. In addition, with policies on an individual rather than group basis, the adverse selection problem is more serious, leading to the expense of evaluating individual risks. This cost structure can be readily seen in the current market context by contrasting group and individual life and medical insurance policies. Thus, one aspect of individual insurance would be its high cost, leading some individuals rationally to reject insurance.

Now let us consider the demand side of individual insurance. There are a number of issues in individual demand which result in a divergence of the market outcome from various definitions of an idealized norm. First, the information needed to evaluate insurance alternatives is difficult and expensive to obtain and interpret. Information on the magnitude of death and health risks for the general public is not something at everyone's fingertips. If this were the only problem, public provision of information might be easily envisaged. However, an individual's risks will vary significantly from aggregate measures, depending on his personal characteristics, particularly past health and disease exposure. Adjusting general statistics for individual risks involves both information acquisition and sophistication in its use, which are not generally present. In addition, risks need to be adjusted for choice of occupation and employer, requiring further sophistication and information on firm specific risks which may not exist and may well be in the interest of employers to suppress. Thus, on the basis of a model of rational calculation, accurate choice is difficult and expensive. This leaves room for rule of thumb (or best-guess) individual behavior[17] or the use of agents by individuals to decide for them.

---

[16] I also abstract from any possibility of compensation from employers under common law remedies.

[17] Given the low probability of occurrence of many of these risks, there will be no significant improvement in rules of thumb as a consequence of individual experience within a single lifetime.

A second problem in individual evaluation is that statistical concepts and evaluations of risks do not appear to be intuitively natural. There is an experimental literature showing that individuals make large and systematic errors in evaluating random situations (see Tversky and Kahneman, 1974). Thus, there is a further market problem in addition to the difficulties of assembling information.

Now let us turn to decision making per se, rather than the measurement and interpretation of risks. Again, there is an empirical literature evaluating individual choice in laboratory settings and comparing this behavior with axioms for rational choice under uncertainty. The conclusion again is that individual choice differs in a large and systematic way from the rational choice model (see Kahneman and Tversky, 1975). While these conclusions have not been verified in market settings to my knowledge, there is a strong presumption that similar results will hold.[18]

This discussion of attitudes toward risk has not faced the additional psychological reality that the events under discussion are important and unpleasant for the individual decision maker. In an examination of individual choice about smoking, two psychiatrists (see Tumerin and Resik, 1972) divided individuals into those who attempted to make a rational choice and those who avoided rationality (e.g., do not bother me with facts). There is little reason to think that the same absence of individual care in decision making will not be present for some sizeable fraction of the population when considering both the avoidance of job-related risks and the decision to insure.

These difficulties with an individualized market provide a number of different justifications for government intervention in this market, unless voluntary group activities are sufficiently widespread. For one, the use of compulsion on a group basis will hold down the costs of organizing and managing this market. The presence of possibly inappropriate individual decisions on insurance represent a justification for public action, on several grounds. First, since the government picks up some of the costs of the failure to insure (welfare, medicaid, free clinics), compulsory insurance can be part of the government's taxation policy to finance desired expenditures. Second, the costs of a failure to insure fall in large part on others in addition to the decision maker. This is clearest with life insurance where the individual buying insurance on his own life is necessarily not among the recipients of benefits in the event of death. Third, there is the argument of self-paternalism. Individuals concerned with their own abilities to make and stick to certain decisions are desirous of being compelled to fulfill certain conditions. Fourth, there is the conventional paternalism argument which, in this context, cites individual irrationality as a justification for intervention. Whatever the

---

[18] For an analysis of a market setting showing frequent divergences from expected utility maximization, see Kunreuther *et al.* (1976).

normative view taken, for positive analysis of the remainder of this paper, I will take the view that individuals underestimate, undervalue, and under-insure health and safety risks. Naturally, the analysis would take a different form without this assumption.

A number of these problems are sensibly approached by organizations of workers which can obtain group rates and collectively bring expertise to bear on the insurance problem. One activity which is undertaken by unions is group insurance. However, enough of the economy is not unionized as to leave this range of issues as a serious problem. For analysis of the impacts of workers' compensation, I will consider models of competitive industry. This will abstract from both the presence of unions and the presence of monopsony power in particular labor markets.

7. WAGE BARGAINS AND WORKER MISPERCEPTIONS

Let us begin by considering jobs where the risks are determined by the job, being independent of behavior both of workers and employers. For simplicity, assume there are two possible jobs, a safe one having no risk of accident and paying wage w_s and a risky one with probability p of an accident and paying wage w. Assume that employers provide insurance which gives benefits b in the event of an accident and that b is not so large that workers prefer that the accident occur. We also assume that b is large enough so that workers do not buy any further insurance for themselves. We also assume that all workers are the same and that they correctly perceive the probability of risk.

Equilibrium requires that workers be indifferent between the certain wage w_s and the package of wage, risk, and insurance (w, p, b). Writing the indirect utility function of these three variables as V, we have the condition

$$V(w_s, 0, 0) = V(w, p, b). \tag{8}$$

If workers are expected utility maximizers, if an accident results in a complete loss of wages, and if the disutility of labor does not differ with job,[19] then

$$V(w, p, b) = (1 - p)u(w) + pv(b), \qquad V(w_s, 0, 0) = u(w_s). \tag{9}$$

We can relate the equilibrium level of the wage to the level of compensation by implicit differentiation of (8):

$$dw/db = -V_b/V_w \tag{10}$$

[19] If we wanted to consider partial disability, we could complicate this analysis by also having a postaccident wage. This setting holds for total disability, whether permanent or temporary, assuming no savings (self insurance) by workers, with p being the expected fraction of time disabled.

In the expected utility case this is

$$dw/db = -pv'(b)/(1 - p)u'(w) \qquad (11)$$

The total expected cost per unit of labor employed the whole period for firms C is[20] $[(1 - p)w + pb]/(1 - p)$. [Each worker hired is available for the period with probability $(1 - p)$, thus $(1 - p)^{-1}$ workers are hired per unit of labor employed.] Thus, we can calculate the change in costs for a change in benefits

$$\frac{dC}{db} = \frac{dw}{db} + \frac{p}{1 - p} = -\frac{V_b}{V_w} + \frac{p}{1 - p} = \frac{p}{1 - p}\left(1 - \frac{v'(b)}{u'(w)}\right) \qquad (12)$$

in the expected utility case. This equation tells us that the cost minimizing insurance for an employer is the provision of ideal insurance as discussed previously. Whatever the level of insurance provided, the costs to employers of using labor accurately reflects social costs, including the losses to workers from inadequate insurance. This implies that demand is properly allocated between goods having different risks of production.

Now let us consider the possibility that workers do not correctly perceive the risks of accidents.[21] We shall assume that the supply of labor is adequately modeled[22] by replacing the true probability p by a "perceived" probability $\hat{p}$. We assume that the safe job is correctly perceived. Now equilibrium in the labor market is described by

$$V(w_s, 0, 0) = V(w, \hat{p}, b). \qquad (13)$$

Assuming that workers see risks as smaller than they are, $\hat{p} < p$, the wage will be lower than in the case of correct perceptions as long as the indirect utility function decreases as the probability of an accident increases. In the expected utility case, the equilibrium wage is lower with incorrect perceptions as long as utility without an accident is higher than utility with an accident

$$u(w) > v(b). \qquad (14)$$

If we now examine the total cost to firms of an increase in benefits, the cost of benefits paid depends on the true probabilities while the wage response to increased benefits depends on perceived probabilities. In the expected

---

[20] This ignores the sizeable direct cost of accidents to firms over and above worker compensation.

[21] The subsequent analysis parallels that of Spence (1977).

[22] Previously, we discussed misperception of risks. In addition, we discussed inadequate evaluation of risk which may not be modelable as a simple change in probability.

utility case, the derivative of total labor cost with respect to benefits is

$$\frac{dC}{db} = \frac{dw}{db} + \frac{p}{1-p} = \frac{p}{1-p} - \frac{\hat{p}v'(b)}{(1-\hat{p})u'(w)} = \frac{p}{1-p}\left(1 - \frac{\hat{p}(1-p)v'(b)}{p(1-\hat{p})u'(w)}\right). \quad (15)$$

For $\hat{p}$ less than p, $\hat{p}(1-p)/p(1-\hat{p})$ is less than 1. Thus, total costs rise more slowly with underperceived risks than with accurately perceived risks. If firms were selecting the benefit level to minimize costs, they would select a lower level than that which would be selected given correct perceptions.

If we measure the social cost of production using the expected utility of workers measured with correct accident probabilities rather than the lower perceived ones, the social cost of producing the good with the risky technology is higher (relative to the safely produced good) than is private cost. Thus, with a competitive industry structure, we will have too much demand for goods which are risky to produce and too many accidents.

Thus far, we have assumed that all workers are the same. Workers can differ in their relative disutilities from different types of labor, their skills in avoiding accidents, their utility functions given accidents, and in their perceptions of risks. Thus, workers who like conditions in the risky industry, have good safety abilities, or do not mind accidents much will tend to work in the risky industry. Insofar as perceptions are correct this is correctly reflected in both social and private costs. However, those that underestimate risks by more[23] are more likely to work in the risky industry. Formal modeling of this problem would require consideration of the joint distribution of skills and perceptions in the labor force.

Let us measure the divergence between social and private costs of production by comparing the equilibrium cost of production with the cost assuming correct perceptions. We can relate this divergence to the size of benefits. Assuming that $\hat{p} < p$ and that $u'(w) < v'(b)$, we have

$$\left.\frac{dC}{db}\right|_{p=\hat{p}} - \left.\frac{dC}{db}\right|_{p=p} = \frac{p}{1-p}\left(1 - \frac{v'}{u'}\right) - \frac{p}{1-p}\left(1 - \frac{\hat{p}(1-p)v'}{p(1-\hat{p})u'}\right)$$

$$= \frac{p}{1-p}\frac{v'}{u'}\left(\frac{\hat{p}(1-p)}{p(1-\hat{p})} - 1\right) < 0. \quad (16)$$

Thus, increases in benefits decrease the divergence. This result arises because benefits paid in cash are evaluated using correct probabilities while accident costs falling on workers and wage response to benefits are evaluated with incorrect probabilities. An increase in benefits increases the correctly measured accident costs and decreases the incorrectly measured ones. Thus,

---

[23] We have assumed that the safe industry has no risks. Analysis would be more complicated if all industries were risky. Conclusions would depend on the degree of misperception.

increasing benefits up to the level of ideal insurance ($v' = u'$) increases the efficiency of the bearing of accident risks by workers and decreases the social accident cost arising from improperly priced products on the goods market insofar as workers underestimate risks.[24] Except in the case where ideal insurance leaves utility independent of the occurrence of an accident, we will not achieve full efficiency by simply increasing benefits, since worker misperceptions will continue to affect the equilibrium cost of production.

8. CHOICE OF TECHNOLOGY

Now let us consider the case where firms can reduce the risk of accidents p by a suitable choice of technology, although with a varying cost.[25] This question requires analysis of the relation between worker perception of risk and true accident probability. Let us write this relation as

$$\hat{p} = \hat{p}(p). \tag{17}$$

A plausible assumption is that workers see smaller differences between technologies than really exist, i.e.,

$$\hat{p}'(p) < 1. \tag{18}$$

For a given level of benefits we have two equations, labor supply relating wage to perceived safety, (13), and the choice of technology to minimize cost for given output:

$$p \quad \text{minimizes} \quad w + [pb/(1 - p)] + t(p), \tag{19}$$

where $t(p)$ is the cost per worker of technology with risk p ($t'(p) < 0, t''(p) > 0$). Calculating the first-order condition for choice of technology we have[26]

$$\frac{b}{(1 - p)^2} + t'(p) = -\frac{dw}{dp} = \frac{V_p}{V_w} \hat{p}'(p). \tag{20}$$

Assuming the expected utility formulation, we can write this as

$$t'(p) = \frac{u - v}{(1 - \hat{p})u'} \hat{p}'(p) - \frac{b}{(1 - p)^2}. \tag{21}$$

---

[24] One might attempt to construct a "natural selection" argument that has workers observing accidents to themselves and others and switching jobs on that basis. One could then ask whether wages needed to maintain employment would then accurately reflect true probabilities. I know of no study of this question. A similar question for consumer loyalty to defective products has been examined by Smallwood and Conlisk (1974). In their analysis the force of long-run selection depends on the rules of thumb being followed by consumers.

[25] Like the previous section, this discussion is based on the paper by Spence (1977).

[26] We assume that the choice problem is (locally) convex in p, so the first-order condition describes a minimum.

Calculating the socially optimal choice of technology replacing perceived risks with true risks (i.e., replacing $\hat{p}$ by p and $\hat{p}'$ by 1), we have

$$-t'(p) = \frac{u - v}{(1 - p)u'} - \frac{b}{(1 - p)^2}. \tag{22}$$

Since we have assumed $u > v$, $\hat{p} < p$, and $\hat{p}' < 1$, we have

$$\frac{u - v}{(1 - \hat{p})u'}\hat{p}' < \frac{u - v}{(1 - p)u'}, \tag{23}$$

implying that the chosen technology is too risky.

It is natural, again, to ask whether an increase in b toward the ideal level increases the safety of the chosen technology. Given a well-behaved choice problem, p will increase in b if the second derivative of total costs with respect to b and p is positive. Calculating this derivative, we have the expression

$$\frac{\partial^2 \text{ cost}}{\partial p \, \partial b} = \frac{1}{(1 - p)^2} + \frac{\partial^2 w}{\partial p \, \partial b}. \tag{24}$$

From the labor supply equation, for expected utility maximization the change in the wage satisfies

$$\frac{\partial^2 w}{\partial p \, \partial b} = -\frac{v'}{(1 - \hat{p})u'}\hat{p}'. \tag{25}$$

With $v'(b) < u'(w)$, $\hat{p} < p$, and $\hat{p}' < 1$,

$$\frac{\partial^2 w}{\partial p \, \partial b} > \frac{-1}{1 - p},$$

implying a positive second derivative of costs. Thus, greater benefits, by making firms calculate a larger share of costs at true probabilities, lead to an increase in safety.

9.   VARIATION AMONG WORKERS

We have singled out one reason for misallocation—that workers might underperceive both risks and improvements in safety. We saw that this dampened firm willingness to provide insurance, and led to too little invest-ment in safety and prices for risky products which were too low, given social costs. Increases in workers' compensation benefits improved resource alloca-tion, when benefits were below both the ideal insurance level and the level that equated utilities with and without the accident. In this section and the next we shall consider two ways in which increased benefits could decrease efficiency. In the next section we shall consider incentives for workers to take care on the job. In this section we shall return to the issue of differences among workers in their ability to avoid accidents, and in their utilities given an accident.

Let us start with two polar cases. First, assume that workers insure themselves for accident risks, and that insurance companies are aware of both personal and firm characteristics that determine risks. Then workers will have the full incentive of social benefits to seek out the jobs in which they have comparative advantage, including the comparative advantage of dealing with risk. Since the seeking process is costly, this produces a reasonable tradeoff between the cost of search and the benefits of better allocation of workers.[27] The conclusion is unchanged when firms pay for insurance, but are aware of worker differences and offer different workers different wages. More commonly, uniform wages are paid within a skill class, with firms trying to hire the best people available. Unless this greatly decreases worker search, the allocation of workers to jobs may be fairly similar.

In contrast to this efficient case we can consider the situation where workers are fully aware of their own capabilities, but firms are unable to distinguish workers at all (ex ante or ex post) and, by law, firms must provide insurance.[28] Assume, in addition, that insurance makes workers indifferent to the occurrence of accidents. Now workers have no incentive to seek out circumstances where they can exploit their comparative advantage and workers are randomly allocated across jobs, resulting in considerable mis-allocation and sizeable redistributions of income relative to the circumstance of perfect discrimination. This problem arises both between industries and among firms in a single industry which might have technologies of different riskiness.

These polar cases are very extreme. The actual circumstances probably reflect a partial ability of firms to distinguish worker comparative advantage (either at hiring or after a short working experience); an ability of insurance companies to distinguish risks among workers, given their jobs, which is probably slightly worse, on average, than the ability of firms to distinguish; limitations on the abilities of workers to be aware of their own risk-handling capabilities; and a compensation system which still leaves workers strongly preferring the absence of accidents (and thus a wage system that partially reflects job risks).

Given these factors we can evaluate the importance of workers' compensation in lessening the efficiency of worker allocation to jobs. Insofar as firms can distinguish among workers, having firms rather than workers bear the

---

[27] Since equilibrium from the search process depends on search of all workers and relocation of some, the optimality properties of this allocation are unclear.

[28] This case parallels the analysis of product liability by Oi (1973a).

insurance cost does not change the allocation except for any effect on the intensity of worker search if wages are uniform. Insofar as workers purchase insurance and insurance companies cannot distinguish among workers more accurately than firms can,[29] having firms bear the insurance cost does not change the allocation. Insofar as workers are risk neutral and do not insure and cannot distinguish their own risks any better than firms can, having firms bear the insurance cost does not change the allocation of workers. Combining these elements, a decrease in workers' compensation benefits improves the allocation of workers to jobs only to the extent that workers do not insure, are aware of risk capabilities and firm differences, and take more care to find the right job as a consequence of an increase in the loss of utility from an accident due to decreased benefits. Combining these elements, the issue of the improved allocation of workers to jobs as a consequence of their bearing greater accident costs and so seeking safer jobs may well be of little consequence and is obtained only at a cost of less insurance for workers and so, given risk aversion, a loss in social efficiency.

10.   ON-THE-JOB SAFETY

We shall now ignore differences among both workers and firms to examine the incentives of both for safety on the job given the set of workers and firms in an industry.[30] Let us denote by x the efforts of a typical firm to avoid accidents on the job. For example, this might represent expenditures for safety equipment, expenditures for safety-related items such as lighting, on-the-job training of workers, and employment of safety experts. Let us denote by y the efforts of a typical worker to avoid accidents. For example, this might include being well rested, concentrating more on his work, personal expenditures on safety equipment, off-the-job training in safety. We shall focus on private incentives for these two accident avoidance efforts which we shall call care. We shall relate these incentives to the assignment of the cost of accidents to firms (as with workers' compensation) or to workers (if they insure themselves or self-insure).

We shall start with a particularly extreme set of assumptions to set up the type of analysis to be done. Assume that the number of workers and number of firms are given, and that all workers and all firms are the same. The only costs of accidents are assumed to be those which are compensated

---

[29] We are assuming that insurance companies are aware of firm specific risks when insuring individuals—which is a poor assumption. As it is not true, a shift of costs to workers decreases the incentives to seek safe jobs at uniform wages since insurance companies bear part of the additional costs of risky jobs.

[30] This analysis parallels that of Diamond and Mirrlees (1975).

by workers' compensation, if it exists. For either allocation of accident costs the wage is independent of the level of accidents. Whoever bears accident costs insures them, with the insurance premium exactly equaling the expected value of accident costs, and correctly varying with the degree of care taken to avoid accidents.

Let $A(x)$ be the aggregate cost of having firms take care level x. Let x^0 be the level of care which minimizes[31] $A(x)$. Let $B(y)$ be the aggregate cost of having workers take care level y. Let y^0 be the level which minimizes $B(y)$. Let $C(x, y)$ be the expected value of accident costs given care levels x and y. We assume that the care taken by a worker does not affect the accident costs of other workers. Total social costs S are the sum of these three elements:

$$S(x, y) = A(x) + B(y) + C(x, y) \qquad (26)$$

If firms bear the accident costs C (i.e., there is a workers' compensation system), then workers will choose the care level y^0 and total costs for firms are $A(x) + C(x, y^0)$. Let us write the optimizing level of care for these costs as x^*. Thus, equilibrium occurs at the pair (x^*, y^0). If there is no workers' compensation, firms will choose the care level x^0 and workers will face the costs $B(y) + C(x^0, y)$. Let us write the level of care which minimizes these costs as y^*. Thus, equilibrium is at the pair (x^0, y^*). To evaluate the efficiency implications[32] of workers' compensation, we want to compare the efficiency of these two points, i.e., compare $S(x^0, y^*)$ with $S(x^*, y^0)$. It is straightforward to see that placing these costs on the party whose expenditures (above the self-protection levels, x^0 and y^0) are more efficient results in the more efficient equilibrium. For example, if firms are more efficient than workers in making additional cost avoidance expenditures

$$S(x^0 + t, y^0) \leq S(x^0, y^0 + t), \qquad (27)$$

then the equilibrium occurring when firms bear these costs is the more efficient equilibrium[33]; that is,

$$S(x^*, y^0) \leq S(x^0, y^*). \qquad (28)$$

Of course, neither of these equilibria is fully efficient since only one party will bear these costs, and for full efficiency both parties would need to pay attention to total accident costs. Note that x^* is the socially optimal level of care, given that workers take the care level y^0.

---

[31] x^0 might be zero. However, some accident avoidance expenditures, such as lighting, also affect productivity. Thus, the optimal x^0 need not be zero since A is cost net of productivity gains.

[32] Of course, there are important distributional effects too. In this simple case workers gain $B(y^*) + C(x^0, y^*) - B(y^0)$ and firms lose $A(x^*) + C(x^*, y^0) - A(x^0)$ from the adoption of workmen's compensation.

[33] For a formal proof see Diamond and Mirrlees (1975).

If insurance firms cannot monitor individual workers, but can base premiums only on the average benefits paid to all workers, each worker individually has no incentive to take care beyond y^0. Thus, the two equilibria are (x^0, y^0) without workers' compensation and (x^*, y^0) with it. The latter is clearly more efficient. If firms are not experience rated,[34] and there are enough firms in each category that any one of them feels that its safety record will not affect its premiums, then the equilibrium is again at (x^0, y^0), whoever pays the premiums for accident costs. The role of experience rating is to provide safety incentives for the firm. This will improve efficiency if firms respond to this financial incentive. If workers do not insure these costs, when they are allocated to workers, then they will take more care than y^0. However, from the social perspective, the accident costs are not the same when borne by the two parties if we make the plausible assumption that workers are risk averse. The tradeoff of getting more care from workers at the cost of having them bear accident costs without insurance may be a poor one.

Returning to the assumption that each party purchases insurance for these accident costs and that premiums vary with care taken, we can introduce further accident costs for both workers and firms, in addition to those covered by workers' compensation. In the absence of compensation, costs to firms now depend on worker care, since accidents inflict costs. Thus, we write costs as $A(x, y)$. Similarly, in the presence of compensation, workers still bear some accident costs, so we write their costs as $B(x, y)$. Equilibrium with workers' compensation now occurs in the simultaneous solution of the two cost minimization problems[35]

$$
\begin{aligned}
x^* \quad &\text{minimizes} \quad A(x, y^0) + C(x, y^0), \\
y^0 \quad &\text{minimizes} \quad B(x^*, y).
\end{aligned}
\tag{29}
$$

Similarly, without workers' compensation equilibrium occurs at the pair x^0, y^* satisfying

$$
\begin{aligned}
x^0 \quad &\text{minimizes} \quad A(x, y^*), \\
y^* \quad &\text{minimizes} \quad B(x^0, y) + C(x^0, y).
\end{aligned}
\tag{30}
$$

It is now somewhat more complicated to check if it is more efficient to have workers' compensation (i.e., incentives for firms are more important than those for workers). Assuming that workers would take more care if firms took less, the following two conditions are sufficient to ensure that adoption

---

[34] Or if benefits are financed by taxation which does not vary with accident experience.

[35] We have now introduced an additional possible element—workers or firms might be aware that the safety behavior of the other depends on their own safety precautions. This is implausible for workers since there are many workers to whom a firm responds. For the present we ignore this possibility for firms, although we will return to it later.

of workers' compensation improves efficiency[36] for all t,

$$S(x^0 + t, y^0) \le S(x^0, y^0 + t), \tag{31}$$

and

$$\frac{\partial}{\partial t}(A(x^0 + t, y^0) + C(x^0 + t, y^0)) \le \frac{\partial}{\partial t}(B(x^0, y^0 + t) + C(x^0, y^0 + t)). \tag{32}$$

In addition to assuming that expenditures by firms are more efficient we need to assume that firms have larger incentives to make expenditures for care when they bear compensable accident costs. As we complicate the model, it becomes more difficult to compare the efficiency of different cost allocations.

Now let us turn to the determination of the equilibrium wage. Generally, one would expect the wage to depend upon the levels of care being taken by workers and firms, and also on the allocation of accident costs. We shall write the wage when firms bear accident costs as $w_1(x, y)$. When workers bear accident costs, we shall write it as $w_2(x, y)$. Considering only efficiency we want to know the determinants of the levels of care x and y and so the level of accidents.[37] If we allowed the numbers of workers or firms to vary we would have additional efficiency conditions, but these have already been examined.[38]

The major issue, as with insurance premia, is whether each economic agent thinks that the wage varies with the care that he individually takes. If there is a uniform wage in the industry and each worker and firm is suffi-ciently small relative to the industry so he thinks that his behavior will not affect the wage in the industry, we are back in the previous analysis. The equilibria are still (x^*, y^0) and (y^0, x^*) as described there, and the analysis of efficiency is unchanged. At the other extreme, each firm might feel that it could pay less than the industry wage if it had a better safety record. In addition, workers, while knowing that each one individually cannot affect the wage, know that they do affect it collectively. In some circumstances, it may occur that the social structure of the labor force is such that workers behave as if each worker affects the wage in the way that the average care of all workers affect the wage. To carry this frictionless model to its extreme, we can assume that all parties are aware of the true relationship between

---

[36] For a proof, see Diamond and Mirrlees (1975).

[37] Of course, the differences between w_1 and w_2, evaluated at the suitable equilibria levels of care, have distributional implications. We ignore the possibility that firms voluntarily provide insurance for these costs as part of the compensation package of workers.

[38] To interpret this model as it stands, i.e., without imbedding it into a demand–supply model for labor and ouput, we might consider the firms to be local governments hiring a fixed number of employees.

wage and care, and that the difference in wage functions under different cost allocations is just equal to the magnitude of insurance premiums (i.e., the expected cost of accidents):

$$w_1(x, y) + C(x, y) = w_2(x, y). \tag{33}$$

In this case, equilibrium care levels are independent of the existence of workers' compensation. [This can be seen by noting that without workers' compensation workers care about $w_2(x, y) - B(x, y) - C(x, y)$, while with workers' compensation workers care about $w_1(x, y) - B(x, y)$. Under the hypothesis (33), these expressions are the same. The same conclusion follows for the behavior of firms.] The interest of this example lies not in its plausibility, but in the strength of assumptions which were needed to reach the conclusion.

By specifying different equilibrium wage functions and different degrees of perception of these functions by workers and firms, one could trace out different possible equilibria and seek conditions under which workers' compensation improves on-the-job safety. I shall explore only one simple case, since it brings out the major elements. Let us assume that workers do not perceive their accident avoidance behavior as affecting either their wages or their insurance premia. Then, with or without workers' compensation, workers select

$$y^0(x) \quad \text{to minimize} \quad B(x, y). \tag{34}$$

We assume[39] that y^0 is decreasing in x. With workers' compensation, and firms ignorant of the effect of their care on worker care, firms select x^* to minimize $A(x, y^0) + C(x, y^0) + nw_1(x, y^0)$, where n is the number of workers per firm and y^0 equals $y^0(x^*)$. Without workers' compensation, firms select x^0 to minimize $A(x, y^0) + nw_2(x, y^0)$ with y^0 at the level $y^0(x^0)$. Thus, firms will have greater incentives for care with workers' compensation[40] if

$$\frac{\partial}{\partial x}(C(x, y) + nw_1(x, y)) \le \frac{\partial}{\partial x}(nw_2(x, y)). \tag{35}$$

Naturally, the amount of care taken depends on the responsiveness of the wage functions to care, rather than the levels of the two functions. If we assume that firms are aware of the relationship $y^0(x)$, the condition for firms to take more care would be

$$\frac{d}{dx}(C(x, y^0(x)) + nw_1(x, y^0(x))) \le \frac{d}{dx}(nw_2(x, y^0(x))). \tag{36}$$

---

[39] It is also assumed that there is a unique, stable equilibrium.
[40] And, thus, will take more care in equilibrium, under the stability and uniqueness assumptions that have been made.

In either case, when firms take more care, workers take less and it is necessary to evaluate which equilibrium is more efficient.

Given that the response of workers to their environment is described by the function by $y^0(x)$, we can evaluate the efficiency of equilibria by evaluating the function $S(x, y^0(x))$ at the equilibrium levels of care. When firms are aware of worker response the comparison is simpler. Netting out the costs $A + C$, we can evaluate the efficiency of equilibria by comparing the social incentives $B(x, y^0(x))$ with the private incentives $nw_1(x, y^0(x))$ or $nw_2(x, y^0(x)) - C(x, y^0(x))$. If $S(x, y^0(x))$ and costs of firms with different cost assignments are convex in x, then workers' compensation improves on-the-job safety if safety incentives for firms are less without compensation than with and if private incentives are smaller than social incentives. This will occur when wages without compensation less compensable costs vary less with firm care than do the wages with compensation, and the latter varies less with care than does uncompensated costs. Phrased alternatively, we have compensation varying more with care than does the difference in wages,

$$n \frac{d}{dx}(w_2(x, y^0(x)) - w_1(x, y^0(x))) \le \frac{d}{dx} C(x, y^0(x)), \qquad (37)$$

and wages with compensation varying less than uncompensated losses,

$$n \frac{d}{dx} w_1(x, y^0(x)) \le \frac{d}{dx} B(x, y^0(x)). \qquad (38)$$

Such a pattern might reasonably follow from a failure of workers to perceive the full degree of accident dependence on circumstances, although I have not seen a fully developed model.

In the case where firms are not aware of worker responsiveness, the analysis is more complicated since we are comparing the social costs $S(x, y^0(x))$ as a function of x with the private costs $A(x, y^0) + C(x, y^0) + nw_1(x, y^0)$ or $A(x, y^0) + nw_2(x, y^0)$. Again, examination of these three functions gives us a comparison of equilibrium care levels.

11. CONCLUDING REMARKS

Separately, we have examined the effects of workers' compensation on the pricing of products produced under job-related risk, the choice of safety technology, the allocation of workers with different safety skills to different firms and industries, and the level of on-the-job safety under plausible assumptions. Workers' compensation appeared more likely to improve efficiency in the economy than to worsen it. To draw any more concrete conclusion one would need to have empirical evaluation of the magnitudes of the responsiveness of the various efficiency elements to the shifting of accident costs. Analysis of efficiency when many market imperfections are present is too difficult to base policy on simple theoretic analysis.

REFERENCES

Arrow, K. J. (1968). Further Comment, *American Economic Review* **58**, 531–539.

Boland, V. F. (1965). Comment, *American Economic Review* **55**, 1172–1179.

Calabresi, G. (1970). *Costs of Accidents.* New Haven, Connecticut: Yale Univ. Press.

Diamond, P., and Mirrlees, J. (1975). On the Assignment of Liability: the Uniform Case, *Bell Journal of Economics* **6**, 487–516.

Kahneman, D., and Tversky, A. (1975). Value Theory: An Analysis of Choices under Risk, paper presented at *ISRACON Conference on Public Economics, Jerusalem.*

Kunreuther, H., *et al.* (1976), Limited Knowledge and Insurance Protection: Implications for Natural Hazard Policy, Report of an NSF-RANN project.

Lees, D. S., and Rice, R. G. (1965). Comment, *American Economic Review* **55**, 140–154.

Oi, W. (1973a). The Economics of Product Safety, *Bell Journal of Economics and Management Science* **4**, 3–28.

Oi, W. (1973b). Workmen's Compensation and Industrial Safety, in *Supplemental Studies for the National Commission on State Workmen's Compensation Laws*, U.S. Govt. Printing Office, Washington, D.C.

Pauly, M. (1968). Economics of Moral Hazard: Comment, *American Economic Review* **58**, 531–539.

Pauly, M. (1968, 1974). Overinsurance and Public Provision of Insurance, *Quarterly Journal of Economics* **88**, 44–62.

Smallwood, D. E., and Conlisk, J. (1974). Product Quality in Markets Where Consumers Are Imperfectly Informed and Naive, Discussion paper 74-7, Department of Economics, Univ. of California, San Diego.

Spence, M. (1977). Consumer Misperceptions, Product Failure, and Producer Liability, *Review of Economic Studies* (Forthcoming).

Tumerin, J., and Resik, H. (1972). Risk Taking by Individual Option—Case Study: Cigarette Smoking, *Perspectives on Benefit-Risk Decision Making*, Nat. Acad. Eng., Washington, D.C.

Tversky, A., and Kahneman, D. (1974). Judgement under Uncertainty: Heuristics and Biases, *Science.* 1124–1131.

Multiperiod stochastic dominance with one-period parameters, liquidity preference, and equilibrium in the log-normal case

HAIM LEVY

UNIVERSITY OF FLORIDA
GAINESVILLE
and
THE HEBREW UNIVERSITY
JERUSALEM

1. INTRODUCTION

The pioneer works of Markowitz (1952, 1959) and Tobin (1958, 1965) in the field of decision making under uncertainty and particularly of portfolio selection have recently been extended by several authors. Tobin and Markowitz used the well-known mean-variance analysis while Hadar and Russell (1969, 1971), Rothschild and Stiglitz (1970a, b), and Hanoch and Levy (1969) developed the concept of stochastic dominance of one portfolio (or one bundle of assets) over another for a wide class of utility functions. Nevertheless, relatively few papers deal with the relationship between the one-period and multiperiod efficient sets. Among those few papers one should mention the work of Tobin (1965), Hakansson (1971), Merton and Samuelson (1974), Samuelson (1971), and Merton (1973).

The analysis of the relationship between the "one-period" and multiperiod efficiency analysis can be done by assuming that the investor maximizes expected utility of terminal wealth after n periods, with the constraint

The author wishes to acknowledge the helpful comments of F. D. Arditti and Yoram Kroll.

that he can revise his portfolio at most n times (i.e. a discrete model), when the length of each one-period is a function of transaction cost, the indivisibilities of the investment, etc. Another possibility is to assume like Merton (1977) and Merton and Samuelson (1974) that each one-period is instant. Under this assumption, the investor maximizes his terminal wealth but revises his portfolio continuously in time. Merton has found that when investors can trade continuously in time, prices at time T distribute log normally even though T is finite. Moreover, Merton showed that under some conditions the relationship between expected return and risk given by the Capital Asset Pricing Model derived by Sharpe (1964) and Lintner (1965) still holds, but without the need to assume a quadratic utility function or normal distribution.

Section 2 reexamines Tobin's results regarding the relationship between the one-period and multiperiod efficient sets. In Section 3, the one-period and multiperiod efficiency criteria are analyzed when the multiperiod distributions are *assumed* to be log normal. In the preceding analysis, unlike Merton and Merton and Samuelson, we assume that the investor can revise his portfolio a finite number of times. Namely, a discrete model rather than a continuous model is assumed. Taking into account the existence of transaction cost, it seems that a discrete model is more appropriate than a continuous one. However, by relaxing the assumption of continuous revisions we have to assume that investors think that the n-period portfolios are lognormally distributed even though it might be that the returns do not obey the log-normal law precisely. In Section 4 the properties of the efficient portfolios, liquidity preference, diversification, and equilibrium are analyzed in terms of one-period parameters.

2. ASSUMPTIONS AND NOTATIONS

Following Tobin (1965), independence of the returns over time of the portfolio is assumed throughout. Thus,

$$f(R_1, R_2, \ldots, R_n) = f_1(R_1)f_2(R_2) \cdots f_n(R_n),$$

where R_i is the portfolio return in period i, and f denotes a density function.[1] In some parts of this paper we also assume stationarity over time, i.e.,

$$f_1(R) = f_2(R) = \cdots = f_n(R).$$

All investors are assumed to maximize expected utility when the utility function is defined on terminal wealth. All utility functions are nondecreasing with $u'(w) > 0$ and $u''(w) < 0$, i.e., risk aversion is assumed.

---

[1] There is some empirical evidence indicating that returns in the stock market are independent over time. For details see Cootner (1967).

Like Tobin (1965) we use uniform strategies[2] only; the investor chooses a portfolio strategy and adheres to it for the whole period under consideration. If the investor wishes to switch to another portfolio after a given investment period, he should start the whole procedure described in this paper again, after the first investment period has elasped.

DEFINITION 1   Portfolio x dominates portfolio y $(x\,D\,y)$ for a given class of utility functions U, if $Eu(x) > Eu(y)$ for all $u \in U$.

DEFINITION 2   Using a given investment rule, one can divide all possible portfolios into two mutually exclusive sets: the *efficient* set and the *inefficient* set. Portfolio y is eliminated from the efficient set, or included in an inefficient set, if the efficient set includes at least one portfolio x such that $x\,D\,y$. Portfolio x is included in the efficient set if there is no other portfolio which dominates it [see Markowitz (1952), Tobin (1965)].

Clearly, our aim should be to minimize the efficient set for given information (or assumptions on the utility functions). For a given set of assumptions or information, one can construct several investment rules which do not violate the basic set of assumptions. However, the *optimal* investment rule is the one that does not contradict the set of assumptions regarding the utility functions, and utilizes *all* the information and hence induces the smallest possible efficient set. An investment *strategy* will be called efficient if it leads to the choice of a portfolio which is included in the efficient set.

Finally, we denote the expected *rate* of return by μ and the expected return by $E = 1 + \mu$. $\hat{\mu}$ denotes the expected value of $\log x$. The variance of the random variable x will be denoted, as usual, by σ^2 or σ_x^2 and the variance of the random variable $\log x$ will be denoted by $\hat{\sigma}^2$. The return is denoted by x and the rate of return is R where $x \equiv 1 + R$.

Let the rate of return in period i be R_i. Thus, the overall n-period rate of return is given by R, where $(1 + R) = \prod_{i=1}^{n}(1 + R_i)$.

Using the independence assumption, the expected return E and variance σ^2 of the n-period distribution are given by

$$E = 1 + \mu = \prod_{i=1}^{n}(1 + \mu_i), \qquad \sigma^2 = \prod_{i=1}^{n}\left[\sigma_i^2 + (1 + \mu_i)^2\right] - (1 + \mu)^2,$$

where μ_i and σ_i denote expected rate of return and the variance, respectively, in the ith period, and μ is the expected rate of return of the portfolio. Under the assumption of stationarity over time (i.e., for a given prospect, the investor

---

[2] Tobin proved that only uniform strategies are optimal in the multiperiod case. Stevens (1972) has shown by a counterexample that Tobin's assertion does not generally hold. However, Stevens does not offer any other policy which in general dominates all uniform strategies. In this paper we confine ourselves only to uniform strategies.

is confronted every year by an identical probability distribution), we obtain

$$\mu_1 = \mu_2 = \cdots = \mu_n \equiv \bar{\mu}, \qquad \sigma_1^2 = \sigma_2^2 = \cdots = \sigma_n^2 \equiv \bar{\sigma}^2.$$

Hence,

$$E = (1 + \bar{\mu})^n, \qquad \sigma^2 = [\bar{\sigma}^2 + (1 + \bar{\mu})^2]^n - (1 + \bar{\mu})^{2n}. \tag{1}$$

From (1), Tobin concludes, first, that

> any portfolio that is efficient for one-period investment is also efficient
> for multiperiod investment,

and second, that

> Some portfolios of low expectation that are not efficient for one-period
> investment (involving less expectation than can be achieved at given
> risk) will be efficient for multiperiod investment. This is because the
> n-period variance is an increasing function of the one-period expectation
> as well as the one-period risk. The n-period risk can be reduced to a
> certain extent by accepting expectations lower than the level corre-
> sponding to the minimum one-period risk (Tobin, 1965, p. 46).

Thus, according to Tobin, $S_n \supseteq S_1$, where S_n is the mean-variance efficient
set constructed for n periods, and S_1 is the one-period mean-variance efficient
set. Therefore, one *cannot* construct the efficient set out of the one-period
parameters $(\bar{\mu}, \bar{\sigma})$ of different portfolios, but should examine first the investors'
economic horizon n. Hence, according to Tobin, one may add some elements
to the efficient set as the horizon increases.

Before examining Tobin's statement and analyzing the relationship
between one-period and multiperiod efficiency analyses, we need the following
theorems:

THEOREM 1   Let $F(x)$ and $G(x)$ be the cumulative distributions of two
alternative prospects. Then a necessary and sufficient condition for $E_F u(x) >
E_G u(x)$ for all concave utility functions $u(x)$ (i.e., $u'(x) > 0$, $u''(x) < 0$) is
$\int_{-\infty}^{x} [G(t) - F(t)] \, dt \geq 0$ for all values of x, and a strict inequality holds for
some x_0. For proof see Hader and Russell (1969), Hanoch and Levy (1969),
and Rothschild and Stiglitz (1970a).

THEOREM 2   Let $F^n(x)$ and $G^n(x)$ be two n-period cumulative distributions. Then a sufficient condition for $E_{F^n} u(x) > E_{G^n} u(x)$ for all concave u
is

$$\int_{-\infty}^{x_i} [G_i(t) - F_i(t)] \, dt \geq 0 \qquad \text{for all } x_i \quad (i = 1, 2, \ldots, n)$$

with at least one strong inequality for some x_{i_0}. G_i and F_i are the cumulative distributions of return for the ith one-period, and returns are independent over time.[3] Note that F^n and G^n are the distributions of final wealth after an investment duration of n periods, and there is no restriction on the shape of these distributions.

TABLE I

One Period

Prospect F_1 (F_2)		Prospect G_1 (G_2)	
Outcome (x)	Probability	Outcome (x)	Probability
10	1/2	1	1/2
11	1/2	3	1/2
$\mu(x)$:	10 1/2	2	
$\sigma^2(x)$:	1/4	1	

Let us examine Tobin's results in light of Theorems 1 and 2. Obviously, the mean-variance rule is an optimal efficiency rule only if returns are normally distributed, and $u(x)$ is concave (Tobin 1958; Hanoch and Levy, 1969). In this case, the one-period mean-variance rule and the rule given in Theorem 1 (which implicitly assumes one-period analysis) coincide, and will provide identical efficient sets. However, examining Theorem 2 and the multiperiod mean-variance rule offered by Tobin yields contradictory results. Following Tobin, we assume stationarity of the distributions of returns. Clearly, every portfolio which is eliminated from the one-period efficient set by Theorem 2 will be eliminated from the n-period efficient set as well. Hence, $S_n \subseteq S_1$, the exact opposite to Tobin's results. Let us illustrate by a simple example (see Table I). F_1 dominates G_1 by the mean-variance rule (and, hence, F_2 dominates G_2), since F_1 has higher expected value and lower variance. Assuming independence, one can easily derive the two-period distributions shown in Table II. Consequently, though F_1 dominates G_1 by the mean-variance rule (and, of course, F_2 dominates G_2), F^2 does not dominate G^2 for the two-period case and both are included in the mean-variance efficient set.[4] This example clarifies Tobin's second argument. However, using Theorem 2, it is clear that

---

[3] The proof of this theorem is given by Levy (1973a). Note that we assume independence over time of the distributions of returns, but not stationarity.

[4] Note that F_2 and G_2 denote the second-period distributions and F^2 and G^2 denote the two-period distribution.

TABLE II

Two Period

F^2		G^2	
Outcome	Probability	Outcome	Probability
100	1/4	1	1/4
110	1/4	3	1/4
110	1/4	3	1/4
121	1/4	9	1/4
$\mu(x)$: 110 1/4		4	
$\sigma^2(x)$: 55 3/16		9	

$E_{F^2}u(x) \geq E_{G^2}u(x)$ for all concave u[5] since $F_1(x) \leq G_1(x)$ for all x and hence $\int_{-\infty}^{x_i} [G_i(t) - F_i(t)]\, dt \geq 0$ for all x_i ($i = 1, 2$) and a strict inequality holds for some x_0. To sum up, according to Tobin's analysis, in the preceding case S_1 includes one portfolio and S_2 includes two portfolios, while according to Theorems 1 and 2 both S_1 and S_2 include only one portfolio.

The contradiction between the results of stochastic dominance procedure (Theorem 2) and those of mean-variance procedure stems from the different assumptions underlying each approach. Both assume that the utility function is concave and defined on terminal wealth. However, the mean-variance analysis is restricted to normal distributions while no such restriction is imposed in Theorems 1 and 2. It is well known that if the distribution is normal, the two approaches yield the same results. Thus, the contradiction stems from the fact that one cannot assume normality for all investment periods simultaneously. If the distribution of one-period returns is assumed to be normal, it is clear that the two-period returns given by $X = x_1 x_2$ are *not* normally distributed. Even if the mean-variance rule is optimal (and coincides with Theorem 1) for each one-period analysis, it is no longer optimal for the multiperiod case since the normality assumption is violated. However, the rule given in Theorem 2 is optimal for any horizon n since it is independent of the shape of the distribution of returns. We may, therefore, assume that for some investment horizon, the appropriate distributions are normal. For this specific horizon the mean-variance rule and stochastic dominance rule coincide. Any deviation from this specific investment horizon might lead to contradiction and to two different efficient sets.

---

[5] In the above specific example one can conclude that F^2 dominates G^2 not only for all risk averters but for all nondecreasing utility functions. See Hadar and Russell (1969), Hanoch and Levy (1969), and Quirk and Saposnik (1962).

In order to analyze the properties of the multiperiod distributions, one must examine the random variable $\prod_{i=1}^{n} x_i$. For a finite n, it is difficult to specify the distribution of this term even if each x_i is normally distributed. On the other hand, for very large n, Merton and Samuelson (1974) showed that one cannot use the Central Limit Theorem and substitute the log-normal density function for $f(x)$ in $Eu(x) = \int u(x)f(x)$. However, Merton and Samuelson show that if a continuous model is assumed, one can use the log-normal distributions instead of $f(x)$.

In the rest of the paper we rule out the possibility of continuous portfolio revision, but assume that for any horizon n, which satisfies $n > n_0$, returns can be approximated by the log-normal distribution. Thus, we relax the restriction that investors revise their portfolio continuously, but *assume* that the n-period distributions are log-normal rather than *prove* that they are log normal, as has been done in the continuous model. Thus, we assume that investors behave "as if" the distributions are log normal.

3. COMPARISON OF THE NORMAL AND THE LOG-NORMAL EFFICIENCY FRONTIERS

Before analyzing the relationship between the multiperiod and the one-period efficient sets, we need the following:

THEOREM 3   Let Y be log-normally distributed. Then the necessary and sufficient conditions for $E_F u(Y) > E_G u(Y)$ for all u, with $u' > 0$ and $u'' < 0$, are

(a) $E_F(Y) \geq E_G(Y)$,
(b) $\hat{\sigma}_F^2 \equiv \text{var}_F(\log Y) < \text{var}_G(\log Y) \equiv \hat{\sigma}_G^2$,

where F and G denote two alternative distributions. For proof see Levy (1973b).

From the preceding formulation it can be seen that one has to minimize var(log Y) for a given expected return rather than var(Y) as is being done in the Sharpe–Lintner model. Examining the conditions of Theorem 3 it is hard to compare the log-normal efficient set with the well-known mean-variance efficient set. However, a small modification in Theorem 3 yields the desired comparison.

THEOREM 4   Let Y be log-normally distributed. Then, necessary and sufficient conditions for $E_F u(Y) > E_G u(Y)$ for all u with $u' > 0$, $u'' < 0$ are

$$\text{(a)} \qquad E_F(Y) \geq E_G(Y),$$
$$\text{(b)} \quad \sigma_F(Y)/E_F(Y) < \sigma_G(Y)/E_G(Y). \tag{2}$$

(Note that the parameters are defined in terms of Y rather than log Y.)

Proof Condition (a) of Theorem 4 is identical to condition (a) of Theorem 3. What is left to show is that condition (b) of Theorem 4 is also identical to condition (b) of Theorem 3. But this is straightforward since $\hat{\sigma}_F{}^2 < \hat{\sigma}_G{}^2$ if and only if $[\exp(\hat{\sigma}_F{}^2) - 1] < [\exp(\hat{\sigma}_G{}^2) - 1]$. But recalling that Y is lognormally distributed, the first two moments are given by (see Aitchison and Brown, 1963)

$$E(Y) = \exp(\hat{\mu} + \tfrac{1}{2}\hat{\sigma}^2), \qquad \sigma^2(Y) = \exp(2\hat{\mu} + \hat{\sigma}^2)\cdot[\exp(\hat{\sigma}^2) - 1].$$

The inequality $[\exp(\hat{\sigma}_F{}^2) - 1] < [\exp(\hat{\sigma}_G{}^2) - 1]$ holds if and only if[6]

$$\sigma_F(Y)/E_F(Y) < \sigma_G(Y)/E_G(Y). \tag{3}$$

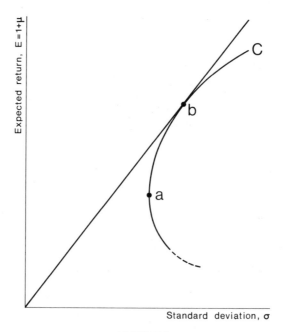

FIGURE 1

The *relevant* frontier for the log-normal case is a subset of the mean-variance frontier. To illustrate, let us denote the log-normal risk measure by M ($M = \sigma/E$). Since the frontier can be described by $\sigma = f(E)$, one can write

[6] Note that we compare means and coefficients of variance of given portfolios which are log-normally distributed. On the construction of these portfolios, see Section 4.

the risk measure as $M = f(E)/E$. All portfolios which are efficient in the log-normal case must yield

$$\partial M/\partial E > 0, \qquad \text{i.e.,} \qquad [Ef'(E) - f(E)]/E^2 > 0,$$

which implies that

$$f'(E) > f(E)/E = \sigma/E. \tag{4}$$

The formulation given in (4) is convenient if one puts σ on the vertical axis and E on the horizontal axis. However, if we put the expected return on the vertical axis and the standard deviation on the horizontal axis, it is more convenient to describe the relevant frontier by

$$E/\sigma > 1/f'(E). \tag{5}$$

In Figure 1, equation (4) or (5) implies that only the segment bc is efficient in the log-normal case, while it is well known that in the one-period case the efficient $M-V$ frontier is larger, namely, the segment ac. In order to measure the magnitude of the reduction in the efficient frontier as a result of using the coefficient of variation rather than the variance itself as a measure of risk, the efficient set has been constructed in the $E-\sigma$ space and the $(E-\sigma/E)$ space for ten stocks listed on the Israeli Stock Exchange.[7] The efficient set has been constructed by raising E by $\Delta E = 0.5\%$ each time.[8] The mean-variance relevant frontier is given by the segment ac in Figure 2a, which includes 23 efficient portfolios. In the log-normal case the investor is limited to the bc segment which includes only eight efficient portfolios. The segment bc in the $E-\sigma$ space is given by the segment b^1c^1 in the $E-\sigma/E$ space in Figure 2b. Note that b^1 represents the portfolio with the minimum *coefficient of variation*, while point a in Figure 2a denotes the portfolio with minimum variance. It is obvious from the preceding analysis that in the log-normal case investors tend to diversify their portfolios but invest in more risky securities.

In the next section we assume that the distributions of the n-period terminal wealth are log-normally distributed and that investors are allowed to revise their portfolios n times. They can include riskless assets in their portfolios, but the terminal value of these riskless assets is not certain since the proportion invested in the riskless assets is changed each period (by some uniform investment strategy) as a function of the observed rates of return on the risky assets included in the portfolio.

---

[7] The basic data used in finding the efficiency frontier are given in the Appendix.

[8] Increasing E by 0.5% is, of course, arbitrary. However, the basic results are invariant to the chosen ΔE.

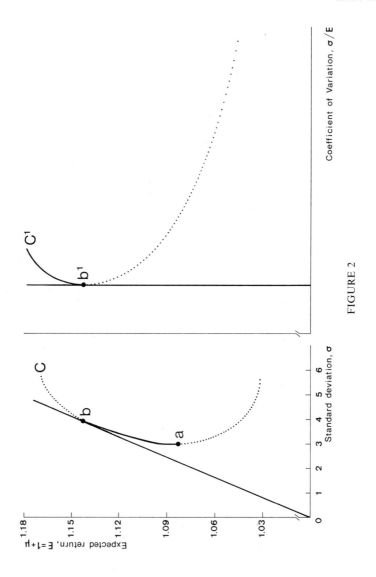

FIGURE 2

4.   EQUILIBRIUM AND LOG-NORMAL EFFICIENCY ANALYSIS WITH ONE-PERIOD PARAMETERS

Assuming that Y is log-normally rather than normally distributed, one can use the mean coefficient of variation investment criterion instead of the mean-variance criterion. However, one cannot analyze liquidity preference and equilibrium relationships when Y is log-normally distributed. The reason, as Feldstein (1969) correctly claims, is that any linear combination of random variables, where each of the elements is log-normally distributed, does not distribute according to the two-parameter log-normal distribution. Moreover, even a combination of a random variable, which is log-normally distributed, with a constant (cash) is not log-normally distributed. Feldstein suggests that investors make a "statistical mistake" [see Feldstein (1969, p. 10)] in assuming that all distributions of return are stable,[9] even though it is statistically obvious that the log-normal distribution is not a stable one.

Feldstein's notion of statistical mistake is employed here with some modification. Let Y, the terminal wealth after n periods be log-normally distributed. The investor is allowed to revise his portfolio n times. Suppose that every period he puts proportion p of his assets in x_1 and $(1 - p)$ in x_2. His final wealth after n periods is

$$Y = \prod_{i=1}^{n} [px_{1i} + (1 - p)x_{2i}] = \prod_{i=1}^{n} z_i;$$

namely, it is assumed that for $n > n_0$, $\log Y = \sum_{i=1}^{n} \log z_i$ is normally distributed (and hence $\prod_{i=1}^{n} z_i = Y$ is log-normally distributed). The investor might shift from one log-normal distribution to another by choosing different linear combinations of the *one-period* random variables. While it is known that a linear combination of $(\pi z_i)_1$ and $(\pi z_i)_2$ will not provide a log-normal distribution, it is possible that a linear combination of x_1 and x_2 (in each period) does provide a log-normal distribution of *final wealth*. The above assertion is correct even if *one* of the assets yields a constant (or zero) rate of return.

Nevertheless, even with this technique one does not overcome all difficulties and has to assume that investors do make a "statistical mistake" and assume log normality implicitly, even though by pure statistical rules it is known that not all portfolio combinations yield log-normal distributions. Thus, even if it is given that Y is log-normally distributed, it is possible to show that there are other n-period distributions which are not precisely log normal, but may be approximately log normal. Indeed Lintner has shown that a

---

[9] A distribution is called stable if each linear combination of the variables belongs to the same family of distributions of the variables themselves.

linear combination of log-normal distributions is very close to a log-normal distribution, especially for long horizons (6–12 months).[10]

Thus, we assume that investors think that for a reasonably long period the distributions of terminal wealth are log-normally distributed, even though some of the distributions are not precisely log normal. After all, in order to find equilibrium prices it is more important what the investor thinks the distribution looks like rather than what the precise statistical rules are.

The relationship betweeen the multiperiod investment decision and the one-period investment decision is given in Theorem 5:

THEOREM 5   Let $[E_{F_1}(x), \sigma_{F_1}(x)]$ and $[E_{G_1}(x), \sigma_{G_1}(x)]$ be the one-period expected return and variance of two alternative prospects. The necessary and sufficient conditions for $E_{F^n}u(x) > E_{G^n}u(x)$ for all concave utilities u are

$$E_{F_1}(x) \geq E_{G_1}(x), \qquad \sigma_{F_1}(x)/E_{F_1}(x) < \sigma_{G_1}(x)/E_{G_1}(x),$$

where F_1 and G_1 denote the *one-period* distributions and F^n and G^n denote the *n*-period distributions which are derived from F_1 and G_1 (by uniform diversification strategies) and are assumed to be approximately log normal.

In other words, this theorem claims that instead of looking at the *multiperiod* mean coefficient of variation rule one can use the *one-period* mean coefficient of variation rule, even though the one-period distributions are *not* log-normally distributed.

Proof   The proof is straightforward: The multiperiod expected return and variance are given by

$$E_{F_n}(Y) = (E_{F_1})^n, \qquad \sigma_{F_n}^2(Y) = [\sigma_{F_1}^2(x) + (E_{F_1}(x))^2]^n - (E_{F_1}(x))^{2n},$$

and the *n*-period coefficient of variation is

$$\frac{\sigma_{F_n}^2(Y)}{E_{F_n}(Y)^2} = \frac{[\sigma_{F_1}^2(x) + (E_{F_1}(x))^2]^n - (E_{F_1}(x))^{2n}}{(E_{F_1}(x))^{2n}} = \left[\frac{\sigma_{F_1}^2(x)}{(E_{F_1}(x))^2} + 1\right]^n - 1$$

(the parameters of distribution G_n are defined similarly). Thus,

$$E_{F_1}(x) > E_{G_1}(x) \qquad \text{if and only if} \qquad E_{F_n}(Y) > E_{G_n}(Y),$$

$$\frac{\sigma_{F_n}(Y)}{E_{F_n}(Y)} < \frac{\sigma_{G_n}(Y)}{E_{G_n}(Y)} \qquad \text{if and only if} \qquad \frac{\sigma_{F_1}(x)}{E_{F_1}(x)} < \frac{\sigma_{G_1}(x)}{E_{G_1}(x)}.$$

[10] Lintner hypothesizes that "investors assess the distributions of returns on individual stocks 'as if' they were jointly lognormal" and they "treat portfolios distributions 'as if' they were lognormally distributed." Note, that in order to find equilibrium in the stock market the relevant information is what the investors think the distributions look like and not the precise statistical distribution law. For more details see Lintner (1972).

But since the mean coefficient of variation is an optimal criterion for log-normal (multiperiod) distributions, this implies that the one-period mean coefficient of variation is the optimal criterion for all risk averters who invest for n periods.

Theorem 5 establishes the relationship between the efficiency frontiers constructed in terms of the one-period and the multiperiod portfolio parameters. Note that this theorem dealing with the log-normal distributions confirms the claim (see Section 2) that $S_n \subseteq S_1$. In other words, it is *not* possible that for some concave u_1, $E_{F^n}u_1(x) < E_{G^n}u_1(x)$ and for another concave u_2, $E_{F^n}u_2(x) > E_{G^n}u_2(x)$ (i.e., F^n and G^n are included in the risk averter's efficient set), in spite of the fact that in the one-period case[11]

$$E_{F_1}(x) \geq E_{G_1}(x), \qquad \sigma_{F_1}(x) < \sigma_{G_1}(x). \tag{6}$$

Thus, unlike Tobin, we maintain that if option F_1 dominates option G_1 in the one-period case, the last prospect cannot revert to the efficient set as n increases. Moreover, the efficient set might decrease over time which implies that $S_n \subset S_1$. This follows from the numerical example given in Section 2. $S_n \subset S_1$ may also hold in the log-normal case since (6) implies that the conditions of Theorem 5 hold, but (5) does not imply (6). Suppose that $E_{F_1}(x) > E_{G_1}(x)$ and $\sigma_{F_1}(x) > \sigma_{G_1}(x)$, F_1 and G_1 are included in the one-period mean-variance efficient set. This does not rule out the possibility that

$$E_{F_1}(x) \geq E_{G_1}(x) \qquad \text{and} \qquad \sigma_{F_1}(x)/E_{F_1}(x) < \sigma_{G_1}(x)/E_{G_1}(x)$$

which means that portfolio G_1 should be eliminated from the multiperiod efficient set (i.e., $S_n \subset S_1$ might hold). Thus, all risk averters are faced with the same one-period mean-coefficient of variation frontier, even though they may differ in their investment horizon n.

If one assumes no riskless assets, it is obvious that a portfolio which includes cash is an efficient portfolio in the log-normal case. To demonstrate, suppose that there is a *one-period* portfolio which does not include cash with expected return $(1 + \mu_m)$ and standard deviation σ_m. Now let us blend this portfolio with cash such that proportion p of our wealth is invested in this portfolio and $(1 - p)$ is held in cash. The new portfolio parameters will be

$$1 + \mu_y = p(1 + \mu_m) + (1 - p), \tag{7}$$

$$\sigma_y = p\sigma_m. \tag{8}$$

Obviously $1 + \mu_m > 1 + \mu_y$, but

$$\frac{\sigma_m}{1 + \mu_m} > \frac{p\sigma_m}{p(1 + \mu_m) + (1 - p)} \equiv \frac{\sigma_y}{1 + \mu_y},$$

[11] Note that Hakansson (1971) implies that the conditions of Theorem 5 hold.

and hence, the portfolio without cash, m, does not dominate the portfolio which includes cash (see Theorem 5). In other words, diversification between risky assets and cash represent an efficient portfolio in the long run. However, if one includes the possibility of one-period riskless bonds, cash will be eliminated from all efficient portfolios since

$$Ey_1 \equiv 1 + \mu(y_1) = p(1 + \mu_m) + (1 - p),$$
$$Ey_2 \equiv 1 + \mu(y_2) = p(1 + \mu_m) + (1 - p)(1 + r),$$

where y_1 is the portfolio which includes the risky portfolio m plus cash, and y_2 includes the same risky portfolio m plus riskless bonds; μ_m is the expected rate of return on the risky portfolios and r is the riskless interest rate. But,

$$\sigma_{y_1} = \sigma_{y_2} = p\sigma_m \qquad \text{and} \qquad Ey_2 > Ey_1 \qquad (\text{since } r > 0);$$

consequently

$$\sigma_{y_2}/[1 + \mu(y_2)] < \sigma_{y_1}/[1 + \mu(y_1)],$$

and hence portfolio y_2 dominates portfolio y_1. This result which is derived in the mean coefficient of variation framework is similar to the well-known result of the one-period mean-variance model in which the demand for money vanishes once one is ready to assume the existence of riskless bonds.

In order to analyze multiperiod diversification strategies, let us assume that the investor is faced with two securities x and y, where for the one-period $Ex > Ey$ and $\sigma_x < \sigma_y$, and the correlation coefficient is given by $R(xy)$. We shall examine whether diversification might be an efficient strategy in the log-normal case where n revisions are allowed. Let us first rule out the possibility of holding riskless bonds and cash.[12] Clearly, no one will specialize in security y since $Ex > Ey$ (see Theorem 5). Diversification is an efficient strategy in the log-normal case if and only if the following inequality holds:

$$\frac{p_1^2\sigma_x^2 + p_2^2\sigma_y^2 + 2p_1p_2R_{(xy)}\sigma_x\sigma_y}{[p_1(1 + \mu_x) + p_2(1 + \mu_y)]^2} < \frac{\sigma_x^2}{(1 + \mu_x)^2} \tag{9}$$

(see Theorem 5), where p_1 is the investment proportion in the first security and $p_2 = 1 - p_1$ is the proportion invested in the second security. After substituting $1 - p_1$ for p_2 and rearranging terms, one can rewrite (9) as[13]

$$p_1 > \frac{\sigma_y E_x - \sigma_x E_y}{\sigma_y E_x - \sigma_x E_y + 2[E_x E_y \sigma_x^2 - R_{(xy)}\sigma_x\sigma_y E_x^2]}. \tag{10}$$

---

[12] If one takes inflation into account, even cash should be considered as a risky asset. Thus, calculating the parameters in real terms, no riskless asset exists. For more details see Sarnat (1972).

[13] Note that $1 + \mu_x = E_x$ and $1 + \mu_y = E_y$ by definition.

Clearly, (10) should hold for $0 < p_1 < 1$ in order to assure that that diversification would be an efficient strategy. If (10) holds only for $p_1 > 1$, diversification is an inefficient strategy since the only *feasible* solution to (10) is $p_1 = 1$, and the investor would choose to invest only in x. As can be readily seen, $p_1 < 1$, and (10) hold simultaneously, if

$$E_x E_y \sigma_x^2 > R_{(xy)} \sigma_x \sigma_y E_x^2 \tag{11}$$

or

$$R_{(xy)} < (E_y/\sigma_y)/(E_x/\sigma_x) < 1. \tag{12}$$

In the case of nonpositive correlation, diversified portfolios are included in the efficient set of all risk averters since (12) holds. For a positive correlation (but not necessarily a perfect one) diversification might be ruled out and the optimal portfolio for all risk averters would be the undiversified portfolio x. For example, suppose that $E_y/\sigma_y = 1$ and $E_x/\sigma_x = 2$. Note that $E_x/\sigma_x > E_y/\sigma_y$ as required by the assumption. If $R_{(xy)} = 0.60$, diversification is an inefficient strategy for every risk averter provided that the n-period distributions are indeed log normal. Graphically, this is shown in Figure 3. The slope $1/f'(E)$ of the frontier YY_1X is always larger than the slope of the straight line $0X$; i.e., the inequality $E/\sigma > 1/f'(E)$ never holds on the curve YY_1X and diversification is an inefficient strategy. If $R_{(xy)} = +1$, diversification would not take place for the same reasons. It is interesting to note that these results have

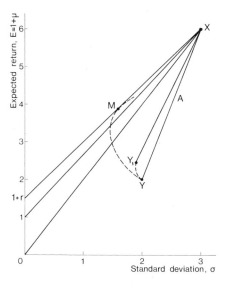

FIGURE 3

no counterpart in the one-period mean-variance portfolio analysis. For one-period investors, any diversified portfolio which lies on the curve Y_1X, or even on the straight line YAX (i.e., if $R_{(xy)} = +1$), is an efficient portfolio and cannot be ruled out from the efficient set.

Let us now relax the assumption that all assets are risky and allow the investors to hold cash or even riskless assets. This will enhance the previous results and the probability that one will rule out diversification increases. Since the slope of line OX is smaller than $1/f'(E)$ for each point on the curve YY_1X, this holds a fortiori for the line $1X$ and the line $(1 + r, X)$ which represent holding security X and cash, and holding security X and riskless bonds respectively. Thus, in the case of riskless assets, or cash, the multiperiod results coincide with the mean-variance results since no one-period risk averter will be a diversifier in the above case [see Sharpe (1964), Lintner (1965)].

In the case where investors are allowed to borrow and lend for the next one-period at the riskless interest rate r, the equilibrium relationships between expected return and risk are exactly like those derived by Sharpe and Lintner, even though we deal with (multiperiod) log-normal distributions rather than normal distributions, and the investment horizon n is not necessarily identical for all investors. No matter what n is, all investors will have the same efficient set given in terms of the one-period parameters, i.e., the line $(1 + r, X)$ given in Figure 3. On this line, $E/\sigma > 1/f'(E)$ and hence all multiperiod risk averters will choose the same risky portfolio M mixed with different proportions of riskless assets. Thus, one can use Tobin's Separation Theorem and the same technique that Sharpe and Lintner used in their model to derive the equilibrium market prices as well as the relationship between expected return and risk. Similar results hold in the continuous case [see Merton (1977)].

Samuelson (1967) and Hadar and Russell (1971) analyze the conditions under which diversification is an optimal strategy. Diversification is called an optimal investment strategy if for every concave utility function u, $Eu(p) > Eu(x_i)$, where x_i are specialized strategies (one security in the ith portfolio), and p represents some linear combination of the specialized portfolios. The results of Samuelson and Hadar and Russell are easily achieved (and more generally) if one is ready to assume that the multiperiod distributions are log normal.

THEOREM 6   Let $(x_1x_2\cdots x_m)$ be m one-period identically independently distributed variates. Then, diversification is an optimal strategy for all risk averters,[14] provided that the multiperiod distributions are log normal.

[14] For a similar theorem see Samuelson (1967), and Hadar and Russell (1971).

Proof   The proof is a simple application of Theorem 5. Let us denote the diversified portfolio by x_p, where $x_p = \sum_{i=1}^{m} p_i x_i$ and $\sum_{i=1}^{m} p_i = 1$ and that for at least two x_i, $p_i > 0$. Since $Ex_1 = Ex_2 = \cdots = Ex_m = E_0$ and $\sigma_{x_1} = \sigma_{x_2} = \cdots = \sigma_{x_m} \equiv \sigma_0$ by assumption, then $Ex_p = E_0$. All that remains to prove is that $\sigma_{x_p}/E_0 < \sigma_0/E_0$ in order to establish the claim that every risk averter would choose a diversified portfolio (see Theorem 5). But the strategy $(p_1 \cdots p_m) = (1/m, \ldots, 1/m)$ minimizes the portfolio variance and is therefore the optimal one for all risk averters.

Samuelson drops the assumption of independence and assumes instead that the joint distribution function is symmetric in its arguments. Under these conditions diversification is again optimal, and the optimal strategy is given by $(p_1 \cdots p_m) = (1/m, \ldots, 1/m)$. One may waive the independence assumption in our model and show that diversification indeed pays in the long run. The precise conditions are given in Theorem 7:

THEOREM 7   Let $x_1 \cdots x_m$ be one-period random variables with identical means and variances and correlation $R_{ij} \le 1$ with $R_{ij} < 1$ for at least one pair (i, j). If the *multiperiod* distributions are log normal, then diversification is optimal.

Proof   Since $Ex_1 = Ex_2 = \cdots = Ex_m \equiv E_0$ by assumption, the portfolio with the minimum variance is the optimal one (see Theorem 5). However,

$$\sigma_p{}^2 = \sum_{i=1}^{m} p_i{}^2 \sigma_i{}^2 + 2 \sum_{i=1, j>i}^{m} p_i p_j R_{ij} \sigma_i \sigma_j,$$

where p represents a diversified portfolio. Since $\sigma_1 = \sigma_2 = \cdots = \sigma_m \equiv \sigma_0$ by assumption,

$$\sigma_p{}^2 = \sigma_0{}^2 \left(\sum_{i=1}^{m} p_i{}^2 + 2 \sum_{i=1, j>i}^{m} p_i p_j R_{ij} \right),$$

since $R_{ij} < 1$ for at least one pair (i, j)

$$\sum_{i=1}^{m} p_i{}^2 + 2 \sum_{i=1, j>1}^{m} p_i p_j R_{ij} < 1,$$

and $\sigma_p < \sigma_0$ which implies that $\sigma_p/E_0 < \sigma_0/E_0$. Thus, all specialized portfolios are inefficient, and all risk averters would diversify their investment.

COROLLARY 1   If $R_{ij} = +1$ for all pairs (i, j), long-run risk averters (such as one-period investors) cannot gain from diversification. This is straightforward since under the assumption of the theorem and the corollary

$$\sigma_p^2 = \sum_{i=1}^{m} p_i^2 \sigma_i^2 + 2 \sum_{i=1, j>i}^{m} p_i p_j \sigma_i \sigma_j R_{ij} = \sigma_0^2 \left(\sum_{i=1}^{m} p_i^2 + 2 \sum_{i=1, j>i}^{m} p_i p_j \right)$$

$$= \sigma_0^2 \left(\sum_{i=1}^{m} p_i \right)^2 = \sigma_0^2.$$

Since $Ex_1 = Ex_2 = \cdots = Ex_m \equiv E_0$, the investor cannot gain from diversification; $Ex_p = Ex_0$ and $\sigma_p^2 = \sigma_0^2$, hence $\sigma_p/Ex_p = \sigma_0/E_0$.

COROLLARY 2   Suppose that $R_{ij} = R_0 < 1$ for all pairs (i, j). Under the assumptions of Theorem 6, diversification is optimal and the optimal strategy is $(p_1, p_2, \ldots, p_m) = (1/m, 1/m, \ldots, 1/m)$.

Proof   Since the expected return of all linear combinations of $(x_1 \cdots x_n)$ yields the same value E_0, the aim is to minimize the portfolio variance, subject to the constraint

$$\sum_{i=1}^{m} p_i = 1.$$

But it is easy to show that the strategy $(p_1, p_2, \ldots, p_m) = (1/m, 1/m, \ldots, 1/m)$, minimizes the variance and hence also minimizes the coefficient of variation of the portfolio.

COROLLARY 3   Let x and y be two one-period random variables with common means, finite (not necessarily identical) variances, and with log-normal distributions. Then diversification is optimal if $R(xy) \leq 0$.

Since $R(xy) \leq 0$, one can always reduce the variance by diversification, and by Theorem 5 the portfolio with minimum variance is the optimal one. The optimal investment strategy is

$$p_1 = \frac{\sigma_2^2 - R\sigma_1\sigma_2}{\sigma_1^2 + \sigma_2^2 - 2R\sigma_1\sigma_2}$$

and

$$p_2 = \frac{\sigma_1^2 - R\sigma_1\sigma_2}{\sigma_1^2 + \sigma_2^2 - 2R\sigma_1\sigma_2}, \qquad (p_1 + p_2 = 1).$$

However, if $R(xy) > 0$ (even smaller than 1), one cannot be certain that diversification provides an optimal, or even an efficient strategy. One counterexample will suffice: Let $\sigma_1 = 1$, $\sigma_2 = 2$. Then $p_1 = (4 - 2R)/(5 - 4R)$. If

$R(xy) \geq \frac{1}{2}$, diversification will not provide an optimal policy or even an efficient strategy since $p_1 > 1$, the the feasible solution is, of course, $p_1 = 1$ (i.e., a specialized portfolio).

5. CONCLUDING REMARKS

Assuming risk aversion and normal distributions, the mean-variance rule coincides with the investment rule which is appropriate for all risk averters regardless of the distributions feature. However, the multiperiod mean-variance rule leads to a nondecreasing efficient set as the investment horizon increases, while the multiperiod risk-aversion criterion leads to a non-increasing efficient set. The two rules do *not* coincide in the multiperiod case, and the mean-variance rule fails since the normality assumption is violated.

Assuming that the distributions of prices are log normal rather than normal does not change the investment frontier. However, the relevant frontier in the log-normal case is a subset of the relevant frontier in the normal case since the mean-variance rule is replaced by the mean coefficient of variation rule.

Liquidity preference, diversification, and equilibrium can be explained if one assumes that investors' best estimate is that the multiperiod distributions are log normal and that they can revise their portfolio by some uniform strategy n times. The same equilibrium relationship has been shown to be true [see Merton (1973)] without the necessity to assume log normality, but with the constraint that the investors revise their portfolio continuously.

If investors act "as if" the terminal wealth is log-normally distributed, portfolios which include cash as well as risky assets are efficient for all long-run risk averters. If one calculates the portfolio return in real terms, cash should be considered as a risky asset. In this case, unlike the one-period case, diversification might be an inefficient strategy for all risk averters.

In case of m identical and independent variables, the optimal long-run strategy is to invest $1/m$ in each security. If all m variables have the same mean and variance, and the correlation coefficient is $R_{ij} = R_0 < 1$ [for all (i, j)], the optimal strategy is again to invest $1/m$ in each security. For two securities with identical means and finite variances, diversification is optimal if $R \leq 0$. However, if $R > 0$ (even less than $+1$), diversification might be an inefficient strategy.

Finally, we also obtained some operative results. These were derived quite easily, but at the cost of making assumptions: most of the results presented in this paper are based on the independence over time assumption, and in order to achieve other results we also had to assume stationarity over time.

APPENDIX

Security no.	Mean-rate of return (%)	Standard deviation
1	14.7	5.1
2	15.3	4.7
3	13.1	4.4
4	12.9	5.4
5	10.8	5.3
6	3.6	4.7
7	6.9	3.7
8	18.0	3.8
9	13.4	4.1
10	9.1	4.1

Security	1	2	3	4	5	6	7	8	9	10
	1.00									
2	0.57	1.00								
3	0.82	0.68	1.00							
4	0.65	0.61	0.71	1.00						
5	0.58	0.65	0.68	0.87	1.00					
6	0.34	0.45	0.44	0.74	0.71	1.00				
7	0.38	0.13	0.38	0.34	0.31	0.34	1.00			
8	0.41	0.44	0.41	0.32	0.30	0.19	0.35	1.00		
9	0.65	0.51	0.70	0.65	0.67	0.49	0.46	0.45	1.00	
10	0.67	0.67	0.76	0.18	0.66	0.48	0.37	0.49	0.67	1.00

REFERENCES

Aitchison, J., and Brown, J. A. C., (1963). *The Lognormal Distribution*. London and New York: Cambridge Univ. Press.

Cootner, P. H. (ed.) (1967). *The Random Character of Stock Market Prices*, rev. ed., Cambridge, Massachusetts: MIT Press.

Feldstein, M. S. (1969). Mean-Variance Analysis in the Theory of Liquidity Preference, *Review of Economic Studies* (January).

Hadar, J., and Russell, W. R. (1969). Rules for Ordering Uncertain Prospects, *American Economic Review* (March).

Hadar, J., and Russell, W. R. (1971). Stochastic Dominance and Diversification, *Journal of Economic Theory*.

Hakansson, N. (1971). Multi-Period Mean-Variance Analysis: Toward a General Theory of Portfolio Choice, *Journal of Finance* (September).

Hanoch G., and Levy, H. (1969). The Efficiency Analysis of Choice Involving Risk, *Review of Economic Studies* (July).

Levy, H. (1973a). Efficiency Criteria and Efficient Portfolio: The Multi-Period Case, *American Economic Review* (December).

Levy, H. (1973b). Stochastic Dominance among Log-Normal Prospects, *International Economic Review* (October).

Lintner, J. (1965). Security Price, Risk, and Maximal Gains from Diversification, *Journal of Finance* (December).

Lintner, J. (1972). Equilibrium in a Random Walk and Lognormal Securities Market, Discussion Paper, No. 235, Harvard Inst. of Econ. Res. (July).

Markowitz, H. M. (1952). Portfolio Selection, *Journal of Finance* (March).

Markowitz, H. M. (1959). *Portfolio Selection.* New York: Wiley.

Merton, R. C. (1971). Optimum Consumption and Portfolio Rules in a Continuous-Time Model, *Journal of Economic Theory* (December).

Merton, R. C. (1973). An Intertemporal Capital Asset Pricing Model, *Econometrica.*

Merton, R. C., and Samuelson, P. A. (1974). Fallacy of Log-Normal Approximation to Optimal Portfolio Decision Making over Many Periods, *Journal of Financial Economics* (May).

Quirk, J. P., and Saposnik, R. (1962). Admissibility and Measurable Utility Functions, *Review of Economic Studies.*

Rothschild, M., and Stiglitz, J. E. (1970a). Increasing Risk: I. A Definition, *Journal of Economic Theory* (September).

Rothschild, M., and Stiglitz, J. E. (1970b). Increasing Risk: II. Its Economic Consequences, *Journal of Economic Theory.*

Samuelson, P. A. (1967). General Proof That Diversification Pays, *Journal of Financial and Quantitative Analysis.*

Samuelson, P. A. (1971). The Fallacy of Maximizing the Geometric Mean in Long Sequences of Investing or Gambling, *Proceedings of the National Academy of Science USA* (October).

Sarnat, M. (1972). Purchasing Power Risk, Portfolio Analysis and the Case for Index Linked Bonds, *Journal of Money Credit and Banking*

Sharpe, W. F. (1964). Capital Assets Prices: A Theory of Market Equilibrium under Conditions of Risk, *Journal of Finance.*

Stevens, G. V. G. (1972). On Tobin's Multiperiod Portfolio Theorem, *Review of Economic Studies* (October).

Tobin, J. (1965). The Theory of Portfolio Selection, in *The Theory of Interest Rates*, (F. H. Hahn and F. P. R. Brechlings, eds.). New York: Macmillan.

Tobin, J. (1958). Liquidity Preference as Behavior towards Risk, *Review of Economic Studies* (February).

Adverse selection and optimum insurance policies

EYTAN SHESHINSKI

THE HEBREW UNIVERSITY
JERUSALEM

1. INTRODUCTION

We describe here how an insurance company decides on the price schedule for insurance contracts against certain accidents (or medical needs) which it offers on the basis of the choices made by the customers themselves regarding the contracts that they purchase. The return from an insurance contract is a random variable which depends on the accident probability of the individual customer. While an individual may generally be assumed to be well-informed about his accident probability, the insurance firm has only imperfect information about this probability and, consequently, can only observe the relation between the type of insurance bought by different customers and their accident frequencies. This paper is concerned with the effect of such self-selecting information devices on the policy chosen by a profit maximizing firm.[1]

This work was supported by National Science Foundation Grant SOC 74-11446 at the Institute for Mathematical Studies in the Social Sciences, Stanford University, Stanford, California.

[1] Insurance firms also look, of course, for objective characteristics (health, age, etc.) which are correlated with accident probabilities, but these (costly) screening devices generally still leave a great deal of variability *within* each group. For simplicity, we disregard the problem of optimum investment in such examinations of customers' status.

We consider an insurance firm that establishes a price schedule for insurance contracts and allows customers indiscriminantly to determine the size of the contract. Accident-prone individuals are expected to purchase relatively large insurance policies, and may typically be willing to pay a higher price for them. It has thus been argued that this "*adverse selection*" aspect will induce firms to charge proportionately higher prices for large contracts. This argument disregards, however, the effect of the *distribution* of customers (by accident probabilities) on the optimum policy. If a sufficiently large number of customers is concentrated in the high-probabilities range, it may be profitable, depending on demand characteristics, not to charge too high a price for large contracts.

We first consider a simple case in which the firm chooses a profit-maximizing linear policy, setting a quantity constraint on the size of permitted policies. The policy chosen by the monopoly is then compared with a policy of the same type that maximizes social welfare, defined as the sum of individuals' expected utilities. It is shown that the monopoly chooses to provide a lower return on contracts, or sets a lower quantity constraint, or both, compared with the social optimum.

A second example provides an explicit solution for the profit-maximizing nonlinear schedule chosen by the firm. This example suggests that the schedule need not be convex throughout, due to the interaction of demands and the distribution of customers.

The performance of markets when buyers or sellers have imperfect information concerning some relevant attributes has been of much recent interest. The implications for general equilibrium of contingent insurance contracts are discussed by Rothschild and Stiglitz (1976). Other cases involving labor markets are discussed by Spence (1974), Arrow (1973), and Salop and Salop (1976). This paper extends these works by allowing for nonlinear price schedules (including quantity constraints). The results, however, pertain only to special cases and can therefore be regarded only as illustrative.

In solving the nonlinear problem, we make use of the methods developed to solve a similar problem in the theory of optimum income taxation [see Mirrlees (1971) and Sheshinski (1976)].

2. THE GENERAL PROBLEM

Consider a group of individuals, all of whom have some risk of suffering an accident, which, if it occurs, does the same damage to each person. In the absence of insurance, all individuals are assumed to have the same income in each state: y_0 ($y_0 > 0$) if no accident occurs and y_1 ($y_1 > 0$) if an accident occurs. An insurance firm offers insurance contracts specifying that if a premium x ($x > 0$) is paid, the insured receives nothing if no accident occurs and receives $x + s(x)$ ($s(x) \geq 0$) if an accident occurs. Thus, $s(x)$ is the compensation, above the premium, paid in case of an accident.

Individuals choose their optimum insurance contracts by maximizing expected utility U. We assume that all individuals have the same strictly concave von Neumann–Morgenstern utility function $u(\cdot)$, but differ with respect to the probability with which they suffer accidents. We call an individual with an accident probability of p ($1 \geq p \geq 0$), a p-*individual*. Individuals are assumed to know their accident probabilities accurately. Thus, the p-individual maximizes his expected utility

$$U(p, x) = (1 - p)u(y_0 - x) + pu(y_1 + s(x)) \tag{1}$$

with respect to x.

We assume that the utility function $u(\cdot)$ is twice differentiable and $u' > 0, u'' < 0$ for all $x \geq 0$. Further, in order to ensure that individuals choose to have a positive consumption in both states, we assume that $u'(0) = \infty$. Suppose, finally, that the insurance policy $s(\cdot)$ is also twice differentiable, with $s' > 0$ for all $x \geq 0$.

The first-order condition for a maximum of (1) is then

$$-(1 - p)u'(y_0 - x) + pu'(y_1 + s(x))s'(x) \leq 0,$$
$$[-(1 - p)u'(y_0 - x) + pu'(y_1 + s(x))s'(x)]x = 0. \tag{2}$$

The second-order condition for a unique global maximum is assumed to hold

$$(1 - p)u''(y_0 - x) + pu''(y_1 + s(x))s'(x)^2 + pu'(y_1 + s(x))s''(x) < 0 \tag{3}$$

for all $1 \geq p \geq 0$ and $y_0 > x \geq 0$. From (2) and (3) it is seen that the optimum x is increasing with p. Hence, given our assumptions, there exists a number $\underline{p}$, $1 > \underline{p} > 0$, defined by the condition

$$-(1 - \underline{p})u'(y_0) + \underline{p}u'(y_1)s'(0) = 0 \tag{4}$$

such that the optimum of the p-individual $x(p)$ is given by

$$x(p) = \begin{cases} 0 & \text{if } p < \underline{p}, \\ \hat{x}(p) & \text{if } p \geq \underline{p}, \end{cases} \tag{5}$$

where $\hat{x}(p)$ is determined by the condition

$$-(1 - p)u'(y_0 - \hat{x}) + pu'(y_1 + s(\hat{x}))s'(\hat{x}) = 0. \tag{6}$$

By (3), (4), and (6), $\hat{x}(\underline{p}) = 0$ and $d\hat{x}/dp > 0$ for $p > \underline{p}$; that is, the size of the optimum policy continuously increases with the probability of accident.

The basic assumption concerning the imperfect information available to the insurance firm is that it cannot distinguish among individuals according to their accident probabilities, except by their market behavior. Any policy offered is therefore open to all individuals in the market without discrimination.

For a given policy $s(\cdot)$, expected profits of the firm from a p-individual, $R[p, s(\cdot)]$, are

$$R[p, s(\cdot)] = (1 - p)x(p) - ps(x(p)),\tag{7}$$

where $x(p)$ is given by (5).

Let there be $f(p)$ ($f \geq 0$) p-individuals in the market. Normalizing the size of the potential customer population to unity, we may regard $f(p)$ as a density function. Total expected profits of the firm, $R[s(\cdot)]$, are then given by

$$R[s(\cdot)] = \int_0^1 R[p, s(\cdot)]f(p)\,dp.\tag{8}$$

The insurance firm is assumed to have information on individuals' behavior $x(p)$ and on the density function $f(p)$, and its objective is to find the policy $s(\cdot)$ that maximizes (7).

Methods of the calculus of variations can be applied to solve this problem. The standard theory, however, has to be extended in order to take into account the constraint imposed by (2). The structure of this problem is similar to the problem of the choice of an optimum income tax function [see Mirrlees (1971) and Sheshinski (1976)]. As in that problem, the first-order conditions for the appropriate maximization do not provide much insight into the method or the properties of the optimum function. We shall therefore proceed to consider special cases for which an explicit solution can be found. The first case restricts the policy chosen by the firm to be linear with a ceiling on size. The other cases allow nonlinear policies but restrict the form of the utility function.

3. THE OPTIMUM LINEAR POLICY
WITH A CEILING

Suppose that the insurance firm offers a policy which is in fixed proportion β ($\beta > 0$) to the premium paid, provided the size of the premium does not exceed a certain level, say, $\bar{x}$.[2] Thus,

$$s(x) = \begin{cases} \beta x, & x \leq \bar{x}, \\ \beta\bar{x}, & x > \bar{x}. \end{cases}\tag{9}$$

---

[2] This violates our assumption that $s(x)$ is differentiable at x, but the required modification is incorporated in equation (10).

If the quantity constraint $\bar{x}$ is effective, then, by (2)–(5), there exist numbers $\bar{p}$ and $\underline{p}$, $1 > \bar{p} > \underline{p} > 0$, defined by

$$-(1 - \bar{p})u'(y_0 - \bar{x}) + \bar{p}u'(y_1 + \beta\bar{x})\beta = 0, \tag{10}$$

$$-(1 - \underline{p})u'(y_0) + \underline{p}u'(y_1)\beta = 0. \tag{11}$$

The optimum of the p-individual is now given by

$$x(p) = \begin{cases} 0 & \text{if} & p \le \underline{p}, \\ \hat{x}(p) & \text{if} & \bar{p} > p \ge \underline{p}, \\ \bar{x} & \text{if} & p \ge \bar{p}, \end{cases} \tag{12}$$

where $\hat{x}(p)$ is determined by (6),

$$-(1 - p)u'(y_0 - \hat{x}) + pu'(y_1 + \beta\hat{x})\beta = 0. \tag{13}$$

By (10) and (13), $\hat{x}(\bar{p}) = \bar{x}$. Total expected profits $R(\beta, \bar{x})$ are given by

$$R(\beta, \bar{x}) = \int_{\underline{p}}^{\bar{p}} [(1 - p)\hat{x}(p) - p\beta\hat{x}(p)]f(p)\,dp + \int_{\bar{p}}^{1} [(1 - p)\bar{x} - p\beta\bar{x}]f(p)\,dp. \tag{14}$$

Using (10), (11), and (13), the first-order conditions for an interior maximum of (14) w.r.t. β and $\bar{x}$ are, respectively,

$$\frac{\partial R}{\partial \beta} = \int_{\underline{p}}^{\bar{p}} (1 - p - p\beta)\frac{\partial \hat{x}}{\partial \beta}f(p)\,dp - \int_{\underline{p}}^{\bar{p}} p\hat{x}(p)f(p)\,dp - \bar{x}\int_{\bar{p}}^{1} pf(p)\,dp = 0 \tag{15}$$

$$\frac{\partial R}{\partial \bar{x}} = \int_{\bar{p}}^{1} (1 - p)f(p)\,dp - \beta\int_{\bar{p}}^{1} pf(p)\,dp = 0. \tag{16}$$

Differentiating (13), we have

$$\frac{\partial \hat{x}}{\partial \beta} = \frac{-p[u'(y_1 + \beta\hat{x}) + u''(y_1 + \beta\hat{x})\beta\hat{x}]}{(1 - p)u''(y_0 - \hat{x}) + pu''(y_1 + \beta\hat{x})\beta^2}. \tag{17}$$

Substituting (17) into (15), using (13), we obtain

$$\frac{\partial R}{\partial \beta} = \int_{\underline{p}}^{\bar{p}} \left[\frac{u'(y_0 - \hat{x}) - u''(y_0 - \hat{x})\hat{x} - (u'(y_1 + \beta\hat{x}) + u''(y_1 + \beta\hat{x})\beta\hat{x})}{(1 - p)u''(y_0 - \hat{x}) + pu''(y_1 + \beta\hat{x})\beta^2} \right]$$

$$\times p(1 - p)f(p)\,dp - \bar{x}\int_{\bar{p}}^{1} pf(p)\,dp = 0. \tag{18}$$

Equations (10), (11), (16), and (18) determine the profit-maximizing values of $\bar{p}$, $\underline{p}$, $\bar{x}$, and β. Notice that for small β, the second term in (18) is small, and the sign of (18) is then the same as the sign of $u'(y_1) - u'(y_0)$, which is positive, assuming that $y_0 > y_1$.

Obviously, depending on y_0, y_1 and the function $f(p)$, conditions on $u(\cdot)$ may have to be imposed to ensure the existence of an interior optimum and the second-order conditions. We shall explore these conditions for a special case of the above model.

Let $u(z) = \log z$. For this case, by (13), $\hat{x} = py_0 - [(1 - p)y_1/\beta]$. By (10) and (11), we have

$$p = y_1/(\beta y_0 + y_1), \qquad \bar{p} = (y_1 + \beta \bar{x})/(\beta y_0 + y_1), \qquad (19)$$

and the first-order condition (18) becomes

$$\frac{\partial R}{\partial \beta} = \int_{\underline{p}}^{\bar{p}} \left[\left(\frac{1 - p}{\beta} \right)^2 y_1 - p^2 y_0 \right] f(p)\, dp - \bar{x} \int_{\bar{p}}^{1} pf(p)\, dp = 0. \qquad (20)$$

Equations (16), (19), and (20) determine the optimum values of p, $\bar{p}$, $\bar{x}$, and β. From (20), the optimum β satisfies

$$\beta = \left[\frac{y_1 \int_{\underline{p}}^{\bar{p}} (1 - p)^2 f(p)\, dp}{y_0 \int_{\underline{p}}^{p} p^2 f(p)\, dp + \bar{x} \int_{\bar{p}}^{1} pf(p)\, dp} \right]^{1/2}. \qquad (21)$$

In order to have $\beta > 0$, it is necessary (as assumed) that $y_1 > 0$. It can be shown that there are values of y_0 and y_1 which yield an interior solution and that satisfy the second-order conditions.

4. COMPARISON WITH THE SOCIALLY OPTIMAL POLICY

We want to compare the insurance policy chosen by the monopoly with a policy which is socially optimal under the same informational structure. Thus, the social planner, as the firm, cannot identify individuals by their accident probability, but knows the aggregate distribution $f(p)$ and the relation $\hat{x}(p)$. We adopt the utilitarian objective, where social welfare W is given by the sum of individuals' expected utilities:

$$W = \int_0^1 U(p)f(p)\, dp = \int_0^{\underline{p}} [(1 - p)u(y_0) + pu(y_1)]f(p)\, dp$$

$$+ \int_{\underline{p}}^{\bar{p}} [(1 - p)u(y_0 - \hat{x}) + pu(y_1 + \beta \hat{x})]f(p)\, dp$$

$$+ \int_{\bar{p}}^{1} [(1 - p)u(y_0 - \bar{x}) + pu(y_1 + \beta \bar{x})]f(p)\, dp. \qquad (22)$$

Consider the problem of maximizing (22) w.r.t. β and $\bar{x}$, subject to a budget constraint

$$\int_{\underline{p}}^{\bar{p}} [(1 - p)\hat{x}(p) - p\beta \hat{x}(p)]f(p) + \int_{\bar{p}}^{1} [(1 - p)\bar{x} - p\beta \bar{x}]f(p)\, dp - \bar{R} = 0 \qquad (23)$$

for a given $\bar{R} \geq 0$. To make the socially optimal policy comparable with the monopoly's policy, $\bar{R}$ should be equal to the maximum value of (14).

Using (10)–(13), the first-order conditions for an interior maximum can be written

$$\frac{\partial W}{\partial \beta} = \mu \frac{\partial R(\beta, \bar{x})}{\partial \beta} + \int_{\underline{p}}^{\bar{p}} u'(y_1 + \beta \hat{x})\hat{x}pf(p)\,dp + u'(y_1 + \beta \bar{x})\bar{x}\int_{\bar{p}}^{1} pf(p)\,dp = 0,$$
(24)

$$\frac{\partial W}{\partial \bar{x}} = \mu \frac{\partial R(\beta, \bar{x})}{\partial \bar{x}} + \int_{\bar{p}}^{1}\left[-(1-p)u'(y_0 - \bar{x}) + pu'(y_1 + \beta \bar{x})\beta\right]f(p)\,dp = 0,$$
(25)

where $\mu > 0$ is a constant (Lagrange multiplier).

In order to compare the socially optimum values of β and $\bar{x}$ determined by the system (10), (11), (13), (24), and (25) with the values chosen by the monopoly, we need to determine the sign of $\partial^2 R/\partial \beta \,\partial \bar{x}$. By (16),

$$\frac{\partial^2 R}{\partial \beta \,\partial \bar{x}} = (\beta \bar{p} + \bar{p} - 1)f(\bar{p})\frac{\partial \bar{p}}{\partial \beta} - \int_{\bar{p}}^{1} pf(p)\,dp.$$
(26)

Since $\partial^2 R/\partial \bar{x}^2 = (\beta \bar{p} + \bar{p} - 1)f(\bar{p})\,\partial \bar{p}/\partial \bar{x} < 0$ and, by (10), $\partial \bar{p}/\partial \bar{x} > 0$, it follows that $\beta \bar{p} + \bar{p} - 1 < 0$. Now, differentiating (10), we obtain

$$\frac{\partial \bar{p}}{\partial \beta} = \frac{-\bar{p}[u'(y_1 + \beta \bar{x}) + u''(y_1 + \beta \bar{x})\beta \bar{x}]}{u'(y_0 - \bar{x}) + u'(y_1 + \beta \bar{x})\beta}.$$
(27)

Hence, the sign of (26) is negative provided $\partial \bar{p}/\partial \beta \geq 0$. The latter holds, by (27), when $u''(z)z/u'(z) \leq -1$.

Assume, therefore, that $\partial^2 R/\partial \beta \,\partial \bar{x} < 0$. Since the last two terms in (24) and the last term in (25) are positive, the position of the curves $\partial W/\partial \beta = 0$ and $\partial W/\partial \bar{x} = 0$ relative to the curves $\partial R/\partial \beta = 0$ and $\partial R/\partial \bar{x} = 0$, is as indicated in Figure 1. (The way in which these curves intersect is determined by second-

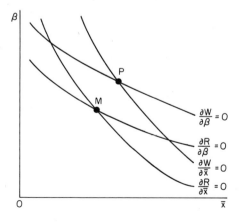

FIGURE 1

order conditions.) The monopoly optimum is indicated by M and the social optimum by P.

It is seen that the social optimum provides a higher marginal return β, *or* a higher ceiling $\bar{x}$, *or both*, compared with the policy chosen by the monopoly. Clearly, the social optimum cannot have a lower marginal return and a lower ceiling than the monopoly's policy.

5. A NONLINEAR EXAMPLE

We shall now consider a case in which, for a particular class of utility and density functions, an explicit nonlinear optimum policy can be derived.

Let $u(y) = y^{1/2}$ and define Y and S to be

$$Y = (y_0 - x)^{1/2}, \qquad S = (y_1 + s(x))^{1/2}. \tag{28}$$

Expected utility is then

$$U = (1 - p)Y + pS. \tag{29}$$

In the YS plane indifference curves are straight lines with slope $\pi \equiv (1 - p)/p$. Since Y and S are strictly monotone functions of x, one can write S uniquely in terms of Y, $S = S(Y)$. For the individual to have a unique optimum, the function $S(Y)$ has to be strictly concave. We shall have to check later whether the optimum solution satisfies this condition.

The p-individual's maximization condition is

$$S'(Y) = -\pi, \tag{30}$$

which, together with the constraint $S = S(y)$, solves for the optimum pair $(S(\pi), Y(\pi))$. From (30),

$$dS/d\pi = -\pi \, dY/d\pi. \tag{31}$$

By (7), (8), and (28), expected profits are given by

$$R[s(\cdot)] = \int_0^\infty [y_0\pi + y_1 - Y^2(\pi)\pi - S^2(\pi)]g(\pi)\,d\pi, \tag{32}$$

where $g(\pi)\,d\pi = -pf(p)\,dp$. Since $y_0\pi + y_1$ is not controlled by the firm, its objective can be restated as

$$\min_{S(Y)} \int_0^\infty [Y^2(\pi)\pi + S^2(\pi)]g(\pi)\,d\pi \tag{33}$$

subject to (11). Forming the Lagrangean function, the Euler equations with respect to $S(\pi)$ and $Y(\pi)$ are

$$\frac{d}{d\pi}[\lambda(\pi)g(\pi)] = 2S(\pi)g(\pi), \tag{34}$$

$$\frac{d}{d\pi}[\lambda(\pi)\pi g(\pi)] = 2Y(\pi)\pi g(\pi), \tag{35}$$

where $\lambda(\pi)$ is the "shadow-price" function. Combining (34) and (35), we may write these as

$$(d/d\pi)[(Y(\pi) - S(\pi))\pi g(\pi)] = S(\pi)g(\pi). \tag{36}$$

Equations (36) and (31) form two first-order differential equations which may be solved for $Y(\pi)$ and $S(\pi)$, once $g(\pi)$ is specified.

As an example, consider the density function $g(\pi) = 1/\pi$. By definition, this implies that $f(p) = 1/(1 - p)p^2$, which is a U-shaped density with concentration of individuals at the two extremes. Condition (36) becomes

$$(dY/d\pi) - (dS/d\pi) = S/\pi. \tag{37}$$

Substituting (31) in (37), we have

$$1/S \, dS/d\pi = -1/(1 + \pi) \tag{38}$$

with solution

$$S(\pi) = a/(1 + \pi) \tag{39}$$

for some constant $a > 0$. From (19) and (11),

$$dY/d\pi = a/\pi(1 + \pi)^2 \tag{40}$$

with solution

$$Y(\pi) = b + \frac{a}{1 + \pi} + a\log\left(\frac{\pi}{1 + \pi}\right) \tag{41}$$

for some $b > 0$. When $\pi \to \infty$ ($p \to 0$), $Y(\pi) \to b$. Since $p \to 0$ implies $x \to 0$ and hence $Y(\pi) \to y_0^{1/2}$, it follows that $b = y_0^{1/2}$.

To make sure that $Y > 0$ ($y_0 > x$), we assume that there is a positive lower bound on π, denoted π_0, which satisfies $Y(\pi_0) > 0$.

The final step is to minimize (33) with respect to a, but we shall delete this condition.

Notice also that the concavity of $S(Y)$, required for the uniqueness of the individual maximization solution (30), is satisfied. By (39) and (40), $d^2S/dY^2 = -a/\pi(1 + \pi)^2 < 0$.

Equations (39), (31), and (28) determine implicitly the optimum policy $s(x)$. Differentiating, using (28), (38), and (40), we obtain

$$\frac{ds}{dx} = \frac{ds/d\pi}{dx/d\pi} = -\frac{S(\pi)\,dS/d\pi}{Y(\pi)\,dY/d\pi} = \frac{S(\pi)\pi}{Y(\pi)} > 0. \tag{42}$$

Also, using (39)–(42), we have

$$\frac{d}{d\pi}\left(\frac{ds}{dx}\right) = \frac{S(\pi)}{Y^2(\pi)(1+\pi)}\left[Y(\pi) - \frac{a}{1+\pi}\right] = \frac{S(\pi)}{Y^2(\pi)(1+\pi)}\left[Y(\pi) - S(\pi)\right]$$

$$= \frac{S(\pi)}{Y^2(\pi)(1+\pi)}\left[(y_0 - x)^{1/2} - (y_1 + s(x))^{1/2}\right]$$

$$= \frac{S(\pi)}{Y^2(\pi)(1+\pi)}\left[b + a\log\left(\frac{\pi}{1+\pi}\right)\right]. \tag{43}$$

Since $dx/d\pi < 0$, we have from (43) that d^2s/dx^2 has the opposite sign of $Y - S = (y_0 - x)^{1/2} - (y_1 + s(x))^{1/2}$. Assume that $y_0 > y_1$ (income in case of accident lower than with no accident). If individuals choose to have in case of accident an income inclusive of insurance premium that does not exceed income net of insurance payment in case of no accident, then $Y - S \geq 0$. It would then follow that $d^2s/dx^2 < 0$. However, one can find parameter values in the above example that will induce individuals with high accident probability (small π) to choose to insure themselves for a higher income in case of an accident than their income in the absence of one. In such a case, d^2s/dx^2 is positive at large x (and negative at smaller x).

REFERENCES

Arrow, K. J. (1973). Higher Education as a Filter, *Journal of Public Economics* **2**, 193–216.
Mirrlees, J. A. (1971). An Exploration in the Theory of Optimum Income Taxation, *Review of Economic Studies* **38**, 175–208.
Rothschild, M., and Stiglitz, J. E. (1976). Equilibrium in Competitive Insurance Markets: An Essay on the Economics of Imperfect Information, *Quarterly Journal of Economics* **90**, 629–650.
Salop, J., and Salop, S. (1976). Self-Selection and Turnover in the Labor Market, *Quarterly Journal of Economics* **90**, 619–628.
Sheshinski, E. (1976). An Example of Income Tax Schedules Which Are Optimal for the Maxi–Min Criterion, *International Economic Review* (forthcoming).
Spence, M. A. (1974). *Market Signalling*. Cambridge, Massachusetts: Harvard Univ. Press.

GENERAL EQUILIBRIUM SYSTEMS: STABILITY, OPTIMALITY, AND DISTRIBUTION

A difficulty with Keynesian models of aggregate demand

ALAN S. BLINDER

PRINCETON UNIVERSITY

1. STATEMENT OF THE PROBLEM

This paper is addressed to a fundamental problem with the way Keynesian models of aggregate demand[1] treat inventories. In the "Keynesian cross" diagram, for example, attention is focused on the point where the $c + i + g$ schedule cuts the 45° line as the equilibrium. But what drives the economy toward this point?

In the typical scenario that accompanies these models, inventory change is the answer. Specifically, whenever $c + i + g > y$, inventories are falling because spending exceeds production. Hence, it is argued, firms will step up their rates of production. Conversely, whenever $c + i + g < y$, inventories are piling up, which signals firms to cut back production.[2] This story sounds perfectly logical, and seems to provide an argument that $y = c + i + g$ defines a stable equilibrium. However, it does not.

I am indebted to Dwight Jaffee, Martin Hellwig, Edi Karni, and Philip Friedman for comments on an earlier draft. This research has been supported by a grant from the National Science Foundation.

[1] I refer here to models which treat prices as fixed, and act as if output could be determined strictly on the demand side. To me, the most sensible way to interpret such models—including the IS–LM model and the simpler "Keynesian cross" model—is as theories of the determination of the *aggregate demand curve* relating quantity demanded to price.

[2] Descriptions such as this can be found in almost every elementary textbook account of macroeconomic equilibrium. For an example, see Samuelson (1976, pp. 222–225).

In Section 2, I first explain why the conventional dynamic story behind Keynesian models of aggregate demand has serious problems in its treatment of inventory adjustments. In the remainder of Section 2 and in Section 3, I show that correcting this error is a matter of some delicacy. Most of the obvious solutions either retain some illogical feature or render the model unstable. Section 4 offers a model that seems to be both logically consistent and stable, and Section 5 examines some of the properties of this model. I suggest that a model like this—a model reminiscent of some of Metzler's (1941) work—must underlie standard Keynesian analysis.[3] Section 6 summarizes the paper.

2. THE CONVENTIONAL KEYNESIAN MODEL

The conventional Keynesian model defines equilibrium as the national income level at which consumption c and fixed investment i add up to national income y. Writing both c and i as functions of y, equilibrium is defined by[4]

$$y = c(y) + i(y). \tag{1}$$

Behind this equilibrium model, there is a disequilibrium adjustment model which generally asserts that, when out of equilibrium, y changes in response to the excess of final sales,

$$x = c(y) + i(y), \tag{2}$$

over aggregate output,[5] that is,

$$\dot{y} = \lambda(x - y), \qquad \lambda > 0. \tag{3}$$

It is well known, and easy to prove, that this model is stable so long as $c'(y) + i'(y) < 1$.

---

[3] I am adhering to Leijonhufvud's (1968) usage of the terms in distinguishing between Keynesian economics and the economics of Keynes' *General Theory* (1936). In fact, the *General Theory* had rather little to say about inventories. This paper clearly has more to do with the Keynesian tradition of Hicks and Hansen than with Keynes' own writing.

[4] This model can be interpreted either as the Keynesian cross, or as the more sophisticated IS–LM model. In the latter, there is a second equation, $m = L(r, y)$, where m is the real money stock and r the rate of interest. Assuming that $L_r < 0$ and $L_y > 0$, this can be inverted and written as $r = R(y)$, $R'(y) = -L_y/L_r > 0$ for fixed m. (Remember, this is a fixed-price model.) Then if investment depends on both r and y, we have $i = I(r, y) = I(R(y), y) = i(y)$. On this interpretation, the slope $i'(y)$ is $i'(y) = I_r R'(y) + I_y = -(I_r/L_r)L_y + I_y$, which might be positive or negative.

[5] This adjustment mechanism has been conventional at least since Samuelson's *Foundations*. See Samuelson (1947, pp. 276–283). It has appeared in countless places since then.

A model that is almost equivalent can be derived by assuming instead that firms adjust output according to the discrepancy between *expected final sales* and actual output:

$$\dot{y} = \lambda(x^* - y), \tag{3'}$$

and employing some assumption such as adaptive expectations to govern the evolution of expected sales:

$$\dot{x}^* = \beta(x - x^*). \tag{4}$$

If this two-equation system is linearized about its equilibrium, the stability matrix is

$$\Delta_0 = \begin{pmatrix} -\lambda & \lambda \\ \beta(c' + i') & -\beta \end{pmatrix}.$$

Conditions for local stability are $\text{tr}(\Delta_0) < 0$ and $\det(\Delta_0) > 0$, which are true for positive λ and β as long as $c' + i' < 1$.

Unfortunately, both of these stable models—which play so prominent a role in teaching elementary economics—are fundamentally illogical. The reason is that the adjustment mechanism and, indeed, the definition of equilibrium itself is predicated on the notion that firms will react to inventory movements. Under (3), they raise output whenever inventories are disappearing. But why should *inventory movements* be a signal to firms to change their behavior? One reason, presumably, is that they are concerned with the *level of inventory stocks*. Yet neither (3) nor (3') pays any attention to stocks. According to these adjustment equations, if sales (or expected sales) are equal to output, firms will be content with their current production decisions no matter whether inventory stocks are at desired levels, or are double the desired levels, or are half the desired levels! In the terminology introduced by Metzler (1941), inventory policy is completely *passive*.[6]

Another way of seeing the illogical nature of this adjustment mechanism is to observe that (3) asserts that firms increase (decrease) production whenever inventories are being run down (built up), regardless of whether firms wish to reduce (increase) inventory stocks or not. Analogously, (3') asserts that production plans are changed in proportion to the *expected* change in inventories. It seems more logical to assume that firms change their output decision only when *unexpected* inventory change occurs.

---

[6] Formally, this can be seen by noting that equilibrium in these systems [defined by equation (1)] can be achieved for any value of the inventory stock. Inventory policy *would* be passive if firms did not care about the size of their inventories, but simply used inventory fluctuations as an observable indicator of the state of demand. However, given that storing inventories is costly, this is not very likely.

This could be accommodated by adding *intended* inventory investment n to final sales, and rewriting the adjustment mechanism as

$$\dot{y} = \lambda(x + n - y). \tag{3''}$$

If n reacts negatively to the stock of inventories (denoted by N), such a model can be stable.[7] The problem with this specification comes in attaching meaning to intended inventory accumulation in a model in which firms are posited to choose a value for $\dot{y}$ rather than for y. Since by definition $y = x^* + n$, a decision on n is tacitly also a decision on y, given sales expectations. Similarly, since $\dot{y} = \dot{x}^* + \dot{n}$, a decision on $\dot{y}$ is tacitly a decision on $\dot{n}$, that is, a decision on the desired value of $\dot{N}$ rather than of N. The only way out of this box is to abandon the notion that producers consciously form sales expectations, and assume instead that they:

(a) fix a path for y by using the adjustment rule (3'');
(b) fix a path for n by some behavioral function; and then
(c) let expectations be defined implicitly by the identity $x^* = y - n$ at each moment.

While this avoids the purely logical pitfall, it is hardly good economics.

3. AN ALTERNATIVE MODEL OF OUTPUT ADJUSTMENT DECISIONS

There is, however, an alternative specification of output adjustments that is logically consistent. In particular, jettison the adjustment mechanism in (3') and replace it by the hypothesis that firms adjust production rates whenever the stock of inventories departs from the level that is desired given expected sales $N^*(x^*)$; that is,

$$\dot{y} = \theta(N^*(x^*) - N), \qquad \theta > 0, \quad N^{*\prime} > 0. \tag{5}$$

A model consisting of equations (2), (4), (5), and an identity defining inventory change,

$$\dot{N} = y - x, \tag{6}$$

has a steady state which defines a unique income level by equation (1) (the Keynesian cross) and a unique inventory level by the requirement that

$$N^*(y) = N. \tag{7}$$

Unfortunately, this model cannot be stable, as I now show.

---

[7] The corresponding model with x^* replacing x simply is impossible because $y = x^* + n$ by definition.

Linearizing the model around its equilibrium, and using (2), the stability matrix for the differential equation system (4)–(6) is

$$\Delta_1 = \begin{pmatrix} 0 & -\theta & \theta N^{*\prime} \\ 1 - c' - i' & 0 & 0 \\ (c' + i')\beta & 0 & -\beta \end{pmatrix}.$$

The characteristic roots of this equation are defined by the cubic equation

$$0 = r^3 + \beta r^2 + [\theta(1 - c' - i') - \theta\beta N^{*\prime}(c' + i')]r + \theta\beta(1 - c' - i').$$

The roots will all be stable if the Routh–Hurwitz conditions are satisfied [see e.g. Gandolfo (1971, pp. 239–241)]. In this case, the conditions are

$$\beta > 0, \qquad \theta\beta(1 - c' - i') > 0,$$

$$\beta\theta\{1 - c' - i' - (c' + i')\beta N^{*\prime}\} - \beta\theta(1 - c' - i') = -(c' + i')\beta^2\theta N^{*\prime} > 0.$$

While the first two are satisfied so long as $c' + i' < 1$, the last condition is always violated. Thus the model is definitely unstable.

The reason for the instability can be explained intuitively. An increment to y increases x by equation (2), and this raises x^* (with a geometric distributed lag) by equation (4). Rising expected sales increase desired inventories $N^*(x^*)$, and this induces firms to increase y by equation (5). So instability arises for any positive adjustment speeds β and θ and any positive marginal inventory-to-sales ratio $N^{*\prime}(x)$[8] (again, so long as it is positive). This last factor—the desire of firms to increase their inventory levels when sales expand—was highlighted as a potential source of instability many years ago by Metzler (1941) [see also Hicks (1974)].

4.   A MODEL OF OUTPUT LEVEL DECISIONS

It appears, then, that in order to construct a logical model that avoids instability, y must not be treated as a state variable. Instead, (3) or (5) must be replaced by an explicit behavioral equation for production decisions. A simple example is

$$y = x^* + n(N^*(x^*) - N), \qquad n' > 0, \quad n(0) = 0, \tag{8}$$

---

[8] If desired inventories respond negatively to higher interest rates, and if this effect is extremely strong, it is conceivable that the model with (5) modified to read $\dot{y} = \theta(N^*(x^*, r) - N)$, $\partial N^*/\partial r < 0$, could be stable. Intuitively, this could occur because an upward perturbation to y would raise interest rates (by the LM curve), and thus reduce desired inventory levels. However, the effect would have to be strong enough to overwhelm the induced increase in N^* described in the text. As a practical matter, no student of inventory behavior has ever been able to pick up any interest sensitivity. I thank Jonathan Eaton and Mark Gersovitz for raising this question.

where n is now posited to depend on the gap between desired and actual inventories. Equation (8) states that firms produce enough output to meet expected sales and to partially correct any imbalances that might exist in inventory levels.

The model consisting of equations (2), (4), (6), and (8) has the same equilibrium solution as the unstable model of Section 3. In particular, in equilibrium, expectations are correct $(x^* = x)$ by (4) and inventory change is zero $(y = x)$ by (6). Equation (8) then implies equation (7), so inventories are at the desired level. But, unlike the model based on $\dot{y} = \theta(N^* - N)$, this one can be stable, as I now show.

For the reader's convenience, the entire model is repeated:

$$x = c(y) + i(y), \tag{2}$$

$$y = x^* + n(N^*(x^*) - N), \tag{8}$$

$$\dot{N} = y - x, \tag{6}$$

$$\dot{x}^* = \beta(x - x^*). \tag{4}$$

Equations (2) and (8) define x and y as functions of the state variables N and x^* with the derivatives

$$\partial y / \partial N = -n', \qquad \partial y / \partial x^* = 1 + n'N^{*'},$$
$$\partial x / \partial N = -(c' + i')n', \qquad \partial x / \partial x^* = (c' + i')(1 + n'N^*).$$

Thus the linearized differential equation system has the stability matrix

$$\Delta_2 = \begin{pmatrix} -n'(1 - c' - i') & (1 + n'N^{*'})(1 - c' - i') \\ -\beta n'(c' + i') & -\beta[1 - (1 + n'N^{*'})(c' + i')] \end{pmatrix}.$$

The determinant is easily evaluated as

$$\det(\Delta_2) = n'\beta(1 - c' - i'),$$

which is positive so long as $c' + i' < 1$. The trace is

$$\text{tr}(\Delta_2) = -n'(1 - c' - i') - \beta[1 - (1 + n'N^{*'})(c' + i')] \tag{9}$$

which will be negative under the aforementioned condition so long as the following condition also holds:

$$c' + i' < 1/(1 + n'N^{*'}). \tag{10}$$

Looking at (10) we can see how inventory investment can be a potential source of instability. If the product of the marginal inventory–sales ratio $N^{*'}$ times the rate at which inventory discrepancies are eliminated, n', is rather large, then the Keynesian model can be unstable even when the sum of the marginal propensities to consume and invest is less than unity.[9] However, there is at least a reasonable stability condition that is subject to empirical verification.

In a recent article, Feldstein and Auerbach (1976) have suggested that inventory behavior follows a "target-adjustment" model, by which they mean that gaps between desired and actual inventories, $N^* - N$, are closed very quickly, but the desired level of inventories responds very sluggishly to changes in sales. In the context of the present model, these notions translate to the empirical statement that n' is very large while β is very small (since the only role of sales expectations in this model is to define desired inventories). In this case, it is apparent that condition (9) can be satisfied—and thus the system can be stable—even if condition (10) fails to hold.

5. DYNAMIC PROPERTIES OF THE PREFERRED MODEL

The model sketched in the previous section tells the following story about the dynamic adjustments that underlie the Keynesian cross (or the IS curve of the Hicks–Hansen model). When some component of aggregate demand rises, GNP lags behind [by (8)], and inventory stocks start falling [by (6)]. Final sales surge ahead of GNP. At the same time, sales expectations gradually are revised upward [by (4)] to reflect the new realities. Both of these forces—falling inventories and rising sales expectations—induce firms to raise production [by (8)]. As inventory disinvestment slows and gradually turns into inventory investment, GNP starts to catch up to final sales. In the later stages of the adjustment period, inventories are built up toward a level consistent with the new final sales; so GNP growth exceeds growth in final sales. Eventually—in a stable system—a new equilibrium is reached with higher GNP, higher inventory levels, no further inventory change, and correct expectations.

To analyze the dynamic responses of the model more explicitly, it is convenient to develop a phase diagram in (x^*, N) space. The $\dot{N} = 0$ locus is defined by $y = x$, which is just $y = c(y) + i(y)$ by equation (2). Since y depends only on x^* and N by equation (8), the slope of the locus follows from (8):

$$\left.\frac{dN}{dx^*}\right|_{\dot{N}=0} = \frac{1 + n'N^{*\prime}}{n'} > 0.$$

---

[9] While both $N^{*\prime}$ and n' are dependent on the way in which time is measured, the product $N^{*\prime}n'$ is not. $N^{*\prime}$, the marginal inventory–sales ratio, rises as the unit for measuring time shrinks. But n', the adjustment parameter, falls.

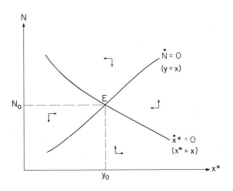

FIGURE 1

The $\dot{x}^* = 0$ locus is defined by the condition that expected and actual final sales are identical, or $x^* = c(y) + i(y)$, where (8) is again used to define y as a function of x^* and N. The slope of this locus is therefore

$$\left.\frac{dN}{dx^*}\right|_{\dot{x}^*=0} = \frac{1 + n'N^{*\prime} - (c' + i')^{-1}}{n'}$$

which is negative whenever condition (10) holds.

Figure 1 depicts a stable equilibrium. Notice that the intersection of the two stationary loci (point E) designates the only point at which

(a)   the economy is at the intersection point in the Keynesian 45° diagram (i.e., on the $\dot{N} = 0$ locus), and

(b)   expectations are correct.

The approach to equilibrium following a perturbation may be either monotonic convergence or damped oscillations, depending on parameter values. In what follows, I concentrate on the monotonic case.

Figure 2 shows what happens if a positive constant, called g, is added to aggregate demand, changing equation (2) to

$$x = c(y) + i(y) + g. \tag{2'}$$

Straightforward algebra shows that both the $\dot{N} = 0$ and $\dot{x}^* = 0$ loci shift to the right, with the latter shifting more.[10] This establishes that both N and x^* (and hence y) eventually rise, which is hardly surprising.

Of more interest are the shapes of the adjustment trajectories. Inventories N fall to a minimum at point A, but eventually rise to a permanently higher

[10] Using (2') and (8) to define x and y as functions of x^* and N, the effect of g on the x^* value along the $\dot{N} = 0$ locus (for fixed N) is $\partial x^*/\partial g = \{(1 + n'N^{*\prime})(1 - c' - i')\}^{-1}$. Similarly, the effect of g on x^* along the $\dot{x}^* = 0$ locus (for fixed N) is $\partial x^*/\partial g = \{1 - (c' + i')(1 + n'N^{*\prime})\}^{-1}$, which is positive in the stable case and larger than the shift in the $\dot{N} = 0$ locus.

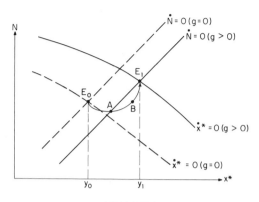

FIGURE 2

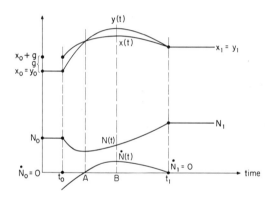

FIGURE 3

level by the time equilibrium is reestablished at point E_1. Production y rises to a maximum at point B *after* the trough in N has been passed, and then declines toward its final equilibrium.[11] Final sales x are tied to y very closely in this simple model by equation (2′). Final sales jump above GNP at first, then grow more slowly so that GNP catches up (at point A), reach their maximum at the same time as output (point B in Figure 2), and decline in the late stages of the adjustment, though not so steeply as GNP. Since $\ddot{N} = \dot{y} - \dot{x} = (1 - c' - i')\dot{y}$, inventory investment also peaks when GNP peaks, and declines thereafter. Figure 3 charts the time paths of y, x, $\dot{N}$, and N following a perturbation (a positive g) at time t_0.

---

[11] Point B is defined as the point where the trajectory shown in Figure 2 has the same slope as the $\dot{N} = 0$ stationary locus. This is because all iso-y lines are parallel to this locus, which is just the particular iso-y line defined by $y = c(y) + i(y)$.

Perhaps the most interesting aspect of this scenario is the finding that GNP *must* overshoot its ultimate target, even if inventory stocks do not, that is, even if there is no inventory cycle.[12] If this mechanism were embedded in a larger model in which the price level responded positively to aggregate demand, the interval of time between B and t_1 would undoubtedly be a period of simultaneous inflation and falling production.[13] Thus a period of stagflation is always part of the aftermath of any stimulus to aggregate demand.

6. RECAPITULATION

I have considered four different Keynesian models of aggregate demand and inventory adjustment. All share the three equations

$$x = c(y) + i(y), \tag{2}$$

$$\dot{x}^* = \beta(x - x^*), \tag{4}$$

$$\dot{N} = y - x, \tag{6}$$

so that $x = x^* = y$ in equilibrium. They differ in their treatment of production decisions.

In the first three models, the specification treats the rate of change of production $\dot{y}$ as the basic decision variable. The first, or conventional Keynesian model, uses the adjustment equation

$$\dot{y} = \lambda(x - y) \tag{3}$$

or

$$\dot{y} = \lambda(x^* - y), \tag{3'}$$

and therefore fails to yield a determinate value for N in equilibrium. In addition, its logic is dubious in that firms are assumed to react only to expected inventory change and never to care about the level of inventories.

All the other models have the same equilibrium comparative statics. The second model replaces (3') by

$$\dot{y} = \lambda(x + n - y), \tag{3''}$$

and therefore defines a determinate equilibrium N by the requirement that intended inventory investment, $n = n(N^*(x^*) - N)$, be zero. However, its logical structure is faulty in that *given expectations* a decision on n implies a decision on y and, conversely, a decision on $\dot{y}$ implies a choice of $\dot{n}$. Thus *either* the implied time structure of decisions is inconsistent *or* the notion

---

[12] In the cyclical case where N overshoots, y would undershoot and gradually return to y_1.
[13] For the full development of such a model, see Blinder (1977).

of expectations is not taken seriously [i.e., equation (4) must be dropped from the model].

In the third model, output is assumed to be changed in response to the *stock discrepancy* between desired and actual inventory levels,

$$\dot{y} = \theta(N^*(x^*) - N), \tag{5}$$

rather than to the *flow rate* of intended or unintended inventory investment. While this model has a coherent logical structure and yields a determinate N in equilibrium, it cannot provide a dynamic foundation for the Keynesian cross because it makes the model unstable.

In sum, none of the models based on a $\dot{y}$ decision seems to work. A different approach is to close the model with the definition that firms produce the sum of expected sales and intended inventory accumulation,[14]

$$y = x^* + n, \tag{8}$$

and determine y via behavioral equations for x^* and n. When expectations are incorrect, there is unintended inventory change. This model determines N in equilibrium, is stable under appropriate parameter values, makes sense as a behavioral assumption, and has a consistent time structure of decisions (i.e., y and n are jointly selected). Thus, it can provide a dynamic foundation for the Keynesian cross and similar models.

In the preferred model, inventory levels move almost countercyclically, except that the trough in N precedes the peak in y. Both final sales and inventory investment reach a peak coincidentally with GNP, though this would obviously no longer be so if lags in the consumption and investment functions were introduced; then x would lag and $\dot{N}$ would lead cyclical turning points in GNP. Since inventory adjustments required an interval of falling production following a surge in aggregate demand, embedding a model such as this one into a larger structure with endogenous prices would have to lead to periods of stagflation—even if price expectations were always correct.

REFERENCES

Blinder, A. (1977). Inventory Behavior, Real Wages and the Short-Run Keynesian Paradigm (mimeo), Inst. for Advanced Studies, Jerusalem (May).
Feldstein, M. S., and Auerbach, A. (1976). Inventory Behavior in Durable-Goods Manufacturing: The Target-Adjustment Model, *Brookings Papers on Economic Activity* **2**.

[14] The models considered in the latter part of Metzler's (1941) classic paper are all based on equation (8). They differ from this paper in the way they specify expectations and intended inventory investment. For expectations, he either assumes that $x_t^* = x_{t-1}$ or that $x_t^* - x_{t-1} = a(x_{t-1} - x_{t-2})$. These are not readily translated into the more convenient continuous time. For n, he assumes either that n_t equals the unintended inventory change of the last period or that n_t equals the gap between desired and actual N. The mechanism used here is more general.

Gandolfo, G. (1971). *Mathematical Methods and Models in Economic Dynamics*. Amsterdam: North-Holland Publ.

Hicks, J. R. (1974). *The Crisis in Keynesian Economics*. New York: Basic Books.

Keynes, J. M. (1936). *The General Theory of Employment, Interest and Money*. New York: Harcourt.

Leijonhufvud, A. (1968). *On Keynesian Economics and the Economics of Keynes*. London and New York: Oxford Univ. Press.

Metzler, L. A. (1941). The Nature and Stability of Inventory Cycles, *Review of Economics and Statistics* **23** (August).

Samuelson, P. A. (1947). *Foundations of Economic Analysis*. Cambridge, Massachusetts: Harvard Univ. Press.

Samuelson, P. A. (1976). *Economics*, 10th ed. New York: McGraw-Hill.

Continuously dated commodities and nontâtonnement with production and consumption

FRANKLIN M. FISHER

MASSACHUSETTS INSTITUTE OF TECHNOLOGY

1. INTRODUCTION: THE PROBLEM OF DATED COMMODITIES

In my earlier paper (1976a), I presented a nontâtonnement model in which production and consumption are allowed to take place out of equilibrium and proved a stability theorem. Among the serious difficulties, implicit in all stability theory but brought to the fore by such an analysis[1] is one involving commodity dating.

Briefly, the problem is as follows [for extended discussion, see Fisher (1976a,b)]. If commodities are distinguished by date, commodity dates will be passed out of equilibrium, since only currently dated commodities can be consumed or used as inputs. Since there are no "pasts" markets, trading in past-dated commodities is suspended. Since participants in such models are typically assumed to believe stupidly that they will be able to complete their transactions, such suspension will come as a surprise and may cause discontinuities in excess demands for other commodities. This will violate Lipschitz conditions which lie at the heart of the mathematics used.

This research was supported by National Science Foundation Grant GS 43185. I am grateful to Hal Varian for many helpful conversations but retain responsibility for error.

[1] Fisher (1976b) presents a relatively nontechnical discussion of such problems as well as a survey of the field. Earlier surveys are given in Negishi (1962) and Arrow and Hahn (1971).

Such discontinuity is not a frequent problem in the real world because of the fact that next year's commodity becomes a perfect substitute for this year's at midnight on December 31. The reason that this eliminates the discontinuity is that the prices of the two commodities typically come together as that moment approaches. *This is an equilibrium statement, however.* There is nothing in the usual price adjustment assumptions in stability models which ensures that it will occur out of equilibrium.

The difficulty is not that arbitrage is not allowed in such models. Arbitrage is allowed (although speculation is not) since participants can store commodities and buy and sell futures. The problem is rather one of assuring that arbitrage will be fully effective by the time the crucial date is passed.

There are a number of possible ways in which one might attempt to get round this problem. The first of these is to assume it away, or, what amounts to the same thing, to assume that commodities are not dated. This is the approach taken by Fisher (1976a). Not only is it clearly unsatisfactory on its own lack of grounds, it also creates or exacerbates a number of inelegant difficulties.

A second possible approach is to suppose that nobody is surprised by discontinuities in the prices. One can proceed by assuming that, as the date on a particular commodity approaches, it becomes harder and harder to trade it so that there are utility or resource losses involved in finding someone with whom to trade. Such an approach can probably deal with the problem, but it seems relatively ad hoc, importing into the model in a special place a realization of disequilibrium that is conspicuously absent from it elsewhere.[2]

Clearly, one cannot hope to have an adequate treatment of the problem without dealing with the process by which prices adjust. Unfortunately, we lack an adequate understanding of this central issue. Microeconomic competitive theory is preeminently an equilibrium theory in which all participants take prices as given and can thus provide little guidance as to how prices change.[3] The device of the fictitious auctioneer has remained behind most price-adjustment processes, in nontâtonnement as well as tâtonnement models. When one seeks to discover more structure in the price-adjustment process, that device fails, for it is hard to gain much insight into adjustment rules based on nobody's behavior.

If one thinks more realistically of individuals as setting their own prices, however, a way around the dated commodity problem becomes apparent.

---

[2] Fisher (1977) shows one way in which quantity constraints on trading taken into account by agents can be incorporated into Hahn Process models. It might be possible to adapt that analysis to have upper and lower bounds on trading on any dated commodity which come together as its date is reached.

[3] This was pointed out by Koopmans (1957) among others.

If the same household or firm is selling and posting prices for both this year's and next year's toothpaste, it will be to that entity's interest to avoid a discontinuity as the date passes by not posting what in effect are two different prices for the same thing and encouraging arbitrage at its own expense.

If one pursues this line, one can deal with a closely related awkwardness. It is unnatural in models which work in continuous time to have commodities distinguished only by discrete dates. There may in fact be good reasons of convenience and transaction costs why futures markets arise only for discrete dates,[4] but these probably ought to be dealt with explicitly rather than being assumed into the basic nature of the commodities. (I somewhat accommodate such considerations below.) It thus seems natural to work with continuously dated commodities and to think of prices as price profiles extending over future time. If prices for different dates are set by different people using different rules, the continuity of such profiles in the commodity date cannot be assured;[5] if individuals set such profiles—the terms on which they stand ready to deliver (buy) at different times—then such continuity will be a natural consequence of the self-interest of the price-setters.

The present paper, then, extends the work of Fisher (1976a) by building such a model with continuously dated commodities in which continuous price profiles are continuously adjusted. Such continuity can be thought of as stemming from individual price adjustment, as in my earlier paper (1972), but this is not made explicit.[6] Although many of the inelegancies of Fisher (1976a) are avoided by this treatment, it remains true that the interest of the paper may lie chiefly in exposing the serious difficulties which remain to be overcome in this sort of work.

2. THE HAHN PROCESS AND MONEY

The basic adjustment process used is the Hahn Process[7] which assumes that there cannot be simultaneously (after trade) unsatisfied demanders and unsatisfied buyers of the same commodity. This implies that any unsatisfied individual excess demand is of the same sign as aggregate excess demand for

---

[4] On this, see e.g., Foley (1970) and Hahn (1971).

[5] Note, however, that such continuity is stronger than is strictly necessary. The really important thing is to assure continuity of the price profile at the current time, that is, as futures prices become spot prices. Continuity in future dates is convenient but not essential.

[6] Such individual price adjustment creates its own serious problems. See Fisher (1970, 1972, 1973, 1976b).

[7] So named by Negishi (1962). The basic paper is Hahn and Negishi (1962). Further developments can be found in Arrow and Hahn (1971, Chapter XIII) and Fisher (1972, 1974, 1976a, 1977).

the same commodity. Since aggregate excess demands push prices, every participant in the model finds that the things he wishes to buy are becoming more expensive, while the things he wishes to sell are becoming cheaper. As a result, the profits which firms expect to make if they complete their transactions (target profits) and the utilities which households expect to achieve if they can complete their transactions (target utilities) are declining out of equilibrium. These declines are reinforced by the irreversible actions involved in consumption and production.

The sum of target utilities can then be used as a Lyapounov function, which seems natural if we think of the process as one in which inconsistent expectations are revised downward until equilibrium is reached.

All this makes sense only if demanders have something of value to offer. Following Arrow and Hahn (1971, Chapter XIII), it is customary to assume that there is a particular commodity, "money," which serves as the sole medium of exchange. "Target demands" from utility maximization become "active demands" only when backed up with money. One must then assume that no one ever runs out of money.[8] I shall implicitly assume all this, but I shall not give money an explicit notational treatment nor shall I distinguish between active and target demands. This will simplify the treatment substantially.

3. TOPOLOGICAL ISSUES

Before proceeding with the formal model, we digress to discuss the issues surrounding the choice of space and norm. We shall take consumption, inputs, outputs, and the like to be continuous profiles defined on $[0, \infty)$ and lying in some normed linear space. Prices will then be taken to lie in the normed dual of that space. At the level of generality at which we shall be working, however, no direct use will be made in the proofs of the particular properties of the chosen space and its normed dual.[9] Hence there is little reason to restrict ourselves to a particular space. Rather, all results should be read as applying to any choice such that our other assumptions are satisfied.

That is not to say, however, that the choice of a normed linear space is a matter of no consequence, for, of course, the interpretation of assumptions and results depends on what space is chosen. In the present paper, this matters in three areas, the third of which is somewhat subtle.

---

[8] For discussion of the relation of this No Bankruptcy Condition to individual price adjustment, see Fisher (1972, 1976b).

[9] Although particular choices, together with rather restrictive assumptions would lead to proofs of boundedness, as will be discussed.

3.1. Differentiability and Continuity

Utility and production functionals are assumed Fréchet differentiable in their arguments. Moreover, the optimization problems faced by households and firms are assumed sufficiently regular that their solutions are weak* continuous in the prices. What such assumptions mean depends on the choice of a normed space in which to work. On the other hand, the plausibility of such assumptions seems about the same for a large number of such choices.

3.2. Boundedness

It is important to the proof of stability that prices lie in a compact set. The natural way to go about this is to work with prices in the weak* topology, show or assume closure and boundedness, and apply the Alaoglu theorem [see e.g., Luenberger (1969, p. 128)]. As it turns out, the difficult issue here is boundedness.

Now boundedness of prices, while plausibly assumed, is at best awkward to prove in models of this sort even with a finite number of commodities [see Fisher (1976a) for details]. Moreover, while such proofs will carry over to the present case, they are less useful here, because they allow the proof of boundedness only for particular choices of norm, in particular the square root of the integral of squared price or, alternatively, the essential supremum. Unfortunately, such results do not appear readily to extend to other choices of norm.

One might therefore suppose that the sensible thing to do is to choose the original commodity space as L_2 or L_1, so as to have prices turn out to lie in L_2 or L_∞, respectively, with the norms those to which the boundedness proofs apply. While such choices are possible ones, however, one gains from them only the ability to prove boundedness of prices using assumptions that are pretty restrictive and not obviously much more plausible than the direct assumption of boundedness itself.[10] Moreover, it turns out that one loses a good deal in the interpretation of the results with these particular choices, for they suffer from what I shall call the "vanishing norm property."

3.3. Vanishing Norm

In a notation restricted to the present section, let q be a quantity profile (consumption, input, etc.) defined over $[0, \infty)$ and lying in a normed linear space X. [For present purposes $q(\theta)$, $\theta \in [0, \infty)$, can be taken to be a scalar,

---

[10] Since the only purpose of assuming or proving boundedness is to obtain weak* compactness, and since weak* convergence of prices is not the strongest result one could wish, one might ask why we do not go ahead and simply assume compactness for prices in some stronger topology. The answer is that it is hard to see why such an assumption is particularly plausible unless it is equivalent to closure and boundedness.

to simplify matters.] For any $\lambda > 0$, define q_λ in X as[11]

$$q_\lambda(\theta) = \begin{cases} 0 & \text{for } 0 \leq \theta \leq \lambda, \\ q(\theta) & \text{for } \theta > \lambda. \end{cases} \tag{3.1}$$

DEFINITION 3.1 X will be said to have the *vanishing norm property* if and only if for every q in X, $\lim_{\lambda \to \infty} \text{norm}(q_\lambda) = 0$.

Heuristically, a space with the vanishing norm property is one in which differences between profiles which occur far in the future are given less and less weight. Examples are easy to come by. All the L_p spaces possess the vanishing norm property for $1 \leq p < \infty$, although L_∞ does not. In particular, L_1 and L_2, the two spaces which turned up in the discussion of boundedness, have it.

Now the reason that the vanishing norm property is an inconvenience is related to the fact that economic activity is occurring during the adjustment process. Hence, just through the passage of time, some prices—those for commodities whose dates have been passed—become fixed. One hardly wants to have this fact alone mean that prices converge, but this is essentially what happens if quantity differences later in time get less and less weight.[12]

More precisely, let X^* be the normed dual of X. Let $\bar{p}$ in X^* be the actual time path of *spot* prices, so that for any θ, the value of $\bar{p}(\theta)$ is the closing price for the single commodity dated θ which actually obtained at θ. For any $\lambda > 0$, let p_λ in X^* be a profile such that $p_\lambda(\theta) = \bar{p}(\theta)$ for $0 \leq \theta \leq \lambda$. We can think of p_λ as a profile which shows actual closing prices for commodities dated up to λ and the futures prices obtaining at λ for commodities dated after λ. It is now easy to prove:

LEMMA 3.1   If X has the vanishing norm property, then, provided that $\bar{p}$ and the p_λ lie in a bounded set, the sequence of the p_λ converges weak* to $\bar{p}$ as λ goes to ∞.

Proof   Since p_λ and $\bar{p}$ lie in a bounded set,

$$\left| \int_0^\infty (p_\lambda(\theta) - \bar{p}(\theta)) q(\theta) \, d\theta \right| = \left| \int_\lambda^\infty (p_\lambda(\theta) - \bar{p}(\theta)) q(\theta) \, d\theta \right|$$

$$= \left| \int_0^\infty (p_\lambda(\theta) - \bar{p}(\theta)) q_\lambda(\theta) \, d\theta \right| \leq \text{norm}(p_\lambda - \bar{p}) \, \text{norm}(q_\lambda)$$

$$\leq K \, \text{norm}(q_\lambda), \tag{3.2}$$

---

[11] It is assumed that q_λ is in X. If the possible discontinuity at $\theta = \lambda$ prevents this, we could easily overcome it by having $q_\lambda(\theta)$ go continuously from 0 at λ to the value of $q(\theta)$ at some θ slightly greater than λ.

[12] Note, however, that such heuristics can be a little misleading. It turns out that the crucial issue as to trivial convergence of prices is whether the *commodity* space X has the vanishing norm property. It does not matter whether the price space (the normed dual of X) does.

where K is some finite positive scalar independent of λ. Since X has the vanishing norm property, the extreme right-hand side of (3.2) approaches zero as λ goes to infinity, proving the lemma.

Note that such a result is far stronger than that of the Alaoglu theorem which would merely show (given closure as well as boundedness) that the sequence of the p_λ has a convergent subsequence.

It is obviously unattractive to have prices converge weak* just because of boundedness and the fact that one has chosen a particular norm (although the fact that the limit involved is a competitive equilibrium is not trivial), particularly because the same result can be achieved in a far from trivial way.

We now proceed to the formal model.

4. BEHAVIOR OF HOUSEHOLDS

There are n commodities, of which the nth, called "money," is the numéraire. Each commodity is dated continuously. Commodity dates are most often denoted by θ. As of time t, the vector of price profiles for the n commodities is denoted by $p(\cdot, t)$. Thus, the value of a particular element of $p(\theta, t)$ for a particular $\theta \geq t$ is a futures price for a particular commodity. For technical reasons, however, it is convenient to think of $p(\theta, t)$ as defined for all θ in $[0, \infty)$, where 0 is some arbitrary starting date, even though trading is not permitted for $\theta < t$. For such past dates, the prices involved remain fixed at levels corresponding to the spot prices which obtained at θ. Each element of $p(\cdot, t)$ is a continuous function.

For a number of reasons, it is inconvenient explicitly to allow money to be distinguished by date so as to have different prices for different times in the future. We assume that money, whenever dated, has price equal to unity, so that the nth component of $p(\cdot, t)$ is a function always equal to unity. There is no market on which future money trades for present money at par, but money can always be stored. The consequent elimination of credit and interest, however, is only apparent. We may think of the n currently dated commodities as including commodities called "bonds." A particular bond is characterized by a specific maturity period. Included in the opportunities open to participants is the ability to place such bonds in storage at time t and to have each unit so stored turn into one unit of money at the end of the maturity period. (For reasons of boundedness some credit limit must be imposed on the ability of any one entity to engage in bond transactions, however.)

I shall not make any of this notationally explicit. Indeed, it will simplify the notation greatly to adopt a notation throughout which treats money in a way parallel to the other commodities as is already done in $p(\theta, t)$. In order to do this, however, one must interpret integrals such as $\int_0^\infty m(\theta, t)\, d\theta$, where

$m(\cdot, t)$ is some profile of money, as equal to the amount of spot money involved, even though $m(\theta, t) = 0$ for $\theta > t$. This occurs in particular for integrals showing the amount of money paid in purchase transactions and for profits and dividends. I apologize for the slight awkwardness involved. This really does make the exposition much simpler.[13]

Households will later be subscripted h, but the subscript will be omitted until needed. Each household has an n-vector of consumption profiles $c(\cdot, t)$, defined over $[0, \infty)$. For $\theta \leq t$, the corresponding values of $c(\theta, t)$ represent actual consumption, while for $\theta \geq t$, they represent consumption planned at t to take place at θ. (It is assumed that these coincide for $\theta = t$, which involves assuming that households are not so mistaken about their possessions and transactions that they plan to consume out of current transactions which do not materialize. I shall return to this later.)

The household attempts to vary the parts of $c(\cdot, t)$ which are not already fixed to maximize a utility *functional* $U(c(\cdot, t))$. Note that, since consumption does take place during the adjustment process, the situation is one in which the thing being currently maximized is altered by past consumption activities. $U(\cdot)$ is assumed Fréchet differentiable and strictly quasi concave.[14]

We denote by $r(\cdot, v, t)$ an n-vector of purchase profiles. Here, a particular value of an element of $r(\theta, v, t)$ denotes the amount of a commodity dated θ which the household, as of time t, plans to purchase at time v. Purchases are measured positively.

Obviously, this definition only makes sense for $\theta \geq v$. We set $r(\theta, v, t) = 0$ for $v > \theta$, and take $r(\theta, v, t)$ for $v \leq t$ to be *actual* purchases made at time v which will also be denoted $\bar{r}(\theta, v)$. It is not assumed that planned and actual purchases coincide at $v = t$; this is what disequilibrium is all about.

As stated, the household assumes $p(\cdot, t)$ to be independent of t.[15] It therefore faces the budget constraints[16]

$$\int_v^\infty p(\theta, t) r(\theta, v, t) \, d\theta = 0 \qquad \forall v \geq t. \tag{4.1}$$

Although all trades must take place for money, this is not made explicit.

---

[13] Some (though not all) of the simplification can be seen on comparing the notation of the present paper with that of Fisher (1976a).

[14] It is notationally convenient to have household consumption functions defined over all commodities even though some of them such as intermediate goods or bonds may not affect utility directly. Strict quasi concavity is to be interpreted as applying only to those commodities the Fréchet derivatives of U with respect to which are not identically zero. Similar remarks apply to the case of production functions for firms.

[15] This is one of the reasons why it is inconvenient to have future money explicitly bear a different price than does spot money.

[16] Because of the argument-heavy notation, I have not distinguished transposition of vectors in taking inner products, since the meaning is clear.

At time t, the household expects to have available at time θ a stock of then currently dated commodities. We denote this expected stock by $x(\theta, \theta, t)$, using the repeated first argument to remember that it is the stock of θ-dated commodities expected to be on hand at θ. At time θ, after trade (which we assume to take no time) the household will be able to do one of two things with this available stock. It can either consume it or it can store it, to the extent it is not instantaneously perishable. Accordingly, the household is constrained by

$$x(\theta, \theta, t) = c(\theta, t) + y(\theta, t) \qquad \forall \theta \geq t, \tag{4.2}$$

where $y(\theta, t)$ is the n-vector of the amounts of commodities which the household plans at t to put into storage as of θ. Naturally, only currently dated commodities can actually be stored.

The results of such storage activities are given by a vector of storage functionals, $\phi(y(v, t), \theta, t)$, where $v < \theta$, assumed Fréchet differentiable in $y(v, t)$ and continuous in θ and t. This gives the amounts of the various commodities which will be available from storage at θ if the input plans for storage $y(v, t)$ are carried out. [For $v \leq t$, $y(v, t) = \bar{y}(v, t)$ denotes actual storage inputs, coinciding with planned inputs at $v = t$.]

It is convenient to incorporate in the definition of $\phi(y(v, t), \theta, t)$ rather more than just simple storing of goods, however. We have already done so in discussing bonds. In addition, there is no reason to think of storage as simply placing a good in a warehouse and then taking it out again. Certain commodities, such as labor may be expended in so doing. These are to be thought of as placed in storage with no later output. Perishable commodities can be likewise considered. The appearance of t as an explicit argument in $\phi(\cdot, \cdot, t)$ will be discussed subsequently when considering firms.

Now, the stock of spot goods expected to be available at θ, $x(\theta, \theta, t)$, can come from four sources. First, some of that stock may already have been received from outside by t; we denote that stock by $\bar{x}(\theta, t)$ and consider it further later. Second, it may be acquired through purchase between t and θ. Third, it may be available from storage. For ordinary goods, this exhausts the possibilities; for money, however, it does not because the household may own shares in firms and expect to share in their profits.

Firms, discussed more fully in the next section, earn profits in money and pay dividends in money. Since present and future money have the same price, however, there is no reason why such profits and dividends cannot be paid in future as opposed to present money, although it does not matter. Hence, we define $s(\theta, t)$ as a vector which has identically zero functions for its first $n - 1$ components and has for its nth component a function showing the household's share of the *total* profits earned by the firms in which it owns shares which it expects to receive in money dated θ. Similarly, we denote by

$d(\theta, t)$ a vector which has identically zero functions for its first $n - 1$ components and has for its nth component a function showing the total amount of those profits already paid to the household as of time t in money dated θ. Thus the last component of $s(\cdot, t) - d(\cdot, t)$ shows the household's share of *undistributed* profits which it expects to receive over time. There is no harm, however, in thinking of all this as involving functions which are nonzero only for $\theta = t$, that is, of having profits and dividends only involve current money, so long as one recalls the notational convention already adopted as to integrals involving money.

We can now write the available stock $x(\theta, \theta, t)$ in terms of its sources as

$$x(\theta, \theta, t) = \bar{x}(\theta, t)$$

$$+ \int_t^\theta r(\theta, v, t) \, dv + \phi(y(v, t), \theta, t) + s(\theta, t) - d(\theta, t) \qquad \forall \theta \geq t. \quad (4.3)$$

Combining this with (4.2) gives another set of constraints within which utility maximization takes place.

It remains to describe the origins of the actual acquired stock of goods dated θ on hand as of t, $\bar{x}(\theta, t)$. This consists of the household's actual stock of such good as of some arbitrary starting date, time 0 (this may be thought of as the household's original endowment), plus actual purchases and actual dividends.

$$\bar{x}(\theta, t) = \bar{x}(\theta, 0) + \int_0^t \bar{r}(\theta, v) \, dv + d(\theta, t) - d(\theta, 0). \quad (4.4)$$

Here, $d(\theta, 0)$ is subtracted since any dividends already paid by time zero are already counted in $\bar{x}(\theta, 0)$. $\bar{x}(\theta, t)$ is assumed a continuous profile.

Since current commodities must either be consumed or else "stored" to become future commodities as their date passes, it must be the case that

$$\bar{x}(t, t) + \phi(y(v, t), t, t) = c(t, t) + y(t, t) \quad (4.5)$$

paralleling (4.2). Note that ϕ is not a stock of particular commodities which can be taken only from inventory and used up. Goods left in inventory automatically become other goods because of the change in dates. For $\theta < t$ we define $\bar{x}(\theta, t) = \bar{x}(\theta, \theta)$, the "closing" stock of θ-dated commodities.

The relevant Lagrangian is given by

$$\Lambda_1 = U(c(\theta, t)) - \int_t^\infty \lambda(v, t) \int_v^\infty p(\theta, t) r(\theta, v, t) \, d\theta \, dv$$

$$+ \int_t^\infty \mu(\theta, t) \left\{ \bar{x}(\theta, t) + \int_t^\theta r(\theta, v, t) \, dv + \phi(y(v, t), \theta, t) \right.$$

$$\left. + s(\theta, t) - d(\theta, t) - c(\theta, t) - y(\theta, t) \right\} d\theta, \quad (4.6)$$

where $\lambda(v, t)$ and $\mu(\theta, t)$ are Lagrange multiplier functions (the latter being a vector).

We assume that the maximization problem of the household has a solution, unique as regards $c(\theta, t)$ and $y(v, t)$ [but not as regards $r(\theta, v, t)$], which occurs at a stationary point of (4.6), and which is continuous in θ [recall that $p(\theta, t)$ is so continuous].[16a] It is evident that the optimal consumption profile $c(\cdot, t)$ and the optimal storage profile $y(\cdot, t)$ depend only on prices and on wealth $w(t)$ defined as

$$w(t) \equiv \int_t^\infty p(\theta, t)\{\bar{x}(\theta, t) + s(\theta, t) - d(\theta, t)\}\, d\theta \tag{4.7}$$

rather than on stocks and undistributed profits directly. We shall assume:

ASSUMPTION 4.1   The solution in $c(\cdot, t)$ and $y(\cdot, t)$ to the optimization problem of the household is continuous in $w(t)$ and weak* continuous in $p(\cdot, t)$.

Weak* continuity in the prices seems fairly natural. It essentially says that if a sequence of price profiles approaches a limit in the sense that for every consumption program the net cost approaches what it would be with the limiting price profile, then the optimal consumption and storage profiles must also approach the optimum under the limiting price profile.

Note that all this involves constraints on the storage functional $\phi(y(v, t), \theta, t)$; in particular, it rules out constant returns. This is necessary here as it will be for firms [and was in Fisher (1974, 1976a)], but is of course not so restrictive for households.

Denoting Fréchet derivatives by subscripts in the obvious way, the first-order conditions for a maximum are (ignoring corner solutions, for simplicity)

$$U_c(c(\theta, t)) = \mu(\theta, t), \qquad \theta \geq t, \tag{4.8}$$

$$\lambda(v, t)p(\theta, t) = \mu(\theta, t), \qquad \theta \geq v \geq t, \tag{4.9}$$

$$\int_v^\infty \mu(\theta, t)\phi_y(y(v, t), \theta, t)\, d\theta = \mu(v, t), \qquad v \geq t. \tag{4.10}$$

These have the following direct implications. First, it is clear from (4.9) that $\lambda(v, t)$ is in fact independent of v so that we may write

$$\lambda(v, t) = \lambda(t), \qquad v \geq t. \tag{4.11}$$

This simply reflects the fact that since the household expects prices to remain unchanged it does not care when before θ it makes its purchases of goods dated θ. This fact also means that $r(\theta, v, t)$ is not uniquely determined, a subject to which we shall have to return.

[16a] Note that such continuity in θ will prevent the situation in which the household (or firm, below) plans to purchase only at a momentarily holding low price and sell only at a momentarily holding high one. Such behavior must be continuously approximated. Continuity in θ is needed below to ensure that price profiles remain continuous in θ when adjusted according to excess demands.

Next, combining (4.8) and (4.9), we obtain

$$U_c(c(\theta, t)) = \lambda(t)p(\theta, t) \qquad \theta \geq t, \tag{4.12}$$

which is the expected result of marginal utilities proportional to prices.
Finally, combining (4.9) and (4.10) yields

$$\int_v^\infty p(\theta, t)\phi_y(y(v, t), \theta, t)\, d\theta = p(v, t) \qquad \theta \geq v \geq t, \tag{4.13}$$

which can be interpreted as stating that marginal revenue product equals factor price in the storage activity, so that the household acts as a profit-maximizing firm in this regard.

5. BEHAVIOR OF FIRMS

Firms will later be subscripted f, but the subscript will be omitted until needed. So far as possible, I use a parallel notation for firms and for households for mnemonic convenience. The differences between them are indicated by the different subscripts when necessary.

The firm at time t seeks to maximize its profits, denoted by $\pi(t)$ and given by

$$\pi(t) = -\int_t^\infty \int_t^\theta p(\theta, t)r(\theta, v, t)\, dv\, d\theta + \bar{\pi}(t), \tag{5.1}$$

where $\bar{\pi}(t)$ denotes profits already attained at time t (defined explicitly later) and, as with households, $r(\theta, v, t)$ denotes the purchases of goods dated θ which the firm plans at time t to make at time v.[17]

There is one difference in the notation for firms, however. Since firms keep score as to profits in money, $r(\theta, v, t)$ for a firm always has its nth component zero as does $\bar{r}(\theta, v)$ below.[18]

Actual profits $\bar{\pi}(t)$ are given by

$$\bar{\pi}(t) = -\int_0^\infty \int_0^t p(\theta, v)\bar{r}(\theta, v)\, dv\, d\theta + \bar{\pi}(0), \tag{5.2}$$

where $\bar{r}(\theta, v)$ denotes actual purchases of goods dated θ made at time v.
[Naturally, $\bar{r}(\theta, v) = 0$ for $v > \theta$.]

---

[17] I apologize for departing from the usual convention of measuring outputs positively and inputs negatively, but the experience of Fisher (1974, 1976a) shows that to do otherwise leads to a bewildering array of minus signs.

[18] The firm might also make profits if money can be produced directly by it. It is notationally simpler to ignore this possibility and to assume that money does not enter the production process. Thus, despite the fact, for example, that output vectors are defined to have n components below, the nth component should be taken as 0. Similar remarks apply to other vectors.

In its profit maximization, the firm has access to a production functional:

$$b(\theta, t) = \phi(y(v, t), \theta, t), \tag{5.3}$$

where $b(\theta, t)$ denotes the output of goods expected available at θ as of time t and $y(v, t)$ denotes the profile of inputs to be made at time v for $v \geq t$ or already made at v for $v \leq t$ (these are assumed to coincide at $v = t$). $\phi(y(v, t), \theta, t)$ is assumed Fréchet differentiable with respect to $y(v, t)$ and continuous in θ and t.

It would of course be more natural to have the output of a particular commodity depend on the inputs used in the production of that commodity rather than on total inputs. (This is true for household storage as well.) To do this explicitly would needlessly burden the notation and the appearance of t as an explicit argument in the production functional can be taken to indicate that the firm plans to optimally allocate its future inputs, given the price profile as of t, while it has already optimally allocated its past inputs given its beliefs before t. Hence we can take outputs to depend only on total inputs given the past history of the firm, denoted (rather crudely) by the explicit appearance of t.

The firm is constrained in its maximization process by

$$\bar{x}(\theta, t) + \int_t^\theta r(\theta, v, t)\,dv + \phi(y(v, t), \theta, t) - y(\theta, t) = 0 \qquad \forall \theta \geq v \geq t, \tag{5.4}$$

where $\bar{x}(\theta, t)$ denotes the actual stock of goods dated θ already purchased as of t and is given by

$$\bar{x}(\theta, t) = \bar{x}(\theta, 0) + \int_0^t \bar{r}(\theta, v)\,dv. \tag{5.5}$$

$\bar{x}(\theta, t)$ is assumed continuous in θ.

The relevant Lagrangian for the firm is given by

$$\begin{aligned}
\Lambda_2 = & -\int_t^\infty \int_t^\theta p(\theta, t) r(\theta, v, t)\,dv\,d\theta + \bar{\pi}(t) \\
& + \int_t^\infty \gamma(\theta, t) \left\{ \bar{x}(\theta, t) \right. \\
& + \left. \int_t^\theta r(\theta, v, t)\,dv + \phi(y(v, t), \theta, t) - y(\theta, t) \right\} d\theta,
\end{aligned} \tag{5.6}$$

where $\gamma(\theta, t)$ is a vector of Lagrange multiplier functions.

We assume that the maximization problem of the firm has a solution, unique as regards $y(v, t)$, which occurs at a stationary point of (5.6) and which is continuous in θ. It is evident that the solution in $y(v, t)$ depends only on the prices and on the value of the holdings of the firm, denoted by $w(t)$ and given by

$$w(t) \equiv \int_t^\infty p(\theta, t)\bar{x}(\theta, t)\, d\theta \tag{5.7}$$

rather than on $\bar{x}(\theta, t)$ directly. We further assume:

ASSUMPTION 5.1   The solution in $y(\cdot, t)$ to the optimization problem of the firm is continuous in $w(t)$ and weak* continuous in $p(\cdot, t)$.

As before, this unfortunately rules out constant returns.

The first-order conditions for a maximum are (ignoring corner solutions for simplicity)

$$p(\theta, t) = \gamma(\theta, t), \qquad \theta \ge t \tag{5.8}$$

$$\int_v^\infty \gamma(\theta, t)\phi_y(y(v, t), \theta, t)\, d\theta = \gamma(v, t), \qquad \theta \ge v \ge t. \tag{5.9}$$

Combining these yields

$$\int_t^\infty p(\theta, t)\phi_y(y(v, t), \theta, t)\, d\theta = p(v, t), \qquad v \ge t, \tag{5.10}$$

which parallels (4.13) and has the interpretation that marginal revenue product must equal factor price.

Given its actual profits $\bar{\pi}(t)$, the firm pays out dividends to its owners. In addition, those owners expect to share in the expected profits of the firm not yet earned, that is, in $\pi(t) - \bar{\pi}(t)$. Thus, we denote by $\bar{g}(\cdot, t)$ an n-component vector whose first $n - 1$ components are identically zero and whose last component gives the schedule of dividends already announced at time t paid out or to be paid out over different times. Similarly, $g(\cdot, t)$ denotes an n-component vector differing from $\bar{g}(\cdot, t)$ only in that the last component gives the schedule of *total* dividend payments expected to be made by the firm (announced and unannounced). It will be convenient, though not really essential, to suppose that all shareowners have the same expectations as to the schedule of such payments.

We shall assume that both $g(\cdot, t)$ and $\bar{g}(\cdot, t)$ are continuous in $\pi(t)$, $\bar{\pi}(t)$, and $w(t)$ and weak* continuous in $p(\cdot, t)$. It is further natural to assume that the firm cannot pay out more than it has so that

$$\bar{G}(t) \equiv \int_{-\infty}^\infty p(\theta, t)\bar{g}(\theta, t)\, d\theta \le \bar{\pi}(t), \qquad \int_{-\infty}^\infty p(\theta, t)g(\theta, t)\, d\theta = \pi(t). \tag{5.11}$$

[Of course, $g(\theta, t) = \bar{g}(\theta, t)$ for $\theta < t$.] We shall later show that all profits are distributed in equilibrium, but there is no harm in allowing them to be retained for liquidity purposes during the adjustment process. (Indeed, to do otherwise might require capital levies on the stockholders of a firm.)

We now connect this to the theory of the household by assuming that the hth household owns a fixed share k_{hf} of the fth firm, where $k_{hf} \ge 0$ and

$\sum_h k_{hf} = 1$. (There is no market in shares.) Then, introducing the subscripts in the obvious way,

$$s_h(\theta, t) = \sum_f k_{hf} g_f(\theta, t), \qquad d_h(\theta, t) = \sum_h k_{hf} \bar{g}_f(\theta, t). \qquad (5.12)$$

6. CLOSURE EQUATIONS AND WALRAS' LAW

Since actual sales must be matched by actual purchases for ordinary goods and since money is not produced, we have the closure equations

$$\sum_h \bar{r}_{hi}(\theta, t) + \sum_f \bar{r}_{fi}(\theta, t) = 0 \qquad (i = 1, \dots, n-1)$$

$$\sum_h \int_t^\infty \bar{r}_{hn}(\theta, t)\, d\theta + \sum_f \dot{\bar{\pi}}_f(t) = 0. \qquad (6.1)$$

Further, combining the household's constraints (4.2) and (4.3), premultiplying by $p(\theta, t)$, integrating over θ, summing over households, using the budget constraint (4.1), the distributive equations (5.12), the definition of profits (5.1), and the constraint (5.4), we obtain Walras' law for this economy, namely,

$$\int_t^\infty p(\theta, t) \left\{ \sum_h (c_h(\theta, t) + y_h(\theta, t) - \bar{x}_h(\theta, t) - \phi^h(y_h(v, t), \theta, t)) \right.$$

$$+ \sum_f (y_f(\theta, t) - \bar{x}_f(\theta, t) - \phi^f(y_f(v, t), \theta, t)) \Bigg\} d\theta$$

$$+ \sum_f (\bar{G}_f(t) - \bar{\pi}_f(t)) = 0. \qquad (6.2)$$

Note that the firm's excess demand for money includes its desire to hold retained earnings.

7. THE PRESENT ACTION POSTULATE

We have already observed that participants in this model do not have a uniquely determined schedule of intended purchases, $r(\theta, v, t)$. The reason for this is that each participant expects prices to remain as they are now; hence, while the *total* of his future purchases of each commodity is determined by the solution to his optimization problem, the *timing* of those purchases is not.

When we come to a consideration of the adjustment processes involved in the model, such indeterminacy cannot be allowed to persist. This is because it is the attempt to exercise excess demand which affects price; hence we cannot hope to have an adjustment model which lacks some specification of the way in which planned purchases are reflected in present action.[19]

For our purposes, it is merely necessary to assume that current purchases are determined from future plans in a continuous manner and that nonzero future needs result in some immediate attempt to satisfy them. Thus, denoting the ith component of $r(\theta, v, t)$ by a subscript, we assume:

ASSUMPTION 7.1 (*Present Action Postulate*) For each participant (household or firm), there exists a set of $n - 1$ continuous and sign-preserving functions $F^i(\cdot)$, $i = 1, \ldots, n - 1$, which do not approach zero except as their arguments do, such that[20]

$$r_i(\theta, t, t) = F^i\left(\int_t^\theta r_i(\theta, v, t)\, dv \right). \tag{7.1}$$

Note that we shall interpret $r(\theta, t, t)$ as *posttrade* purchase demand, so that it is an unsatisfied demand. This means that we have assumed that each participant immediately acts so as to satisfy his future needs and does so (with trade taking place instantaneously) until he has either satisfied those needs or is unable to trade further.

This assumption is implicit in all existing stability models. I have elsewhere (1976a,b) discussed it extensively and so shall be somewhat briefer here.

In the first place, the presence of dated commodities makes the Present Action Postulate more palatable than it would otherwise be. This is so even for households where we require that a household expecting to require toothpaste in 1984 now attempt to purchase 1984 toothpaste rather than now attempting to acquire spot toothpaste. It is much more important for firms, however, for it prevents us from having to assume that firms now begin to sell outputs on the spot market which will not be produced for years; further, we can allow a firm to acquire a given commodity for use as an input even though it expects to be a net supplier of that commodity (with a later date) later on. Indeed, the introduction of dating makes the problems associated with the Present Action Postulate essentially no greater for firms than for households.

Nevertheless, those problems are not negligible. Basically, firms and households are indifferent as to the timing of their purchases; we are insisting

---

[19] The recognition of the fact that planned purchases must be translated into actual attempts to buy if they are to affect prices also lies at the heart of the institutional assumptions concerning money and no bankruptcy introduced by Arrow and Hahn (1971, Chapter XIII) into these models and continued here. For a more elaborate discussion, see Fisher (1976b).

[20] *Remark* It is not necessary that present purchase attempts depend only on the integral of future desired purchases, so long as the properties of $F^i(\cdot)$ as a function of that integral are retained; (7.1) gives the simplest version.

that they choose a particular kind of action from a set of equally optimal actions. Why should they do this?

The answer inevitably lies somewhat outside the models of the household and the firm so far given, for the kinds of justification for the Present Action Postulate that come readily to mind require some consciousness of disequilibrium. Thus, for example, present action may be optimal if one realizes that one may not in fact be able to complete ones purchases. More important than this, perhaps, is the fact that experience with attempts to buy just a little will show, given the Hahn Process Assumption (described formally later), that prices are moving perversely so that hanging back from the market is unlikely to be seen as a successful way to speculate. Both these reasons will be reinforced by the realization that trading in goods dated θ must be completed by θ.

Nevertheless, these arguments, however persuasive, import into the motivations of the participants some consciousness of disequilibrium and of uncertainty which is conspicuously absent in their price expectations and in the derivation of their optimal strategies.

8. THE HAHN PROCESS AND TRADING RULES

As already discussed, the basic trading rule we shall use is that of the Hahn Process, which is extremely natural when markets are distinguished by dealers. The basic assumption is that there are not at the same (postinstantaneous trade) time both unsatisfied suppliers and unsatisfied demanders of the same commodity. Formally, define

$$R(\theta, t) = \sum_h r_h(\theta, t, t) + \sum_f r_f(\theta, t, t), \qquad \theta \geq t. \tag{8.1}$$

we assume:

ASSUMPTION 8.1   (*Hahn Process*)   (a)   For all households h and ordinary commodities $i = 1, \ldots, n - 1$, $r_{hi}(\theta, t, t)R_i(\theta, t) \geq 0$, and $r_{hi}(\theta, t, t)R_i(\theta, t) > 0$ unless $r_{hi}(\theta, t, t) = 0$.
(b)   For all firms f and ordinary commodities $i = 1, \ldots, n - 1$, $r_{fi}(\theta, t, t)R_i(\theta, t) \geq 0$, and $r_{fi}(\theta, t, t)R_i(\theta, t) > 0$ unless $r_{fi}(\theta, t, t) = 0$.

It is not necessary to be explicit about the way in which *actual* trades $\bar{r}(\theta, t)$ take place. We need only assume that they do so in a way consistent with the Hahn Process and satisfying appropriate Lipschitz conditions.[21]

---

[21] One example is given by Arrow and Hahn (1971, Chapter XIII).

One other matter needs to be discussed before proceeding, namely, the assumption already made in passing that households and firms are always able to fulfill their consumption, storage, and production plans as regards currently dated commodities. This assumption seems necessary in order to avoid awkward discontinuities caused by the sudden realization that plans cannot be fulfilled. There are (at least) two ways in which it can be violated.

In the first place, since participants expect their transactions to be completed, it might be the case, for example, that a household holds no stock of a particular dated commodity but plans to have its consumption come entirely from current purchases. Since it may not be able to make those purchases, it may find itself suddenly unable to fulfill its consumption plan. (The discontinuities involved here are very similar to those created by dated commodities if continuity of prices is not assured.)

Second, even if a participant does hold buffer stocks with which it expects to fulfill its plans, it might be the case that the stock of one such commodity so held consists of commitments by firms to produce and deliver that commodity by the time its date comes due. Out of equilibrium, however, it is possible that firms may not be able to satisfy those commitments since they may not be able to acquire the necessary inputs.

Obviously, in this latter situation, one might expect the prices for the commodities in question to rise very quickly as short firms attempt to cover their commitments. While it is possible to build such behavior into the price adjustment rules given in the next section (by letting the rate of change of price depend on $\theta - t$), it does not appear particularly simple to ensure that this always results in short positions being covered by the time delivery is due. Further work here is very desirable.

9.   PRICE ADJUSTMENT

We adapt the conventional price adjustment assumptions to the present model. Here, and later, dots denote derivatives with respect to t.

ASSUMPTION 9.1   (*Price Adjustment*)   For each of the nonmonetary commodities $i = 1, \ldots, n - 1$, there exists a continuous and sign-preserving function $H^i(\cdot)$ which does not approach zero except as its argument does, such that for all $\theta \geq t$, $\dot{p}_i(\theta, t) = H^i(R_i(\theta, t))$ unless $p_i(\theta, t) = 0$ and $R_i(\theta, t) < 0$ in which case $\dot{p}_i(\theta, t) = 0$.

Note the feature that it is the *same* function $H^i(\cdot)$ which applies for all values of θ. In fact, this can be generalized to allow continuous dependence on θ. The crucial feature is continuity in θ which allows continuous price profiles to remain continuous. It is hard to see why this should be the case unless the same individual controls price adjustment for a given commodity for all θ. This is, of course, the dated commodities problem with which we began.

Recall that $p(\theta, t)$ becomes fixed as t passes θ.

We assume that the adjustment mechanisms satisfy the appropriate Lipschitz conditions so that there exist solutions to the partial differential equations involved which are continuous in the initial conditions. This assumption is also made as regards the other fundamental variables in the system, acquired stocks, $\bar{x}(\theta, t)$.[22]

10. DECLINE OF TARGET PROFITS

We now return to the theory of the firm and show that target or expected profits $\pi(t)$ decline unless the firm is able to complete all its transactions (with the exception of disposing of free goods).[23]

The proof is in two steps. First, observe that the maximized profits of the firm at time t depend on those things which the firm takes as given. These are, prices $p(\theta, t)$, profits already earned $\bar{\pi}(t)$, and the value of the actual stock of already purchased goods $\bar{x}(\theta, t)$. In addition, the firm is constrained by its own past input and output decisions, that is, by the part of the profile $y(v, t)$ already committed and its consequent effects on $\phi(y(v, t), \theta, t)$. When the firm decides on its optimal program at time t, it takes actions which further constrain its future behavior by choosing $y(t, t)$. We first consider what we shall term "replannable" profits, denoted by $\pi^*(t)$, which differ from target profits $\pi(t)$, in that replannable profits are the profits which could be earned if the firm could continually go back to t and remake its production decision from then on so as to reoptimize its behavior given new prices and new acquired stocks.

We shall refer to a position in which the firm completes all its transactions with the possible exception of disposing of free goods as an equilibrium for the firm.

LEMMA 10.1   For every firm, $\dot{\pi}^*(t) \leq 0$ and $\dot{\pi}^*(t) < 0$ unless the firm is in an equilibrium for it.

[22] Henry (1973a,b) has shown that the restriction of prices to the nonnegative orthant presents no essential problem here, at least for the usual case of a finite number of commodities. [See also Champsaur et al. (1977).] The present case can be regarded as having a continuum of commodities or as involving partial differential equations. It seems clear that Henry's work can be extended to cover this.

[23] That the Hahn Process implies the decline of target profits as well as of target utilities was first observed in Fisher (1974).

Proof By the Envelope Theorem for constrained maximization, we can evaluate $\dot{\pi}^*(t)$ by differentiating the Lagrangian (5.6) with respect to the things not under the firm's control[24]:

$$\dot{\pi}^*(t) = \dot{\Lambda}_2 = -\int_t^\infty \int_t^\theta \dot{p}(\theta, t) r(\theta, v, t)\, dv\, d\theta + \dot{\bar{\pi}}$$
$$+ \int_t^\infty \gamma(\theta, t)\bar{r}(\theta, t)\, d\theta, \tag{10.1}$$

recalling that we are assuming that changes in the production plan of the firm can be readjusted so as to be under the control of the firm.[25]

Differentiating the definition of realized profits $\bar{\pi}(t)$, given in (5.2) and using the first-order conditions (5.8), we find

$$\dot{\bar{\pi}}(t) = -\int_0^\infty p(\theta, t)\bar{r}(\theta, t)\, d\theta = -\int_0^\infty \gamma(\theta, t)\bar{r}(\theta, t)\, d\theta, \tag{10.2}$$

so that

$$\dot{\pi}^*(t) = -\int_t^\infty \int_t^\theta \dot{p}(\theta, t) r(\theta, v, t)\, dv\, d\theta$$
$$= -\int_t^\infty \dot{p}(\theta, t)\left\{\int_t^\theta r(\theta, v, t)\, dv\right\} d\theta. \tag{10.3}$$

By the Present Action Postulate (Assumption 7.1), however, the component of the inner integral on the far right-hand side of (10.3) corresponding to the *i*th commodity ($i = 1, \ldots, n - 1$) has the same sign as $r_i(0, t, t)$. Further, by the Hahn Process Assumption (Assumption 8.1), if $r_i(0, t, t)$ is not zero, it has the same sign as $R_i(0, t)$. Finally, by the Price Adjustment Assumption (Assumption 9.1), that is also the sign of $\dot{p}_i(0, t)$, unless $p_i(0, t) = 0$ and $r_i(0, t, t) < 0$. The lemma is now immediate.

It is now easy to prove:

THEOREM 10.1 For every firm, actual target profits $\pi(t)$ are non-increasing through time and are strictly declining unless the firm is at an equilibrium for it.

Proof Consider a small positive time interval dt. At t, $\pi(t) = \pi^*(t)$, but $\pi(t + dt) \leq \pi^*(t + dt)$, since $\pi(t + dt)$ is the maximum profit which can

---

[24] See Fisher (1976a) for a brief discussion of the extension of the Envelope Theorem to problems involving functionals.

[25] It might be supposed that there would be further terms in (10.1) stemming from the derivatives of the integrals in Λ_2 with respect to the lower limits of integration. In fact, those terms do not appear because all the integrals in (5.6) are items under the control of the firm. This can be verified, if required, by evaluating those terms in the light of the constraint (5.4) and the first-order conditions (5.8).

actually be made at $(t + dt)$ and $\pi^*(t + dt)$ is the maximum profit which could be made at $(t + dt)$ if the firm could go back and redo its production decisions during $[t, t + dt]$. By Lemma 10.1, however, for small enough dt, $\pi^*(t + dt) \leq \pi^*(t)$ with the strict inequality holding unless the position at t is one of equilibrium for the firm. This proves the theorem.[26]

We shall assume $\pi(t)$ bounded below.

11. DECLINE OF TARGET UTILITIES

With this result in hand, we are almost ready to prove the parallel result for target utilities. Before doing so, however, we need to add one more assumption.

We have already assumed in (4.1) that the household believes it can acquire goods by trade at constant prices only by giving up goods of equal value. We now assume that it is correct in this:

ASSUMPTION 11.1   (*No Swindling*) $\int_t^\infty p(\theta, t)\overline{r}(\theta, t)\,d\theta = 0$.

As before, the analysis is divided into two parts. We first consider re-plannable utility U^*, the utility which would be achieved if the household could constantly revise its consumption and storage plans from t onward. U^* depends on prices, stocks received from outside and undistributed profits.

We shall refer to a position in which the household completes all its transactions (with the possible exception of disposing of free goods) as an equilibrium for the household.[27]

LEMMA 11.1   For every household, $\dot{U}^* \leq 0$, and $\dot{U}^* < 0$ unless the household and every firm in which it owns a positive share are in equilibria for them.

Proof   By the Envelope Theorem, we can evaluate $\dot{U}^*$ by differentiating the Lagrangian (4.6) with respect to the things outside the control of the

---

[26] The reason that dt must be taken small is that π^* is defined relative to t and Lemma 10.1 holds only at t. This is because the excess demands which would arise from optimizing π^* will generally differ after t from those which arise in optimizing π itself, and it is the latter which help drive the prices.

[27] Note that an equilibrium for the household cannot occur unless all profits to which it is entitled are distributed. This is because the household behaves as though it has the undistributed profits to spend. Hence it will either be purchasing with them in which case there is an unsatisfied transaction or it will wish to consume or store them. But we have assumed that current consumption and storage plans are satisfied. In either case, profits must be distributed. This will show up again when we define equilibrium and consider the implications of Walras' law (6.2).

household. Thus,

$$\dot{U}^* = \dot{\Lambda}_1 = -\int_t^\infty \lambda(v, t) \int_v^\infty \dot{p}(\theta, t) r(\theta, v, t) \, d\theta \, dv$$

$$+ \int_t^\infty \mu(\theta, t) \{\bar{r}(\theta, t) + \dot{d}(\theta, t) + \dot{s}(\theta, t) - \dot{d}(\theta, t)\} \, d\theta, \quad (11.1)$$

recalling that consumption and storage can be readjusted from t onward.[28]

Using the first-order conditions, (4.8)–(4.11), this becomes

$$\dot{U}^* = -\lambda(t) \int_t^\infty \dot{p}(\theta, t) \left\{ \int_t^\infty r(\theta, v, t) \, dv \right\} d\theta$$

$$+ \lambda(t) \int_t^\infty p(\theta, t) \dot{s}(\theta, t) \, d\theta + \lambda(t) \int_t^\infty p(\theta, t) \bar{r}(\theta, t) \, d\theta. \quad (11.2)$$

The third term in this is zero by the No Swindling Assumption, however, while the integral in the second term is the rate of change of the household's share of profits of the firms it owns [recall that $s(\theta, t)$ has only its nth component nonzero and that $p_n(\theta, t) = 1$]. By Theorem 10.1, this is nonpositive and is strictly negative unless all those firms are in equilibria for them. Since $\lambda(t)$ is obviously positive, it remains only to show that the double integral multiplied by $-\lambda(t)$ in the first term is nonnegative and is strictly positive unless the household is at an equilibrium for it.

This is readily done, however. By the Present Action Postulate (Assumption 7.1), the component of the inner integral corresponding to the ith commodity ($i = 1, \ldots, n - 1$) has the same sign as $r_i(\theta, t, t)$. Further, by the Hahn Process Assumption (Assumption 8.1), if $r_i(\theta, t, t)$ is not zero, it has the same sign as $R_i(\theta, t)$. Finally, by the Price Adjustment Assumption (Assumption 9.1), that is also the sign of $\dot{p}_i(\theta, t)$, unless $p_i(\theta, t) = 0$ and $r_i(\theta, t, t) < 0$. The desired result now follows immediately.

An argument identical to that used to prove Theorem 10.1 from Lemma 10.1 now shows:

THEOREM 11.1 For every household, actual target utility $U(\cdot)$ is nonincreasing through time and is strictly decreasing unless the household and all the firms in which it owns a positive share are in equilibria for them.

We shall assume $U(\cdot)$ bounded below.

12. PROPERTIES OF EQUILIBRIUM

The fundamental variables of the system are prices $p(\cdot, t)$ and acquired stocks $\bar{x}(\cdot, t)$. It will be convenient to adopt a notation for the vector of the latter listing $\bar{x}(\cdot, t)$ for all firms and households (in some definite but not important order). We denote it by $\bar{X}(\cdot, t)$.

[28] A comment similar to that made in the case of firms applies to terms stemming from differentiation with respect to limits of integration.

When discussing equilibria, it will be convenient to suppress the time argument and speak of $p(\cdot)$ and $\bar{X}(\cdot)$.

Now, since consumption, storage, and production take place out of equilibrium, the maximization problem facing each participant changes; that is, past consumption fixes some of the argument in the utility functional to be maximized, while past production and storage decisions affect the constraints within which present optimization takes place. It follows that the set of $(p(\cdot), \bar{X}(\cdot))$ which are equilibria will change over time depending on the production and consumption histories which occur. We thus define:

DEFINITION 12.1 $(p(\cdot), \bar{X}(\cdot))$ is an equilibrium for t if and only if, given the history of the economy at t, with $p(\cdot, t) = p(\cdot)$ and $\bar{X}(\cdot, t) = \bar{X}(\cdot)$, for every household and firm[29]

$$c(\theta, t) + y(\theta, t) - \bar{x}(\theta, t) - \phi(y(v, t), \theta, t) \leqq 0. \tag{12.1}$$

(The same expression holds for households and firms if we set consumption of firms at zero.)

It is easy to prove:

LEMMA 12.1   If an equilibrium for t actually occurs at t, then:

(a)   For all participants and all nonmonetary commodities $i = 1,\ldots,n-1$, $r_i(\theta, t, t) \leq 0$;[30] the strict inequality holds if and only if the corresponding inequality in (12.1) is also strict.

(b)   For all commodities $i = 1, \ldots, n$, a strict inequality in (12.1) implies $p_i(\theta, t) = 0$. Hence a strict inequality never occurs in the nth component of (12.1).

(c)   For every firm, $\bar{G}(t) = \bar{\pi}(t) = \pi(t)$.

Proof   Proposition (a) follows immediately for firms from the constraint (5.4) and the Present Action Postulate. For households, it follows from the constraints (4.2) and (4.3), the Present Action Postulate, and the fact that undistributed profits are nonzero only for money. In other words, (a) simply says that excess demand for ordinary commodities can be satisfied only through purchases.

Proposition (b) and the first equality in (c) follow from examining Walras' law (6.2) and observing that, in view of (12.1) and (5.11), every term in every summation in (6.2) is nonpositive. Hence every term must be zero. The second equality in (c) is evident.

---

[29] I adopt the usual convention for vector inequalities in which $x > y$ means $x_i > y_i$, $x \geq y$ means $x_i \geq y_i$ but $x \neq y$, and $x \geqq y$ means $x_i \geqq y_i$ with $x = y$ permitted.

[30] Note that, in view of the Present Action Postulate (Assumption 7.1), this can be stated equivalently as $\int_t^\infty r_i(\theta, v, t)\,dv \leq 0$.

Note that an equilibrium for t is an equilibrium for every participant. It is important to note that an equilibrium in this model (as in models without production and consumption) is an exhaustion of trading opportunities. All trades are consummated and economic activity thenceforward consists of the carrying out of previously made plans and commitments. It would be interesting to have a stability model in which equilibrium involves continued trading.

On the other hand, it is of course true that there is no guarantee in the convergence proof below that equilibrium is reached in finite time, so that trading may in fact continue indefinitely (although it will disappear asymptotically).

This fact makes it necessary to consider the nature of equilibrium a bit more fully. If an equilibrium for t is actually attained at t, then it will remain an equilibrium for all later time. On the other hand, if an equilibrium for t is not actually attained at t, then the set of equilibria will change. Since convergence can only be established asymptotically, this means that we must think in terms of an asymptotic equilibrium set. This can most easily be done by recognizing that the left-hand side of (12.1) depends on prices $p(\cdot)$, acquired stocks $\bar{X}(\cdot)$, and actual past history. Denote that left-hand side by $z(p(\cdot), \bar{X}(\cdot), \theta, t)$, where the time argument stands for dependence on past history. We can now define:

DEFINITION 12.2 $(p(\cdot), \bar{X}(\cdot))$ is an asymptotic equilibrium if and only if for every participant, all θ, and all commodities $i = 1, \ldots, n$,

$$\limsup_{t \to \infty} z_i(p(\cdot), \bar{X}(\cdot), \theta, t) \le 0. \tag{12.2}$$

We add some remarks. First, it is evident that the results of Lemma 12.1 apply asymptotically. Hence, in particular, for all goods for which $p_i(\theta) \ne 0$, the limit superior in (12.2) can be replaced by an ordinary limit which will in fact be zero. The more complicated statement in (12.2) is due to the fact that the holdings of excess supplies of free goods need not approach a limit.

Second, we shall establish appropriate compactness below and prove that every limit point of the path of prices and acquired stocks is an asymptotic equilibrium. It follows that there is at least one asymptotic equilibrium. This may or may not be an equilibrium for some finite t which is actually attained at that time.

13. BOUNDEDNESS

I have already discussed the issues surrounding the boundedness of prices in an earlier section. I shall now proceed to assume it directly.

ASSUMPTION 13.1 $p(\cdot, t)$ remains in a bounded set.

The other fundamental variables of the system are the acquired stocks $\bar{X}(\cdot, t)$. It turns out not to be necessary directly to assume these bounded, however, instead, it suffices to assume:

ASSUMPTION 13.2   For each participant the value of possessions $w(t)$ remains bounded.

Given the boundedness of prices, this is weaker than assuming stocks themselves bounded. I have elsewhere (1974, 1976a,b) discussed the arguments for the stronger assumption.

14.   COMPACTNESS AND QUASI-STABILITY

We are going to use the decline of target utilities to take the sum of such utilities as a Lyapounov functional and establish quasi stability. In other words, we shall show that every limit point of the path of prices and acquired stocks is an asymptotic equilibrium. This will do little good, however, unless we can show that such a limit point exists and, as it happens, the easiest way to show that appears to be tied up with the proof of quasi stability itself. Hence we discuss both subjects together.

We begin with prices. By Assumption 13.3, $p(\cdot, t)$ remains in a bounded set and we may obviously assume that it remains in the closure of that set. By the Alaoglu theorem, it follows that:

LEMMA 14.1   The time path of prices lies in a set which is weak* compact.

In what follows, any reference to limit points or to compactness is to be understood as being in the weak* topology as involves prices.

Similarly, since the value of possessions $w(t)$ is a scalar, since we have assumed it to lie in a bounded set in Assumption 13.4, and since we can take it to lie in the closure of that set, it follows [denoting the vector of the $w(t)$ for all participants by $W(t)$]:

LEMMA 14.2   The time path of values of possessions $W(t)$ lies in a compact set.

The problem with proceeding directly, however, is that it is not enough to show that the time path of $W(t)$ has a limit point; we must show this (or almost this) for the time path of acquired stocks themselves, $\bar{X}(\cdot, t)$, and here closure and boundedness are not enough. In fact, the time path of $\bar{X}(\cdot, t)$ need not have a limit point, but the exception is inessential.

The exception concerns the treatment of free goods. As prices approach a weak* limit point and $W(t)$ approaches a limit point, there is nothing to determine who holds the excess supplies of the goods which are free at the limiting prices. (We have already met this problem in defining an asymptotic equilibrium, Definition 12.2.) Clearly, however, this is inessential, since the holdings of excess free goods do not affect any consumption, storage, or production decisions. Hence, it is merely necessary to devise a way of conveniently dealing with such holdings.

This we do by defining what we shall call "essential stocks."

DEFINITION 14.1   Given a price profile $p(\cdot)$, the vector of essential stocks relative to $p(\cdot)$ for each participant, household or firm, is denoted by $q(\cdot, t)$ and defined as follows. For every t, θ, and $i = 1, \ldots, n$,

$$q_i(\theta, t) = \bar{x}_i(\theta, t) \qquad \text{if} \quad p_i(\theta, t) \neq 0;$$
$$q_i(\theta, t) = \min\{\bar{x}_i(\theta, t), c_i(\theta, t) + y_i(\theta, t) - \phi_i(y(v, t), \theta, t)\} \qquad (14.1)$$
$$\text{if} \quad p_i(\theta, t) = 0.$$

(Recall that $c(\theta, t) = 0$ for firms.)

We denote the vector which lists essential stocks for all participants by $Q(\cdot, t)$ and, when speaking of equilibria, by $Q(\cdot)$. We shall speak of asymptotic equilibria as involving points in the space of $(p(\cdot), Q(\cdot))$ as:

DEFINITION 14.2 $(p(\cdot), Q(\cdot))$ is an asymptotic equilibrium if and only if $Q(\cdot)$ is defined relative to $p(\cdot)$ and $(p(\cdot), \bar{X}(\cdot))$ would be an asymptotic equilibrium if $\bar{X}(\cdot) = Q(\cdot)$.

In a way, what all this amounts to is assuming free disposal of goods which are free at equilibrium.

We can now prove:

LEMMA 14.3   (a)   The time path of $(p(\cdot, t), W(t))$ has a limit point (the limit being weak* in the case of $p(\cdot, t)$).

(b)   To every limit point of the time path of $(p(\cdot, t), W(t))$, say $(p(\cdot), W)$, there corresponds a limit point to the time path of $Q(\cdot, t)$, say $Q(\cdot)$, where $Q(\cdot, t)$ is defined relative to the limiting prices $p(\cdot)$.

(c)   Every such limit point, $(p(\cdot), Q(\cdot))$ is an asymptotic equilibrium.

Proof   (a) follows immediately from Lemmas 14.1 and 14.2. Now, $c(\cdot, t)$ and $y(\cdot, t)$ are continuous in $w(t)$ and weak* continuous in $p(\cdot, t)$. It follows that, as $(p(\cdot, t), W(t))$ approach $(p(\cdot), W)$ along a convergent subsequence, $c(\cdot, t)$ and $y(\cdot, t)$ approach limits for every participant, say $c(\cdot)$ and $y(\cdot)$. Moreover, utilities are bounded below and nonincreasing. Hence utility for each participant approaches a limit and, by Theorem 11.1, this cannot occur unless for every agent the limit superior of excess demands for each commodity is nonpositive and the limit of excess demand strictly zero for all commodities with a positive price at the limiting $p(\cdot)$. Thus, for all commodities for which the limiting price is positive,

$$\lim \bar{x}_i(\theta, t) = \lim \{c_i(\theta, t) + y_i(\theta, t) - \phi_i(y(v, t), \theta, t)\} \qquad (14.2)$$

and, since the right-hand side of (14.2) exists, $Q(\cdot, t)$ must have a limit point. Evidently, from what has been said, using the sum of target utilities as a Lyapounov functional, every such limit point $(p(\cdot), Q(\cdot))$ must be an equilibrium, and the lemma is proved.

15. GLOBAL STABILITY

We are now nearly in position to prove the principal result of this paper, the global stability of the model. To be able to do this as regards prices, however, requires the following assumption:

ASSUMPTION 15.1 (*Indecomposability*) Let $S(p)$ be the set of dated commodities (including money) which have strictly positive prices. For any asymptotic equilibrium and any proper subset of $S(p)$, say $S'(p)$, there exists a pair of commodities, $i(\theta) \in S'(p)$ and $j(v) \in (S(p) - S'(p))$ such that in the solution to the optimization problem for some participant the marginal rate of substitution between $i(\theta)$ and $j(v)$ is defined, is not at a corner solution, and is equal to the price ratio.

This assumption essentially prevents the possibility that (at equilibrium) the economy breaks down into two or more unrelated subeconomies with agents in one using one set of goods and agents in the other using the remainder, each at corner solutions with respect to the goods not used. It is stated as it is because of the possibility that the technologies of firms (or households in their storage activities) can break down into two or more unrelated parts.

THEOREM 15.1 The model is globally stable; that is, for any set of initial conditions, there exists a price profile $p^*(\cdot)$ and a vector of essential stocks $Q^*(\cdot)$, defined relative to $p^*(\cdot)$, such that:

(a) $(p^*(\cdot), Q^*(\cdot))$ is an asymptotic equilibrium;
(b) $p(\cdot, t)$ converges weak* to $p^*(\cdot)$; and
(c) $Q(\cdot, t)$ converges to $Q^*(\cdot)$.

Note that this implies that consumption, production, and storage profiles also converge in norm. Indeed, this is evident in the course of the proof.

Proof In view of Lemmas 14.1–14.3, we need only show that every limit point of prices and essential stocks is the same. Suppose instead that there are two different limit points which we call * and **. Then there is a sequence of times at which the economy is very close to * and another sequence at which it is very close to **. In what follows, we choose t_1 as a time from the first sequence and $t_2 > t_1$ as a time from the second.

We first consider households. By strict quasiconcavity of $U(\cdot)$, there exists an $\alpha_1 \geq 0$ such that, for any $\varepsilon_1 > 0$, we can choose t_1 and t_2 large enough to make

$$\int_{t_1}^{\infty} (p(\theta, t_1)c(\theta, t_1)\, d\theta \leq \int_{t_1}^{\infty} p(\theta, t_1)c(\theta, t_2)\, d\theta - \alpha_1 + \varepsilon_1, \qquad (15.1)$$

with $\alpha_1 > 0$ unless the limiting consumption profiles, say c^* and c^{**}, coincide for all dates and commodities which have a nonzero price at *.[31]

Moreover, as is evident from common sense or from the implication of the first-order conditions given in (4.13), the storage activity of the household must be profit maximizing if we think of it as buying inputs from its consumption activity and selling back outputs all at current market prices. Hence, there exists an $\alpha_2 \geq 0$ such that, for any $\varepsilon_2 > 0$, we can choose t_1 and t_2 large enough to make

$$\int_{t_1}^{\infty} p(\theta, t_1)\{y(\theta, t_1) - \phi(y(v, t_1), \theta, t_1)\}\, d\theta$$
$$\leq \int_{t_1}^{\infty} p(\theta, t_1)\{y(\theta, t_2) - \phi(y(v, t_2), \theta, t_2)\}\, d\theta - \alpha_2 + \varepsilon_2, \qquad (15.2)$$

where $\alpha_2 > 0$ unless the limiting storage profiles, say y^* and y^{**}, coincide for all dates and commodities with positive prices at *.[32]

However, * is an asymptotic equilibrium so that the sum of the integrals on the left-hand sides of (15.1) and (15.2) approaches the value of actual holdings at *. Further, ** is an asymptotic equilibrium, so the sum of the integrals on the right-hand sides of the same equations becomes asymptotically no greater than the value of the actual holdings at **, both values being in the prices of *. Thus there exists an $\alpha_3 \geq 0$ such that, for any $\varepsilon_3 > 0$, we can choose t_1 and t_2 large enough to make[33]

$$\int_{t_1}^{\infty} p(\theta, t_1)\bar{x}(\theta, t_1)\, d\theta \leq \int_{t_1}^{\infty} p(\theta, t_1)\bar{x}(\theta, t_2)\, d\theta - \alpha_3 + \varepsilon_3, \qquad (15.3)$$

with $\alpha_3 > 0$ unless c^* and c^{**} and y^* and y^{**} (and $\bar{x}^*$ and $\bar{x}^{**}$) coincide as before.

---

[31] The first-order conditions and the fact that prices are continuous in θ make consumption profiles similarly continuous. Otherwise c^* and c^{**} would have to coincide only almost everywhere. A similar remark applies to other optimal profiles below.

[32] Notice that the appearance of t_2 rather than t_1 in the integral on the right-hand side of (15.2) does not affect this. Since $t_2 > t_1$, the household's technical storage opportunities at t_1 include taking those actions it actually took up to t_2 and then having the technical opportunities it actually had at that point. A similar remark holds for firms below, although it is not needed explicitly.

[33] Recall (4.5) and the fact that $\bar{x}(\theta, t) \equiv \bar{x}(\theta, \theta)$ for $\theta < t$.

From (4.4),

$$\bar{x}(\theta, t_2) = \bar{x}(\theta, t_1) + \int_{t_1}^{t_2} \bar{r}(\theta, v)\, dv + d(\theta, t_2) - d(\theta, t_1). \tag{15.4}$$

Moreover, all profits are paid out in equilibrium (Lemma 12.1); further, since profits are nonincreasing (Theorem 10.1) and bounded below, they approach a limit. Hence $d(\theta, t_2)$ and $d(\theta, t_1)$ approach a common limit. Thus there exists an $\alpha_4 \geq 0$ such that, for any $\varepsilon_4 > 0$, we can choose t_1 and t_2 large enough to make

$$\int_{t_1}^{\infty} p(\theta, t_1) \int_{t_1}^{t_2} \bar{r}(\theta, v)\, dv\, d\theta \geq \alpha_4 - \varepsilon_4, \tag{15.5}$$

with $\alpha_4 > 0$ unless all the household's activities at * and ** coincide for commodities with positive prices at * as before.

Now consider firms. Since the optimal program of the firm is profit maximizing,

$$\int_{t_1}^{\infty} \int_{t_1}^{\theta} p(\theta, t_1) r(\theta, v, t_1)\, dv\, d\theta$$
$$\leq \int_{t_1}^{\infty} \int_{t_1}^{t_2} p(\theta, t_1) \bar{r}(\theta, v)\, dv\, d\theta + \int_{t_1}^{\infty} \int_{t_2}^{\theta} p(\theta, t_1) r(\theta, v, t_2)\, dv\, d\theta, \tag{15.6}$$

with the strict inequality holding unless the firm as of t_2 is merely carrying out plans made as of t_1 and successfully carried out in the interim, as regards all dates and commodities with a positive price at t_1. Thus, in the limit, the strict inequality will hold unless the limiting stock profiles of the firm, say $\bar{x}^*$ and $\bar{x}^{**}$, and production profiles, say y^* and y^{**}, coincide in all dated commodities with positive prices at *.[34]

Since * is an asymptotic equilibrium, however, the left-hand side of (15.6) approaches zero, while the second integral on the right-hand side becomes nonpositive. Hence, there exists an $\alpha_5 \geq 0$ such that, for any $\varepsilon_5 > 0$, we can choose t_1 and t_2 large enough to make

$$\int_{t_1}^{\infty} p(\theta, t_1) \int_{t_1}^{t_2} \bar{r}(\theta, v)\, dv\, d\theta \geq \alpha_5 - \varepsilon_5, \tag{15.7}$$

with $\alpha_5 > 0$ unless the activities of the firm at * and ** coincide for positively priced commodities as before.

Now sum (15.5) over households and (15.7) over firms. There exists an $\alpha \geq 0$ such that, for any $\varepsilon > 0$, we can choose t_1 and t_2 large enough to make

$$\int_{t_1}^{\infty} p(\theta, t_1) \int_{t_1}^{t_2} \left\{ \sum_h \bar{r}_h(\theta, v) + \sum_f \bar{r}_f(\theta, v) \right\} dv\, d\theta \geq \alpha - \varepsilon, \tag{15.8}$$

---

[34] Purchase profiles need not coincide at t_1 and t_2 (although they do so trivially at * and **) because the timing of sales and purchases at given prices is not completely determined by the solution to the optimization problem of the firm (and similarly for households).

with $\alpha > 0$ unless for every firm and every household all consumption, storage, production, and stock profiles coincide at * and ** for all positively priced commodities. Since net sales of ordinary commodities by the production sector must be net purchases by the household sector, however, and since actual profits approach a common limit at * and **, the closure equations (6.1) imply that $\alpha > 0$ is impossible.

Thus all profiles coincide for all dated commodities with positive prices at *. It is but a matter of interchanging notation to show that they also coincide for all dated commodities with positive prices at **. It thus remains to show that all positive prices are the same at * as at **.

To do so, observe that the proposition is trivial if money is the only positively priced good at * and **. Suppose, therefore, that there is some other dated commodity with a positive price at one of the equilibria, say *. Then, by the Indecomposability Assumption (Assumption 15.1), there is some dated commodity other than money with a positive price at *, say $i(\theta)$, such that for some participant the marginal rate of substitution between $i(\theta)$ and money is defined, not at a corner solution, and equal to the corresponding price ratio at *. Since all consumption, storage, production, and stock profiles coincide at * and **, however, the marginal rate of substitution in question must be the same at ** as at *, and, since it is not at a corner solution, it must be the case that the price of $i(\theta)$ is the same at ** as at *. If there is now another commodity with a positive price at *, then the Indecomposability Assumption states that there is a commodity with a positive price at *, say $j(v)$, such that the marginal rate of substitution either between $j(v)$ and money or between $j(v)$ and $i(\theta)$ is determined, not at a corner solution, and equal to the corresponding price ratio for some participant. Arguing as before, this means that the price of $j(v)$ must be the same at ** as at *. Evidently we can reach all dated commodities with a positive price at either * or ** in this way; hence all such prices must be the same, and the proof is complete.

REFERENCES

Arrow, K. J., and F. H. Hahn (1971). *General Competitive Analysis*. San Francisco: Holden-Day; and Edinburgh: Oliver & Boyd.

Champsaur, P., J. Drèze, and C. Henry (1977). Stability Theorems With Economic Applications, *Econometrica* **45** (March), 273–294.

Fisher, F. M. (1970). Quasi-Competitive Price Adjustment by Individual Firms: A Preliminary Paper, *Journal of Economic Theory* **2**, (June), 195–206.

Fisher, F. M. (1972). On Price Adjustment without an Auctioneer, *Review of Economic Studies* **39** (January), 1–16.

Fisher, F. M. (1973). Stability and Competitive Equilibrium in Two Models of Search and Individual Price Adjustment, *Journal of Economic Theory* **6** (October), 446–470.

Fisher, F. M. (1974). The Hahn Process with Firms But No Production, *Econometrica* **42** (May), 471–486.

Fisher, F. M. (1976a). A Non-Tâtonnement Model with Production and Consumption," *Econometrica* **44** (September), 907–938.

Fisher, F. M. (1976b). The Stability of General Equilibrium: Results and Problems, in *Essays in Economic Analysis* (*Proceedings of the Association of University Teachers of Economics Annual Conference, Sheffield 1975*) (Artis and Nobay, eds.), pp. 3–29. London and New York: Cambridge Univ. Press.

Fisher, F. M. (1977). Quantity Constraints, Spillovers, and the Hahn Process, *Review of Economic Studies* **44** (October).

Foley, D. K. (1970). Economic Equilibrium with Costly Marketing, *Journal of Economic Theory* **2** (September), 276–291.

Hahn, F. H. (1971). Equilibrium with Transaction Costs, *Econometrica* **39** (May), 417–440.

Hahn, F. H., and T. Negishi (1962). A Theorem on Non-Tâtonnement Stability, *Econometrica* **30** (July), 463–469.

Henry, C. (1973a). An Existence Theorem for a Class of Differential Equations with Multivalued Right-Hand Side, *Journal of Mathematical Analysis and Applications* **41** (January), 179–186.

Henry, C. (1973b). Problèmes d'Existence et de Stabilité pour des Processus Dynamique Considerés en Economie Mathematique. Lab. Econ. Ecole Polytech. (March).

Koopmans, T. C. (1957). *Three Essays on the State of Economic Science*. New York: McGraw-Hill.

Luenberger, D. G. (1969). *Optimization by Vector Space Methods*. New York: Wiley.

Negishi, T. (1962). The Stability of a Competitive Economy: A Survey Article, *Econometrica* **30** (October), 635–669.

An exchange model of bilateral trade

PHILIP FRIEDMAN

BOSTON UNIVERSITY

1. INTRODUCTION

The literature on imperfections in international trade is quite large with a strong emphasis upon tariffs and other price distortions. However, non-tariff distortions have been considered mostly from the viewpoint of their equivalence to tariffs (Bhagwati and Ramaswami, 1963; Lapan, 1976). One source of trade distortion is founded in the restrictions placed upon trading relationships among nations. In particular, a policy of bilateralism has been pursued by many nations in the past, and continues to be discussed as a means of circumventing existing restrictions on trading and capital movements as well as for policy reasons directed at balance of payments equilibrium.

While bilateralism has been discussed, most of the research has been directed toward empirical measurement of the extent (Pryor, 1963; Wiles, 1969; Michaely, 1962) or the costs (Von Brabant, 1973; Friedman, 1976) of bilateral activity. An explicit general model of bilateral trade, and the effects of this constraint on the implied gains from exchange, has not been developed. By employing a simple model of exchange, and constraining the type of bilateral constraint to those that have been actually observed, this paper validates the inference that bilateral trade is generally suboptimal.

I wish to acknowledge the help of Rafael Lusky for suggestions on an earlier draft and Alan Blinder for insightful comments.

2. A GENERAL MODEL OF BILATERALISM

The effects of a restriction to bilateral trade can be conceptualized as the alterations of the solutions of a general exchange model caused by appending the condition of mutually balanced trade as an additional constraint.

Consider a world of K countries, each producing N goods. These countries have "normal" demand functions in that they each demand some of each good. All countries trade freely in all goods.

Let the production frontier for the ith country be represented by $F^i(Y_1^i \cdots Y_N^i)$ for the set of N goods. Let KX_j^i denote the shipments of commodity j from country k to country i, and define the total imports of commodity j by country i by $X_j^i \equiv \sum_{K=1}^{K} KX_j^i$ so that imports include self-importation. "Imports" so defined are identical to consumption. Each country has a utility function with $(\bar{X}_1^i \cdots X_N^i)$ as its arguments, which it maximizes with respect to the X_j^i, subject to the constraints[1]

(i) $\displaystyle\sum_{j=1}^{N} P_j X_j^i - \sum_{j=1}^{N} P_j Y_j^i$ (budget balance),

(ii) $F^i(Y_1^i \cdots Y_N^i)$ (production frontier),

(iii) $X_j^i > 0$ for all i (demand normality).

Where there are no restrictions due to country-by-country trade balances, the Lagrangean is

$$\max L^i = U^i[X_1^i \cdots X_n^i] - \lambda^i \left[\sum_{j=1}^{N} P_j X_j^i - \sum_{j=1}^{N} P_j Y_j^i \right] - \mu^i [F^i(Y_1^i \cdots Y_n^i)]. \quad (1)$$

Differentiation of (1) yields the FOC for maximization:

$$\partial L/\partial X_j^i = \partial U^i/\partial X_j^i - \lambda^i P_j = 0, \quad (1a)$$

$$\partial L/\partial Y_j^1 = \lambda^i P_j - \mu^i \, \partial F^i/\partial Y_j^i = 0, \quad (1b)$$

and two constraint equalities

$$\partial L/\partial \lambda^i = \sum_{j=1}^{N} P_j X_j^i - \sum_{j=1}^{N} P_j Y_j^i = 0, \quad (1c)$$

$$\partial L/\partial \mu^i = F^i(Y_1^i \cdots Y_n^i) = 0, \quad (1d)$$

indicating balanced budgets and efficient production for each of K countries. There are also world market clearing equations:

$$\sum_{i=1}^{K} Y_j^i = \sum_{i=1}^{K} X_j^i \quad (1e)$$

---

[1] All the usual caveats concerning social utility functions apply.

which determine the $N - 1$ relative world prices. By Walras' law only $N - 1$ of these are independent.

Let us now consider an additional constraint which requires countries i and k to have balanced trade vis-a-vis each other. The constraint is applied to a single pair of trading partners, while the rest of the world continues to trade multilaterally. The assumption of bilateralism will lead to the not too surprising conclusion that an exchange model which is constrained by considerations other than budget restrictions produces a second best optimization [see Friedman (1973)].

Assuming that all other prices remain unchanged,[2] we can model the bilateral constraint as

$$\sum_{j=1}^{N} {}^{k}P_j{}^{k}X_j{}^{i} = \sum_{j=1}^{N} {}^{k}P_j{}^{i}X_j{}^{k}.$$

These two countries face their own set of commodity prices via mutual trade.[3] The maximization problem in equation (1) is altered by the presence of an additional constraint:

$$\text{MAX } L^i = U^i(X_1{}^{i} \cdots X_N{}^{i}) - \lambda^i \left[\sum_{j=1}^{N} {}^{k}P_jX_j{}^{i} - \sum_{j=1}^{N} P_jY_j{}^{i} \right]$$

$$- \mu^i[F^i(Y_1{}^{i} \cdots Y_N{}^{i})] - {}^{k}\theta^i \left[\sum_{j=1}^{N} {}^{k}P_j{}^{k}X_j{}^{i} - \sum_{j=1}^{N} {}^{k}P_j{}^{i}X_j{}^{k} \right]. \quad (2)$$

Differentiation of (2) yields the FOC:

$$\partial L/\partial X_j{}^{i} = \partial U^i/\partial X_j{}^{i} - \lambda^i {}^{k}P_j - {}^{k}\theta^i {}^{k}P_j = 0, \quad (2a)$$

$$\partial L/\partial Y_j{}^{i} = -\lambda^i P_j + \mu^i \partial F^i/\partial Y^i = 0, \quad (2b)$$

and the obvious constraint equations

$$\frac{\partial \left[\sum_{j=1}^{N} {}^{k}P_j{}^{k}X_j{}^{i} \right]}{\partial X_j{}^{i}} = \frac{\partial \left[\sum_{j=1}^{N} {}^{k}P_iX_j{}^{i} \right]}{\partial X_j{}^{i}},$$

since $\partial^k X_j{}^{i}/\partial X_j{}^{i} = 1$ and $U^i = \bar{U}i$; that is, there is no preference for goods due to country of origin.

While the production efficiency criteria are unaltered,[4] there are altered equilibrium conditions for traded commodities. If we consider the bilaterally

---

[2] This assumption amounts to a small country argument for both bilateral traders. See Rothschild (1944).

[3] We must assume that the bilaterally trading countries cannot secure the total of their import demands at world prices either because of an ad hoc external constraint or an internal policy to pursue bilateral exchange.

[4] Bhagwati and Ramaswami (1963) point out that in an efficient system, external distortions will effect consumption optimality without effecting production optimality.

trading nations to be simultaneously engaging in multilateral trade with the rest of the world, then they must maximize according to equations (1a) and (2a) for an overlapping set of goods. Since the effects of any good upon utility function is unrelated to the country of origin,[5] we can express the price differences in trading activities between the bilateral partner and the multi-lateral world:

$$P_j/{}^kP_j = (\lambda^i + {}^k\theta^i)/\lambda^i = 1 + ({}^k\theta^i/\lambda^i), \tag{3}$$

where ${}^k\theta^i/\lambda^i$ is the marginal rate of bilateral income substitution (MRBIS) of i trading with k.

We can view the ratio of income constraints from equation (3) as a rate of substitution for income out of free trade and into the bilateral context. This term then represents the relative shadow price of income which is placed under the additional constraint.

Equation (3) generates a relationship between prices of freely traded goods and the same goods priced under a bilateral constraint. Since ${}^k\theta^i$ represents the marginal utility of an additional portion of income being constrained, we expect it to be negative. Higher prices paid for the same goods effectively reduces the available budget and results in a welfare loss.

There are two circumstances when ${}^k\theta^i$ would be zero: first, when there is no trade among bilateral partners, i.e. when $\sum_{j=1}^{N} {}^kX_j^i = 0$; and second, when unrestricted multilateral trade resulted coincidentally in bilateral balance.

When ${}^k\theta^i = 0$, bilateral prices are perforce equal to multilateral prices, the constraint is not binding and trading partners incur no losses. If more than two countries engage in bilateral trade, then optimization occurs under additional constraints. If, universal bilateralism exists, then the overall budget constraint becomes redundant since it is equal to the sum of all the bilateral budget constraints.

When ${}^k\theta^i$ is negative and the bilateral constraint is binding, world prices differ from bilateral prices for the same set of goods. The price differential is directly related to the size of ${}^k\theta^i$; that is, if all goods demanded by country i can be supplied by the rest of the world, then the bilateral constraint is met in the trivial nonbinding sense:

$$\sum_{j=1}^{N} {}^kP_j{}^kX_j^i = \sum_{j=1}^{N} {}^kP_j{}^iX_j^k = 0.$$

If the above holds, then ${}^k\theta^i = 0$ and ${}^kP_j = P_j$. When the constraint is nonzero, some of the demand for X of the bilaterally trading country is not fulfilled in the world markets at P_j.

---

[5] Were we to suspend this assumption, then all of the costs would be ascribed to altered tastes by the country of origin. Defining distortions as preferences appears to be a tautological approach which eliminates policy evaluation.

3. CONCLUSION

Bilateral trade can be optional only in the case of a trivial solution. Since bilateralism effectively constrains the exchange solution, it cannot be a rational policy decision in the absence of preferences for the country of origin of goods and services, or the absence of an external trading restriction.

REFERENCES

Bhagwati, J., and Ramaswami, V. K. (1963). Domestic Distortions, Tariffs, and the Theory of Optimum Subsidy, *Journal of Political Economy* **71**, 44–50.

Friedman, P. (1973). On the Theory and Measurement of Bilateralism, Working Paper No. 73-09, Department of Economics, Univ. of Florida.

Friedman, P. (1976). The Welfare Costs of Bilateralism: German–Hungarian Trade, 1933–1938, *Exploration in Economic History* **13**, No. 1, 113–125.

Lapan, H. E. (1976). International Trade, Factor Market Distortions, and the Optimal Dynamic Subsidy, *American Economic Review* **66**, 335–346.

Michaely, M. (1962). Multilateral Balancing in International Trade, *American Economic Review* **52**, 685–702.

Pryor, F. L. (1963). *The Communist Foreign Trade System.* Cambridge, Massachusetts: MIT Press.

Rothschild, R. W. (1944). The Small Nation and World Trade. *The Economic Journal* **54**, 26–40.

Von Brabant, J. M. P. (1973). *Bilateralism a Structural Bilateralism in Intra-CMEA Trade.* Rotterdam Univ. Press.

Wiles, P. (1969). *Communist International Economics.* New York: Prager.

When it is ethically optimal
to allocate money income
in stipulated fractional shares

PAUL A. SAMUELSON

MASSACHUSETTS INSTITUTE OF TECHNOLOGY

1. INTRODUCTION AND SUMMARY

It is tempting for an egalitarian to recommend equal *money* incomes for all; or, for one who perceives differing degrees of need and deservingness, to stipulate some optimal fractions of total money income to be allocated among Persons $1, 2, \ldots, j, \ldots, J$. Such a rule of invariant fractional money-income shares is known to be, in general, a *shibboleth* incompatible with true continual maximization of a Bergson Social Welfare Function which is defined in terms of the many real goods and services that the various people consume.[1]

I owe thanks to the National Science Foundation for financial aid; also to Kate Crowley and Vicki Elms for editorial assistance. My ancient debts to Abram Bergson and Robert Bishop will be obvious.

[1] See Bergson (1938, n. 15; 1966; Chapter 3 Addendum) and Samuelson (1947, p. 225) for explication of this now obvious general implication of asymmetry among individuals' preferences. Relevant lines from the latter include these:

> ... the rule of equality of income (measured in dollars, numeraire, abstract purchasing power) applied to individuals of different tastes, but made to hold in all circumstances, is actually inconsistent with any determinate, definite W function. Equality becomes a fetish or shibboleth, albeit a useful one, in that the means becomes the end, and the letter of the law takes precedence over the spirit.

The present paper shows that what is in general a shibboleth will be formally optimal in a definable category of cases. In particular, if people have *different* nonstochastic tastes, but all display the same *constant vectoral relative risk aversions* of exact logarithmic or Bernoullian degree, then a Bentham–Bergson–Harsanyi Social Welfare Function will be maximized by the rule of invariant money-income fractional shares. Less singularly, if people have identical nonstochastic tastes and the *same* constant degree of *vectoral relative risk aversion* (not necessarily that of Bernoulli), then invariant money fractions will also be optimal. Also, in Santa Claus cases of Kantian symmetry, equal shares almost trivially obtain at the optimum, a case open to some generalizings.

2   SOCIAL WELFARE FUNCTIONS

DEFINITION *of an individualistic social welfare function*   Suppose there are J persons $(1, 2, \ldots, J)$, who, for simplicity, are free of envy, altruism, and all consumption externalities. The jth person consumes the vector of n goods and services $(x_1^j, \ldots, x_n^j) = \mathbf{x}^j$, the tastes and demands for which are derivable from maximizing a cardinal indicator of utility, $U^j(\mathbf{x}^j) = U^j(x_1^j, \ldots, x_n^j)$.

The most general Bergson Social Welfare Function would involve an ethical norming or ordering of all states of the world, $\mathbf{X} = (x_1^1, \ldots, x_n^1, \ldots, x_1^J, \ldots, x_n^J) = (\mathbf{x}^1, \ldots, \mathbf{x}^J)$, summarizable by a cardinal indicator

$$W = \omega(\mathbf{x}^1, \mathbf{x}^2, \ldots, \mathbf{x}^J) = \omega(\mathbf{X})$$
$$= \omega(x_1^1, \ldots, x_n^1, x_1^2, \ldots, x_n^2, \ldots, x_1^J, \ldots, x_n^J). \tag{1}$$

For the decision of equal incomes as optimal in one situation implies a certain relative well-being as between vegetarians and non-vegetarians; at different relative prices between vegetables and non-vegetables an equal distribution of income can no longer be optimal.

... equality of money income where there is diversity of tastes involves the equality of nothing important. It is in lesser degree like the Anatole France aphorism concerning the equality of the law in its treatment of rich and poor. Before Bergson's treatment one could have sensed, but not analyzed definitively, this subtlety.

What is said about equality of income can as well be said about any non-50–50 invariant fractional shares, $(\alpha_1, \alpha_2, \ldots)$, $\sum \alpha_j = 1$. Actually, this *Foundations* passage involves both an understatement and an overstatement: an understatement because in the singular Bernoulli case discussed here, despite asymmetry of nonstochastic tastes, invariant fractional shares constitute no shibboleth—and similarly for some other generalizations developed here; an understatement because, even when relative prices do not change or are irrelevant, equality at one set of society's endowments need not imply equality at another set (as when wartime scarcity mandates ethical fair-sharing, compatibly with ethical toleration of some inequality in an affluent peacetime).

Note that a lower-case boldface symbol, such as $\mathbf{x}^j$, is an $n \times 1$ column vector; a capital-letter boldface symbol, such as $\mathbf{X}$, is an $n \times J$ rectangular matrix.

When individuals' tastes are to be "respected," Bergson defines an *Individualistic* Social Welfare Function as one with the *weak-separability* or "tree" property[2]

$$W = w[U^1(\mathbf{x}^1), U^2(\mathbf{x}^2), \ldots, U^J(\mathbf{x}^J)], \qquad \partial w/\partial U^j > 0 \qquad (j = 1, \ldots, J). \quad (2)$$

Bergson (1938), Lange (1942), Samuelson (1947), and others have recognized that Bentham's hedonistic additive function represented that special case of (1), and of (2), which takes the form

$$W = \lambda_1 V^1(x_1{}^1, \ldots, x_n{}^1) + \cdots + \lambda_J V^J(x_1{}^J, \ldots, x_n{}^J) = \sum_1^J \lambda_j V^j(\mathbf{x}^j), \qquad \lambda_j > 0. \quad (3)$$

Here $(\lambda_1, \ldots, \lambda_n)$ are, so to speak, ethical weight factors whose respective numerical magnitudes depend on the particular version of the $U^j(\mathbf{x}^j)$ cardinal indicator of the respective persons' utilities suitable to serve as $V^j(\mathbf{x}^j)$'s in (3).

DEFINITION *of a Bentham–Bergson–Harsanyi additive SWF* Harsanyi (1955) has presented persuasive arguments for (3)'s being more than one highly special case of (2), being instead a rather natural extension to the stochastic domain of (2)'s basic philosophy that "individuals' tastes are to be respected."[3] Indeed,

---

[2] See Bergson (1938), Lange (1942), Samuelson (1947), and Graaf (1959) for explicit treatments of *individualistic* social welfare functions. The general idea was much exploited by Pareto around the turn of the century; however, the notion that one should not give far-sighted glasses to myopic people goes back a long way. In the 1930s, Lerner (1934a,b, 1944), Kaldor (1939), Hicks (1939), and other writers, anxious to save something from the rubble of conventional welfare economics left after the positivist attack by Robbins (1932), made implicit (and sometimes confused) use of the *individualistic function* concept. Chipman (1976) has professed to find explicitly in Pareto (1896–1897, 1909, 1913, and earlier writings) the concept of a social welfare function $\omega(\mathbf{X})$ or $w[U^1( ), \ldots, U^J( )]$. This, I believe, involves an act of sympathetic charity since Pareto's many writings are often obscure on what we now call Pareto optimality, and since expressions such as $\theta_1(\delta U^1) + \theta_2(\delta U^2) + \ldots$ are sometimes used by Pareto as positivistic-politics constructs and sometimes as vague Lagrange multiplier expressions relevant to the first-order conditions for being on the ("Pareto-optimal" points of the) utility-possibility frontier. Alas, during Pareto's most productive quarter century, he was able to conduct no dialogue with competent peers and consequently his expositions suffer from impatience, repetition, and obscurity—so that only his genius shines through.

[3] Harsanyi (1955) at first escaped the notice it deserves as a classic. Strotz (1958) was led to somewhat similar results by axiomatizing welfare economics along the lines of the axiomatization of probabilistic inference by Chernoff. See Samuelson (1965, pp. 124–126) for my own belated recognition of the 1955 Harsanyi advance. Diamond (1967) gives a dissenting view (as J. Rothenberg and F. Fisher implicitly had done on other grounds in their 1961–1962 controversy with Strotz).

(a) if individuals' *nonstochastic* tastes are to count, as in (2);

(b) if individuals' *stochastic* tastes are to count, in the sense that when they *all* ex ante prefer one stochastic option to another, so will the Social Welfare Function;

(c) if each individual wants to make stochastic decisions which satisfy the aesthetic *consistency* or independence axioms of Ramsey (1931), Marschak (1950), and Savage (1954) that lead to *maximizing the expected value* of his existent Neumann cardinal utility function defined for all $\mathbf{x}^j$ outcomes

$$\max E\{N^j(\mathbf{x}^j)\}, \quad U^j(x^j) \equiv f_j[N^j(x^j)]; \quad f_j'[\ ] > 0, \quad f_j''[\ ] \gtrless 0; \quad (4)$$

(d) if the ethical observer wishes to make his stochastic decisions so as also to obey the Ramsey–Marschak–Savage consistency (or "sure-thing") axioms, thus acting to achieve

$$\max E\{N(\mathbf{x}^1, \ldots, \mathbf{x}^J)\} = \max E\{N(\mathbf{X})\}, \quad (5)$$

where $N(\mathbf{X})$ is a definable cardinal function unique up to scale and origin constants and representing some stretching of $\omega(\mathbf{X})$ in (1); then it follows from (a)–(d) that the form of (3) must obtain for $N(\mathbf{X})$, namely

$$N(\mathbf{X}) \equiv \sum_1^J \lambda_j N^j(x_1{}^j, \ldots, x_n{}^j) = \sum_1^J \lambda_j N^j(\mathbf{x}^j), \quad (6)$$

where the $N^j(\mathbf{x}^j)$ are observable from revealed personal risk choices and will be strictly concave if people are strictly risk averse.

Combining (a)–(d), we can infer that Harsanyi in effect stipulates the following functional identity on an existent $N[N^1, \ldots, N^J]$ function

$$E\{N[N^1(\mathbf{x}^1), \ldots, N^J(\mathbf{x}^J)]\} \equiv N[E\{N^1(\mathbf{x}^1)\}, \ldots, E\{N^J(\mathbf{x}^J)\}]. \quad (7)$$

When $N^j(\mathbf{x}^j)$ takes only the values a^j and b^j with 50–50 probabilities, (7) becomes

$$\tfrac{1}{2}N[a^1, \ldots, a^J] + \tfrac{1}{2}N[b^1, \ldots, b^J] \equiv N[\tfrac{1}{2}a^1 + \tfrac{1}{2}b^1, \ldots, \tfrac{1}{2}a^J + \tfrac{1}{2}b^J]. \quad (8)$$

Subtract the first term on the left from both sides to find that both sides of the new expression must be independent of $[a^1, \ldots, a^J]$; setting the requisite partial derivatives equal to zero gives

$$\tfrac{1}{2}N_j[\tfrac{1}{2}a^1 + \tfrac{1}{2}b^1, \ldots, \tfrac{1}{2}a^J + \tfrac{1}{2}b^J] \equiv \tfrac{1}{2}N_j[a^1, \ldots, a^J]$$
$$\equiv \tfrac{1}{2}c_j, \quad \text{a constant} \quad (j = 1, \ldots, J), \quad (9)$$

where by notational definition

$$N_j[z_1, \ldots, z_J] \equiv \partial N[z_1, \ldots, z_J]/\partial z_j.$$

Therefore,

$$N[z_1, \ldots, z_J] \equiv c_0 + c_1 z_1 + \cdots + c_J z_J \quad (10)$$

just as (6) asserts when we choose to set arbitrary c_0 inessentially at zero and identify the c's as λ's.

3. CONSTANCY OF RELATIVE RISK AVERSION

Constant (Scalar) Relative Risk Aversion

From various investigations, such as those of Pfanzangl (1959), R. Schlaifer (unpublished), Pratt (1964), Arrow (1964), Samuelson (1969a,b), Merton (1969), and many others, the ordinary concept of constant relative risk aversion is well understood in its application to a single measure of income or wealth. A standard theorem can state the equivalence of any of the following definitions of the term.

THEOREM *on constant (scalar) relative risk aversion*   Any one of the following properties implies all the others:
  (i)   The person acts to maximize

$$E\{(x^\gamma - 1)/\gamma\}, \qquad 1 \geq \gamma,$$

where x is a positive scalar;
  (ii)   he acts to maximize

$$E\{U(x)\},$$

where $xU''(x)/U'(x) = d\log U(x)/d\log x = \gamma - 1 \leq 0$;
  (iii) $\frac{1}{2}U(\beta_H x) + \frac{1}{2}U(\beta_T x) - U(x) \equiv 0$ defines

$$\psi(\beta_H, \beta_T) \equiv \psi(\beta_T, \beta_H) = 1,$$

where $\psi(\beta_H, \beta_T)$ is independent of x and must be expressible in the form

$$\tfrac{1}{2}\exp[\gamma \log_e \beta_H] + \tfrac{1}{2}\exp[\gamma \log_e \beta_T] = 1 \geq \gamma.$$

When $\gamma = 1$, the person is *risk neutral*, with linear utility, $U = a + bx$ and with $\beta_H = 2 - \beta_T$. For $\gamma < 1$, the person is risk averse and $\beta_H > 2 - \beta_T$. As $\beta_H \beta_T \to \infty$, $\gamma \to -\infty$, and the person becomes infinitely risk averse and approximates indefinitely closely to a *minimaxer* (or, more accurately, a maximiner). For $\beta_H = \beta_T^{-1}$, we are in the Bernoulli case of logarithmic utility, $U = a + b\log X$: here, $\gamma = 0$ and $(x^\gamma - 1)/\gamma$ becomes a 0/0 indeterminate form, evaluable by l'Hôpital's rule as $\gamma \to 0$; l'Hôpital's rule applied to (iii)'s final relation also yields $\beta_H = \beta_T^{-1}$ as $\gamma \to 0$. For $\gamma = \frac{1}{2}$, we have Cramer's square-root utility function, which is unbounded above (as with all cases of positive γ). Cross-sectional observations on market trade-offs between securities' mean returns and their risks suggested a negative γ as most realistic, with β_T in $\psi(\beta_H, \beta_T) = 1$ being bounded below by a positive fraction and $(x^\gamma - 1)/\gamma$ being bounded above.

Proof of the theorem is direct The mutual equivalence of (i) and (ii) is immediate. That (i) implies (iii) is immediate. That (iii) implies (ii), and hence its equivalent (i), follows from the fact that it implies

$$\frac{\partial}{\partial x}\left\{-\frac{\partial \beta_H}{\partial \beta_T}\right\} \equiv 0 \equiv \frac{\partial}{\partial x}\left\{\frac{\partial \psi(\beta_H, \beta_T)/\partial \beta_T}{\partial \psi(\beta_H, \beta_T)/\partial \beta_H}\right\}, \tag{11}$$

$$0 \equiv \frac{\partial}{\partial x}\left\{-\frac{\partial \beta_H}{\partial \beta_T} - \log \beta_T + \log \beta_H\right\} \equiv \frac{\partial}{\partial x}\{\log U'(\beta_T x) - \log U'(\beta_H x)\}$$

$$\equiv x^{-1}\left\{\frac{\beta_T x U''(\beta_T x)}{U'(\beta_T x)} - \frac{\beta_H x U''(\beta_H x)}{U'(\beta_H x)}\right\} \equiv x^{-1}\{A(\beta_T x) - A(\lambda \beta_T x)\}, \quad \lambda = \beta_H/\beta_T,$$

where $A(z) = zU''(z)/U'(z)$. For the last brace to vanish for all choices of $(\beta_T x)$ and λ requires that each term in the brace be a constant, or that $zU''(z)/U'(z)$ be a constant as (ii) requires.[4]

Remark It appears that (iii) need not be specified as holding for *all* possible arbitrary choices of β_T. It seems to be enough to require (iii) to hold for a limited number of specified fractional β_T's, perhaps even for only a single value. Thus, set $\beta_T = \frac{1}{2}$, and suppose that β_H is observed always to be $(\frac{1}{2})^{-1}$ independently of x. The identity

$$\tfrac{1}{2}U(\tfrac{1}{2}x) + \tfrac{1}{2}U(2x) - U(x) \equiv 0 \tag{12}$$

has only one monotone-increasing solution for $U(x)$, up to a linear transformation, namely $U(x) = z + b \log x$. A formal solution of (12) would appear to permit our replacing b by an arbitrary function of $\log_{1/2} x$, $\Pi(\log_{1/2} x)$, so long as $\Pi(z)$ is periodic in z with a unit period, $\Pi(z) \equiv \Pi(z \pm 1)$. However, unless $\Pi(z)$ were a strict constant, the derivative of $U(x) = a + \Pi(\log_{1/2} x) \log x$ could not help becoming negative for some sufficiently small value of x: hence $U(x) = a + b \log x$ is the only admissible monotone-increasing solution of (12). The reader may also verify that there is only a linear well-behaved concave solution, $U(x) = a + bx$ of

$$\tfrac{1}{2}U(x - \tfrac{1}{2}) + \tfrac{1}{2}(x + \tfrac{1}{2}) - U(x) \equiv 0. \tag{13}$$

Likewise any specific values for $\bar{\beta}_T$ and $\bar{\beta}_H$ in

$$\tfrac{1}{2}U(\bar{\beta}_T x) + \tfrac{1}{2}U(\bar{\beta}_H x) - U(x) \equiv 0 \tag{14}$$

lead to $a + b[(x^\gamma - 1)/\gamma]$ as admissible solutions for $U(x)$.

---

[4] An alternative proof that (iii) implies (ii) comes from realizing that, when β_H is, from $\frac{1}{2}U(\beta x) + \frac{1}{2}U(f[\beta; x]x) \equiv U(x)$, the most general function of β_T and x, namely $f[\beta_T; x]$, then $-\frac{1}{2}\partial^2 f(1; x)/\partial \beta_T{}^2$ equals $-xU''(x)/U'(x)$. This last expression must be a constant independent of x as in (ii) if $f[\beta_T; x]$ is to be free of x. Q.E.D.

Constant (Vectoral) Relative Risk Aversion

People do not consume scalar money income. They consume a vector of goods and services, $\mathbf{x}^j = (x_1{}^j, \ldots, x_n{}^j)$, for the jth person.

How do we generalize the notion of constant relative risk aversion from a scalar to a vector? Years ago Robert Bishop of MIT pointed out the way. We examine how a person reacts to risk of money incomes spendable at different absolute (and relative) prices. What can be shown to be the same thing, we require that gains and losses expressed as scaled-up or scaled-down intensities of any initial vector of goods and services induce the same decision of preference or indifference when both the initial vector endowment and the intensities of gains and losses are increased in the same proportion.

All this is made definite by the following theorem of Stiglitz (1969) and Samuelson (1969a,b) generalizing the equivalencies already encountered in the case of constant (scalar) relative risk aversion.

THEOREM *on constant (vectoral) relative risk aversion*   Anyone of the following properties implies all the others:

(i)   The person acts to achieve

$$\max E\{[H(x_1, \ldots, x_n)^\gamma - 1]/\gamma\},$$

where $H(\lambda x_1, \ldots, \lambda x_n) \equiv \lambda H(x_1, \ldots, x_n)$ is a first-degree-homogeneous concave function;

(ii)   the person acts to achieve

$$\max E\{U(x_1, \ldots, x_n)\},$$

where $\partial U(x_1, \ldots, x_n)/\partial x_i \equiv U_i(x_1, \ldots, x_n)$ are all homogeneous functions of the same nonpositive degree, namely with

$$\sum_{k=1}^{n} \frac{\partial \log[U_i(x_1, \ldots, x_n)]}{\partial x_k} = \gamma - 1 \leq 0 \qquad (i = 1, \ldots, n);$$

(iii)   the person acts to maximize $E\{U(\mathbf{x})\}$, where

$$\tfrac{1}{2}U(\beta_T \mathbf{x}) + \tfrac{1}{2}U(\beta_H \mathbf{x}) - U(\mathbf{x}) \equiv 0$$

defines $\psi(\beta_H, \beta_T) \equiv \psi(\beta_T, \beta_H) = 1$ independently of $\mathbf{x}$ and where $\psi(\beta_H, \beta_T)$ is expressible in the form

$$\tfrac{1}{2}\exp[\gamma \log_e \beta_H] + \tfrac{1}{2}\exp[\gamma \log_e \beta_T] = 1 \geq \gamma;$$

(iv)   the person acts to maximize the expected value of the Roy *indirect utility* function

$$\max E\{[I^\gamma H^*(p_1, \ldots, p_n)^\gamma - 1]/\gamma,$$

where

$$H^*(p_1/I, \ldots, p_n/I) \equiv \max_{x_i} H(x_1, \ldots, x_n) \qquad \text{s.t.} \quad \sum_1^n (p_k/I)x_k = I$$

$$= \max_{x_i} \frac{H(x_1, \ldots, x_n)}{\sum_1^n(p_k/I)x_k} \equiv IH^*(p_1, \ldots, p_n)^{-1},$$

and where $H^*(\mathbf{p})$ is a concave homogeneous function of degree one;

(v)   the person acts to maximize the expected value of the *indirect utility* function, $U^*(p_1/I, \ldots, p_n/I)$, where the partial derivatives of U^*, $\partial U^*(y_1, \ldots, y_n)/\partial y_i = U_i^*(y_1, \ldots, y_n)$, should all be homogeneous functions of the same nonpositive degree,

$$\sum_{k=1}^n \frac{\partial \log U_i^*(y_1, \ldots, y_n)}{\partial \log y_i} = \gamma - 1 \le 0, \qquad (i = 1, \ldots, n);$$

(vi)   the person acts to maximize the expected value of the Roy *indirect utility* function $U^*(p_1/I, \ldots, p_n I) = U^*(\mathbf{p}/I)$, where

$$\tfrac{1}{2}U^*(\mathbf{p}/\beta_H) + \tfrac{1}{2}U^*(\mathbf{p}/\beta_T) - U^*(\mathbf{p}) \equiv 0$$

defines

$$\psi(\beta_H, \beta_T) \equiv \psi(\beta_T, \beta_H) = 1 \qquad \text{independently of } \mathbf{p},$$

where $\psi(\ \ )$ can be expressed as

$$\tfrac{1}{2}\exp[\gamma \log_e \beta_H] + \tfrac{1}{2}\exp[\gamma \log_e \beta_T] = 1.$$

Proof of the theorem is straightforward   As part of the oral tradition at MIT in the early 1960s, Bishop had posed the problem of (v) in its risk-neutral form (where $\beta_H = 2 - \beta_T$), and had inferred that (v) implied homothetic preference and (i) with $\gamma = 1$. Stiglitz (1969) demonstrated that (vi) implied (i) globally.[5] That (i) implies all the rest is immediate; that (iv) implies (i) and all the rest is immediate once we utilize duality theory. That (ii) and (i) are essentially equivalent follows from integrating the linear partial-differential equations of (ii); likewise to prove the equivalence of (iv) and (v).

[5] The present theorem, due to Stiglitz (1969) and also to Samuelson (1969a,b), has global validity throughout the whole of the nonnegative $(x_1, \ldots, x_n)$ or $(p_1, \ldots, p_n)$ orthant. Stiglitz (1969) also gives more general results of local validity: in the manner of Gorman (1953) or Theil (1954), he considers the risk-neutral case where all the Engel curves are straight lines in certain subregions of the nonnegative orthant for $(x_1, \ldots, x_n)$; however, as argued in Samuelson (1965, n. 2), if the Engel's loci are *always* to be straight lines, they must be straight lines through the origin—which is the homothetic case. Likewise, if constant vectorial risk aversion is to obtain globally, the only solution to the function equations of (iii) or (vi) are those corresponding to homothetic tastes. Since completing this paper, I have chanced on the valuable work of Rothblum (1975), which gives references to numerous writers who have worked independently of the Bishop, Stiglitz, and Samuelson investigations.

The part of a rigorous proof that is at all difficult is the demonstration that either (iii) or (vi) imply all the rest. Actually, from the scalar theorem, we know that (iii) implies there exists a $N(x_1, \ldots, x_n)$ whose expected value is maximized and that takes the form

$$a + bN(x_1, \ldots, x_n) = \theta(x_2/x_1, \ldots, x_n/x_1)$$
$$+ \gamma^{-1}[x_1{}^\gamma \tau(x_2/x_1, \ldots, x_n/x_1) - 1]. \tag{15}$$

Then, for $\gamma < 1$ and for x_1 either large or small, nonconstancy of θ would contradict *every* $\partial N/\partial x_i$ being *always* positive. With θ an ignorable constant, (15) is seen to be essentially of the form given in (i). A similar argument applies dually to show that (vi) implies (v).

4. OPTIMALITY CONDITIONS

The General Case

Suppose we have prescribed totals of each good to allocate among the J persons so as to maximize a Bentham–Bergson–Harsanyi social welfare function:

$$\max_{x_i{}^j} \sum_1^J \lambda_j U^j(\mathbf{x}^j) \quad \text{s.t.} \quad \left(\sum_{j=1}^J x_i{}^j \right) = \sum_1^J \mathbf{x}^j = (\bar{x}_i) = \bar{\mathbf{x}} > 0$$

$$= V(\bar{x}_1, \ldots, \bar{x}_n; \lambda_1, \ldots, \lambda_J) = \sum_1^J \lambda_j U^j(\mathbf{x}^{j*}), \tag{16}$$

where $(\bar{\mathbf{x}}^{j*}) = (x_i{}^{j*})$ satisfy

$$\frac{\partial U^j(\mathbf{x}^{j*})/\partial x_i{}^j}{\partial U^j(\mathbf{x}^{j*})/\partial x_1{}^j} = \pi_i \quad (i = 2, \ldots, n; \quad j = 1, \ldots, J), \tag{17a}$$

$$\frac{\lambda_j \, \partial U^j(\mathbf{x}^{j*})/\partial x_1{}^j}{\lambda_1 \, \partial U^1(\mathbf{x}^{1*})/\partial x_1{}^1} = 1 \quad (j = 2, \ldots, J). \tag{17b}$$

The conditions in (17) are both necessary and sufficient provided some regularity conditions are imposed on the $U^j(\mathbf{x}^j)$ functions—as for example that they all be *strictly* quasi concave, and satisfy strong Inada conditions such that as any $x_i{}^j \to 0$, $\partial U^j(\mathbf{x}^j)/\partial x_i{}^j \to \infty$ and as any $x_i{}^j \to \infty$, $\partial U^j(\mathbf{x}^j)/\partial x_i{}^j \to 0$.

From standard welfare economics and duality theory, we know that the following market-clearing algorithm can provide the solution to (16):

$$\max_{I^j} \sum_1^J \lambda_j U^{j*}(I^j; \bar{p}_1, \ldots, \bar{p}_n) \quad \text{s.t.} \quad \sum_{j=1}^J I^j = \sum_{i=1}^n \bar{p}_i \bar{x}_i$$

$$= \sum_1^J \lambda_j U^{j*}(I^{j*}; \bar{p}_1, \ldots, \bar{p}_n), \tag{18}$$

where the optimal (I^{j*}) are each functions of the given parameters

$$I^{j*} = \Phi^j(p_1, \ldots, p_n; \bar{x}_1, \ldots, \bar{x}_n; \lambda_1, \ldots, \lambda_J) \equiv p_1\Phi^j(1, \mathbf{p}/p_1; \bar{x}; \lambda) \quad (19)$$

and where, by definition of the quasi-concave *indirect dual* utility function,

$$U^{j*}(I^j, p_1, \ldots, p_n) \equiv U^{j*}(1, \mathbf{p}/I^j)$$

$$= \max_{x_i^{\,j}} U^j(x_1^{\,j}, \ldots, x_n^{\,j}) \quad \text{s.t.} \quad \sum_1^n p_i x_i = I^j$$

$$x_i^{j*} = -\frac{\partial U^{j*}(1, \mathbf{p}/I^j)/\partial p_i}{\partial U^{j*}(1, \mathbf{p}/I^j)/\partial I^j} = \Phi_i^j(\mathbf{p}/I^j)$$

and where the $\bar{\mathbf{p}} = (\bar{p}_1, \ldots, \bar{p}_n)$ are market-clearing prices satisfying

$$\sum_{j=1}^J \Phi_i^j([\mathbf{p}/p_1]/[I^j/p_1]) = \bar{x}_i \quad (i = 2, \ldots, n). \quad (20)$$

Relations (19) and (20) are assured to have at least one solution for $(\mathbf{X}^*; \bar{\mathbf{p}}/\bar{p}_1; I^{1*}/\bar{p}_1, \ldots, I^{J*}/\bar{p}_1)$ under our regularity conditions. However, in the general case where the $U^j(\mathbf{x}^j)$ functions do not correspond to homothetic demand and are different for each j, the optimal (I^{j*}/I^{1*}) may give rise to multiple solutions of the general equilibrium problem; only one of these solutions can be the optimal one for $\mathbf{X}^*$. Even if demands are all homothetic, if they differ enough among persons, multiplicity of solution may hamper the practicability of using market pricing to attain the welfare optimum. Indeed, as shown in the Musgrave *Festschrift* piece of Samuelson (1974), the optimal $\mathbf{X}^*$ could correspond to a general equilibrium solution of (19) and (20) that is locally and globally unstable.

As will be discussed in a later section, in the Santa Claus case of perfect symmetry, where $U^j(\mathbf{x}) \equiv U^1(\mathbf{x})$ and $\lambda_j \equiv \lambda_1$, the welfare optimum must be at the Kantian point of perfect symmetry

$$x_i^{j*}/\bar{x}_i \equiv 1/J, \quad I^{j*}\bigg/ \sum_{k=1}^J I^{k*} \equiv 1/J,$$

$$\frac{\bar{p}_i}{\bar{p}_1} \equiv \frac{\partial U^j(\bar{x}/J)/\partial x_i^{\,j}}{\partial U^j(\bar{x}/J)/\partial x_1^{\,j}} \quad (j = 1, \ldots, J; \quad i = 2, \ldots, n). \quad (21)$$

In this case of "balanced income effects," the relevant general equilibrium solution will be unique.

Singular Case of Bernoulli's Logarithmic Risk Aversion

Now assume all people have constant (vectoral) risk aversion of exactly Bernoulli's degree. (The is testable by their being just willing to risk half their chocolates and gloves on the fair toss of a coin provided they are promised twice the amount of their chocolates and gloves when they win: i.e., $\beta_H = \beta_T^{-1}$ in our earlier theorems.)

The relevant optimality problem of (16) now specializes to

$$\max_{x_i^j} \sum_1^J \lambda_j \log H^j(\mathbf{x}^j) \quad \text{s.t.} \quad \sum_1^J \mathbf{x}^j = \bar{\mathbf{x}}$$

$$\equiv \max_{\alpha^j} \sum_1^J \lambda_j \log[(\alpha_j I) H^{j*}(\bar{\mathbf{p}})^{-1}] \quad \text{s.t.} \quad \sum_1^{J} \alpha_j = 1$$

$$\equiv \sum_1^J \lambda_j \log[I H^*(\bar{\mathbf{p}})^{-1}] + \max_{\alpha^j} \sum_1^J \lambda_j \log \alpha_j \tag{22.1}$$

$$\equiv \sum_1^J \lambda_j \log[I H^*(\bar{\mathbf{p}})^{-1}] + \sum_1^J \lambda_j \log\left(\lambda_j \Big/ \sum_1^J \lambda_k\right), \tag{22.2}$$

where

$\qquad H^j(\mathbf{x}^j)$ is first-degree-homogeneous and concave, $\qquad$ (23.1)

$\qquad H^{j*}(\mathbf{p})$ is likewise, being $H^j(\ )$'s "dual" defined by $\qquad$ (23.2)

$$H^{j*}(\mathbf{p}) = \min_{x_i} \frac{\sum_1^n p_i x_i}{H^j(x_1, \ldots, x_n)}, \tag{23.3}$$

$$I = \sum_1^n \bar{p}_i \bar{x}_i, \qquad \alpha_j = I^j/I, \tag{23.4}$$

$\qquad \bar{\mathbf{p}}$ represents market-clearing prices satisfying
$\qquad$ (19) and (20). $\qquad$ (23.5)

The equivalence of (22.2) and (21.1) gives the implied optimality of invariant fractional money-income shares:

$$\alpha_j^* \equiv \lambda_j \Big/ \sum_1^J \lambda_k \quad \text{for all} \quad (\bar{x}_i). \tag{24}$$

This follows from the singular property of the logarithmic function that

$$\sum \log[f_j(\lambda_j, \alpha_j) g_j(\lambda_j, \beta)] \equiv \sum \log g(\lambda_j, \beta) + \sum \log f_j(\lambda_j, \alpha_j) \tag{25}$$

with the implication that the second term's extremum is independent of the variable β. The last term in (22.2) looks much like "entropy" in discussions of information theory and statistical mechanics.

We may summarize this singular Bernoulli case (which is a variant of the Cobb–Douglas case found in Chipman (1974) to be capable of aggregation):

THEOREM[6] *on singular logarithmic risk aversion*   When all persons have constant (vectoral) risk aversion of Bernoulli degree, so each maximizes $E\{\log H^j(\mathbf{x}^j)\} \equiv E\{\log \beta^{-1} H^j(\beta \mathbf{x}^j)]\}$, the optimal allocation of fixed totals of society's goods is achievable by specifying invariant fractional shares of *money* income, $(\alpha_1^*, \ldots, \alpha_J^* = 1 - \alpha_1^* - \alpha_2^* - \cdots)$.

None of this requires similarity of individuals' nonstochastic tastes! Note that x_i^{J*}/x_i^{1*} varies among the goods. However, $\sum_1^n \bar{p}_i x_i^{j*} / \sum_1^n \bar{p}_i x_i^{1*}$ is always the same no matter how the relative components of $(\bar{x}_1, \ldots, \bar{x}_n)$ vary.

Proof of this theorem has already been provided by the demonstrated equivalence of (22.1) and (22.2), by virtue of (25)'s decomposition of the logarithmic expressions.

It follows from this exact theorem that, if all people have relative (vectoral) risk aversions that are never very far from that of constant Bernoullian degree, the optimal income fractions (α_j^*) will alter very little as social endowments change a great deal.

Constant (Vectoral) Relative Risk Aversion and Uniform Tastes

Less singularly, we find another class of cases in which invariant income shares are optimal. Suppose all people have the same nonstochastic tastes; and all have the same constant relative (vectoral) risk aversion, not necessarily of Bernoullian degree, $\beta_H \gtreqless \beta_T^{-1}$.

Now (16) takes the equivalent of the form

$$\max_{x_i^j} \sum_1^J \lambda_j H(\mathbf{x}^j)^\gamma/\gamma \quad \text{s.t.} \quad \sum_1^J \mathbf{x}^j = \bar{\mathbf{x}}$$

$$= \max_{\alpha_j} \sum_1^J \lambda_j \alpha_j^\gamma I^\gamma H^*(\bar{\mathbf{p}})^{-\gamma}/\gamma \quad \text{s.t.} \quad \sum_1^J \alpha_j = 1$$

$$= \left[I^\gamma H^*(\bar{\mathbf{p}})^{-\gamma}/\gamma \right] \max_{\alpha_j} \sum_1^J \lambda_j \alpha_j^\gamma \quad \text{s.t.} \quad \sum_1^J \alpha_j = 1 \quad (26.1)$$

---

[6] I came upon this singular result by chance when giving as an example of a Bergson Social Welfare Function the following parody of Fisher's "ideal index": $w = [\frac{1}{2}x_1^1 + \frac{1}{2}x_2^1]^{1/2}[\frac{1}{2}(x_1^2)^{-1} + \frac{1}{2}(x_2^2)^{-1}]^{-1/2}$. Invariant fractional shares, $\alpha_1^* = \alpha_2^* = \frac{1}{2}$, turned out singularly to be optimal for this "ideal index," whose logarithm is of the Bentham–Bergson–Harsanyi additive form. Curiously, relative prices remain at unity for $\bar{x}_2/\bar{x}_1$ in a wide range around unity; this is because $\exp U^1 = \frac{1}{2}x_1^1 + \frac{1}{2}x_2^1$ happens to be weakly quasi concave, with linear indifference contours. However, for $\bar{x}_2/\bar{x}_1$ large enough, it will be ethically optimal to have Person 1 consume none of the now-scarce first good; even so, the ratio x_2^2/x_1^2 becomes so excessive that $\bar{p}_2/\bar{p}_1$ must fall to get all of the redundant second good demanded. Nonetheless, equal α_1^* and α_2^* stays optimal despite the change in relative prices! At the proofreading stage, I therefore had to alter the final footnote of Samuelson (1977), suggesting that, for $\gamma \neq 0$, $[\frac{1}{2}x_1^2 + \frac{1}{2}x_2^1]^{\gamma-1} + [\frac{1}{2}(x_1^2)^{-1} + \frac{1}{2}(x_2^2)^{-1}]^{-\gamma-1}$, the *non*optimality of invariant α_j^* would obtain. Around equation (29) I return to the subtleties raised by this footnote.

$$= [I^\gamma H^*(\overline{\mathbf{p}})^{-\gamma}/\gamma] \left[\sum_1^J \lambda_j^{1/(1-\gamma)} \right] \Big/ \left[\sum_1^J \lambda_k^{\gamma/(1-\gamma)} \right], \qquad (26.2)$$

where

$H(\mathbf{x})$ is homogeneous-first-degree and concave, $\qquad (27.1)$

$H^*(\mathbf{p})$ is likewise, being H's dual, $\qquad (27.2)$

$$H^*(\mathbf{p}) = \min_{x_i} \frac{\sum_1^n p_i x_i}{H(x_1, \ldots, x_n)}, \qquad (27.3)$$

$$I = \sum_1^n \overline{p}_i \overline{x}_i, \qquad \alpha_j = I^j/I, \qquad (27.4)$$

$\overline{\mathbf{p}}$ represents market-clearing prices satisfying
(19) and (20). $\qquad (27.5)$

The equivalence of (26.2) and (26.1) gives the implied optimality of fractional money-income shares.

$$\alpha_j^* = \lambda_j^{\gamma/(1-\gamma)} \Big/ \left[\sum_1^J \lambda_k^{\gamma/(1-\gamma)} \right]. \qquad (28)$$

For $\gamma \to 0$, l'Hôpital's rule applied to $\log \alpha_j^*$ yields (24) from (28).

We may summarize this case of identical tastes and constant (vectoral) risk aversion.

THEOREM *on uniform tastes and constant (vectoral) risk aversion*   When all people have identical tastes and the same constant relative (vectoral) risk aversion, each acting to maximize $E\{H(\mathbf{x}^j)^\gamma/\gamma\} \equiv E\{H(\theta \mathbf{x}^j)^\gamma \theta^{-\gamma}/\gamma\}$, the social optimum of a Bentham–Bergson–Harsanyi welfare function is achievable by specifying invariant fractional shares of money, $(\alpha_1^*, \alpha_2^*, \ldots, \alpha_J^* = 1 - \alpha_1^* - \alpha_2^* - \cdots)$. Now, with tastes uniform and necessarily homothetic, $x_i^{j*}/x_i^{1*} \equiv (\alpha_j^* \overline{x}_i)/(\alpha_1^* \overline{x}_i) \equiv \alpha_j^*/\alpha_1^*$, for all i

$$\alpha_j^* = \lambda_j^{\gamma/(1-\gamma)} \Big/ \left[\sum_1^J \lambda_k^{\gamma/(1-\gamma)} \right] > 0, \qquad \sum_j^J \alpha_j^* = 1.$$

Any change in the (λ_j/λ_1) coefficients, and hence in the optimal income fractions, will have no effect on relative prices or people's relative consumptions in this case of uniform homothetic tastes.

No further proof of this theorem is needed beyond the recognition that (26.1) is factorable and is thus equivalent to (26.2).

Unlike the singular Bernoulli case with its differences in tastes, the case dealt with in this last theorem is more intuitively understandable. With tastes homothetic and uniform among people, the complexities of a vector as against a scalar essentially evaporate: whatever the composition of endowments totals $(\bar{x}_i)$, mere Pareto optimality will force the relevant equilibrium to involve every person consuming $x_i{}^j/x_1{}^j$ in the same proportions as $\bar{x}_i/\bar{x}_1$.

We are in effect back in the scalar realm, with only α_j variable in $\alpha_j \bar{x}_i = x_i{}^j$. Relative prices are never affected by changes of α_j in $p_i/p_1 = [\partial H(\bar{x}/\bar{x}_1)/\partial x_i]/[\partial H(\bar{x}/\bar{x}_1)\partial x_1]$; and when changes in $\bar{x}/\bar{x}_1$ do alter relative prices, they are altered for everybody in the same way.

Nonoptimality of Invariant Fractional Shares Even When Changes in Relative Prices Do Not Occur or Are Irrelevant

The cited items, Bergson (1966) and Samuelson (1947) both stress the crucial role played by shifting relative prices in making it mandatory that income shares $(\alpha_j{}^*/\alpha_1{}^*)$ alter as social endowments alter. The results of the previous section seem to confirm this emphasis.

Nevertheless, as hinted at in footnotes 1 and 6, nonoptimality of invariant fractions may well occur even in the absence of relative price changes. Indeed, the case mentioned in footnote 6 would involve different optimal values for $(\alpha_1{}^*, \alpha_2{}^*)$ when $\bar{x}_2/\bar{x}_1$ is raised a bit above unity—this despite the fact that $\bar{p}_2/\bar{p}_1$ stays at 1 for sizeable shifts of $\bar{x}_2/\bar{x}_1$ away from 1.

To clinch the point that changes in relative prices do not constitute the whole story, consider the case where

(1)   only scalars of real incomes are involved, chocolates, (x^1, x^2); or

(2)   what is much the same case, where $\bar{x}/\bar{x}_1$ never changes and each person has the same homothetic tastes

$$U^j = f_j[H(x_1{}^j, x_2{}^j)] \qquad (j = 1, 2). \tag{29}$$

In this last case we know that relative prices never change, even when $f''_2[H] \neq f''_1[H]$; and we know that it suffices to solve, for

$$U^j = f_j[x^j H(\bar{x}_1, \bar{x}_2)] \equiv U_j(x^j),$$

the optimality problem

$$\max_{x^j} \sum_1^2 \lambda_j U_j(x^j) \qquad \text{s.t.} \quad x^1 + x^2 = \bar{x}. \tag{30}$$

For fixed (λ_1, λ_2), fixed β, and varying $(\bar{x}_1, \bar{x}_2) = (\bar{x}, \beta\bar{x})$, the optimal solution need not have the property

$$x^{2*}/x^{1*} = \text{constant invariant to changes in } \bar{x}. \tag{31}$$

Thus, let the persons have different degrees of relative risk aversion so that (30) becomes equivalent to

$$\max_{x^j} \left[\lambda_1(x^1)^{1/2} + \lambda_2(x^2)^{1/3} \right] \quad \text{s.t.} \quad x^1 + x^2 = \bar{x}. \tag{32}$$

Then, the larger is $\bar{x}$ the greater for fixed (λ_2/λ_1) will be x_1^*/x_2^*. This violates the optimality of invariant fractional shares.

Actually, if invariant shares are to be optimal for arbitrary choices of λ_2/λ_1 in $\lambda_1 U_1(x^1) + \lambda_2 U_2(x^2)$, it is necessary that the latter belong to the Bergson (1936) CES family, namely

$$\begin{aligned} U^j(\mathbf{x}^j) &= c_j[H(\mathbf{x}^j)^\gamma - 1]/\gamma, \quad 1 > \gamma \\ \sum \lambda_j U^j(\mathbf{x}^j) &= a_\gamma + b_\gamma \sum [b_j H(\mathbf{x}^j)]^\gamma. \end{aligned} \tag{33}$$

In a sense, therefore, the theorems of the last two sections involve necessity as well as sufficiency.

However, as the remaining sections will show, if the vector (λ_j/λ_1) is to be frozen, it is possible to define cases of symmetry, and of symmetry's generalization, where invariant fractional shares do remain optimal.

5.   SYMMETRY SITUATIONS AND GENERALIZATIONS

Perfect Symmetry

To remain a philosopher one must let cowardice keep breaking in. From Kant to Rawls, philosophers have manufactured ethics out of the thin air of disguised symmetry assumptions. Without symmetry, they are at sea without a compass—or, better, at sea where there is no definable magnetic-compass direction. With symmetry (*and* with quasi concavity!) the principle of Sufficient Reason yields a definite optimum at the point of symmetry. Natch.

This may be expressed by the following theorem.

THEOREM *on symmetry*   Let the most general Bergson SWF of (1) have

(a)   symmetry as between persons and
(b)   be quasi concave (i.e., have iso-ω contours in the $n \times J$ x_i^j space that are convex).

Then

$$\max_{x_i^j} \omega(\mathbf{x}^1, \mathbf{x}^2, \ldots, \mathbf{x}^J) \quad \text{s.t.} \quad \sum_1^J \mathbf{x}^j = \bar{\mathbf{x}}$$

$$= \omega(\bar{\mathbf{x}}/J, \bar{\mathbf{x}}/J, \ldots, \bar{\mathbf{x}}^J/J)$$

COROLLARY   For $\lambda_1 = \lambda_2 = \cdots = \lambda_J$ and $U^j(\mathbf{x}) \equiv U(\mathbf{x})$, a quasi-concave function,

$$\max_{x_i^{\,j}} \sum_1^J U(\mathbf{x}^j) \qquad \text{s.t.} \quad \sum_1^J \mathbf{x}^j = \bar{\mathbf{x}}$$

$$= \sum_1^J U(\bar{\mathbf{x}}/J).$$

Remark $U(y_1, \ldots, y_n)$ is quasi concave iff

$$U(y_1, \ldots, y_n) \geq \Lambda \qquad \text{forms a convex set in} \quad (y_1, \ldots, y_n). \qquad (34)$$

When $U(y)$ is strictly quasi concave, the contour defined by $U(y_1, \ldots, y_n) = \Lambda$ is a strictly convex frontier of the convex set. The optimum point with $\alpha_j^* = x_i^{j*}/\bar{x}_i = J^{-1}$ is *unique* when $\omega(\ )$ or $U(\ )$ are *strictly* concave monotonic *strongly* increasing functions.

By (personal) symmetry of a function, we mean

$$\omega(\mathbf{x}^1, \mathbf{x}^2, \ldots, \mathbf{x}^J) \equiv \omega(\mathbf{x}^2, \mathbf{x}^1, \ldots, \mathbf{x}^J) \equiv \omega(\mathbf{x}^J, \mathbf{x}^1, \ldots, \mathbf{x}^2) \qquad (35)$$

and likewise for every permutation of the vectors $(\mathbf{x}^1, \mathbf{x}^2, \ldots, \mathbf{x}^J)$.

Remark   Suppose $\omega(\mathbf{X})$ were convex, as when $\sum U(\mathbf{x}^j)$ and $U(\ )$ possess "increasing marginal utility" and each person displays "risk preference." The point of symmetry is then the *worst* rather than *best* state of the world. The social optimum of maximum Bentham–Bergson–Harsanyi $\omega(\mathbf{X})$ occurs when *all* $\bar{\mathbf{x}}$ is given to one person—*any* person. Invariant fractional income shares are optimal, with $(\alpha_j^*) = (1, 0, \ldots, 0), (0, 1, 0, \ldots, 0)$, etc. [Actually, whatever $x_i^{\,j}$ were initially meted out, such people would spontaneously gamble until, with probability one, laissez faire would entail one victor with all the spoils. To argue that such an outcome is what most would "regret," is in effect to deny that the ethical observer wishes to adhere to the individualistic social welfare concept, preferring to them "paternalism" or what Musgrave calls "merit wants."]

Local First-Order Symmetry

Symmetry is too strong a requirement on $\omega(\mathbf{X})$ for $\alpha^j = J^{-1}$ to be optimal. Writing $\partial \omega(\mathbf{X})/\partial x_i^{\,j}$ as $_j\omega_i(\mathbf{X})$, it suffices that

$$\frac{_j\omega_i(\bar{\mathbf{x}}/J, \ldots, \bar{\mathbf{x}}/J)}{_1\omega_i(\bar{\mathbf{x}}/J, \ldots, \bar{\mathbf{x}}/J)} \equiv 1 \qquad (j = 2, \ldots, n; \quad i = 1, \ldots, n). \qquad (36)$$

Symmetry of $\omega(\mathbf{x}^1, \ldots, \mathbf{x}^J)$ implies (36). But (36) does not actually imply global symmetry; rather (36) merely implies what might be called local first-order symmetry. (*Example*: imagine a 2-good indifference-curve field with slopes of -1 on the 45° line; it need not possess global symmetry around the 45° line. Q.E.D.)

However, once we limit $\omega(\mathbf{X})$ to be of (3)'s Bentham–Bergson–Harsanyi form, symmetry of $\sum \lambda_j U^j(\mathbf{x}^j)$ is necessary as well as sufficient if $\alpha_j \equiv J^{-1}$ is to be ethically optimal for all choices of $(\bar{x}_1, \ldots, \bar{x}_n)$.

It will suffice to consider first the 1-good case, $n = 1$. Now (36) becomes

$$\frac{\lambda_j d[U^j(x)]/dx}{\lambda_1 d[U^1(x)]/dx} \equiv 1, \qquad U^j(x) \equiv a_j + \lambda_j^{-1} U(x),$$

$$\sum_1^J \lambda_j U^j(x^j) \equiv \sum_1^J \lambda_j a_j + \sum_1^J U(x^j). \qquad \text{Q.E.D.}$$

(37)

For the n-good case, we similarly require for every arbitrary vector $\mathbf{x}$

$$\frac{\lambda_j d[U^j(x)]/dx}{\lambda_1 d[U^1(x)]/dx} \equiv 1 \qquad (j = 2, \ldots, J; \quad i = 1, \ldots, n). \qquad (38)$$

Therefore

$$U^j(\mathbf{x}) \equiv a_j + \lambda_j^{-1} U(\mathbf{x}),$$

$$\sum_1^J \lambda_j U^j(\mathbf{x}^j) \equiv \sum_1^J \lambda_j a_j + \sum_1^J U(\mathbf{x}^j). \qquad \text{Q.E.D.}$$

Nonequal Sharings

One nose, one person. So reckons the naive quantum mechanics of philosophical individualism. However, if nutritional requirements for a 6-foot Norwegian differ from those for a 5-foot Malayan, does fair rationing involve equal calories per person or equal "fractions of nutritional need?" Clearly, there arise cases where symmetry analysis must be amplified or generalized.

Thus, let person 1 represent a larger family than any of the rest, being in effect the embodiment of two normal consuming people. If the subutilities of the two inner-people add to form person 1's utility, and if each of them happened to be just like each outer-person $(2, 3, \ldots, j, \ldots, J)$, it must be intuitively obvious that person 1 should receive twice the vector they receive—namely

$$\mathbf{x}^{j*} = \bar{\mathbf{x}}/(J + 1), \qquad (j = 2, \ldots, J), \qquad \mathbf{x}^{1*} = 2\bar{\mathbf{x}}/(J + 1). \qquad (39)$$

Again, the principle of invariant fractional income shares obtains (indeed, obtains in the strong form of all people consuming goods in the same proportions as total endowments).

This far-fetched example alerts us to the following way of generalizing for additive Bentham–Bergson–Harsanyi functions the local first-order symmetry concepts of (38).

THEOREM *on constant (vectoral) fractional shares under generalized symmetry* Suppose

$$U^j(\mathbf{x}^j) \equiv a_j + \lambda_j^{-1} C_j U(\mathbf{x}^j/C_j), \qquad C_j > 0,$$

$$c_j = C_j \bigg/ \sum_1^J C_k \qquad (j = 1, \ldots, J),$$

and $U(\mathbf{x})$ is concave and monotone strongly increasing; then

$$\max_{x^j} \sum_1^J \lambda_j U^j(\mathbf{x}^j) \qquad \text{s.t.} \quad \sum_1^J \mathbf{x}^j = \bar{\mathbf{x}}$$

$$= \sum_1^J \lambda_j a_j + \max_{x^j} \sum_1^J C_j U(\mathbf{x}^j/C_j)$$

$$= \sum_1^J \lambda_j a_j + \sum_1^J C_j U(c_j \bar{\mathbf{x}}/C_j)$$

$$= \sum_1^J \lambda_j a_j + \left(\sum_1^J C_j\right) U(\bar{\mathbf{x}}/\sum_1^J C_k), \tag{40}$$

where

$$x_i^{j*} \equiv c_j \bar{x}_i, \qquad (i = 1, \ldots, n; \quad j = 1, \ldots, J),$$

$$\alpha_j^* = c_j \qquad \text{independently of} \quad (\bar{x}_1, \ldots, \bar{x}_n).$$

To prove this theorem, we solve for the unique roots of the necessary first-order maximizing conditions, involving $\partial U^j(\mathbf{x}^j)/\partial x_i^j = U_i^j(\mathbf{x}^j)$ and $\partial U(\mathbf{z})/\partial z_i = U_i(\mathbf{z})$:

$$1 = \lambda_j U_i^j(\mathbf{x}^j)/\lambda_1 U_i^1(\mathbf{x}^1), \qquad (j = 2, \ldots, J; \quad i = 1, \ldots, n)$$

$$= \frac{C_j^{-1} \lambda_j \lambda_j^{-1} C_j U_i(c_j\{\bar{\mathbf{x}}/\sum_1^J C_k\}/c_j)}{C_1^{-1} \lambda_1 \lambda_1^{-1} C_1 U_i(c_1\{\bar{\mathbf{x}}/\sum_1^J C_k\}/C_1)} = \frac{U_i(\bar{\mathbf{x}}/\sum_1^k C_k)}{U_i(\bar{\mathbf{x}}/\sum_1^k C_k)}. \tag{41}$$

Remark: If we drop the B–B–H additivity requirement and shift attention from (38) to the more general (36), the conditions of this last theorem become sufficient but overly strong to be necessary. Thus, the following example has invariant optimal fractional vectoral shares, $\mathbf{x}^{j*} = \alpha_j^* \bar{\mathbf{x}}$:

$$W = \log H(\mathbf{x}^1) + \log[H(\mathbf{x}^2)^{1/4} H(\mathbf{x}^3)^{1/4} + H(\mathbf{x}^4)^{1/2}]^2$$

$$H(\theta\mathbf{x}) \equiv \theta H(\mathbf{x}), \qquad H(\mathbf{x}) \text{ strictly quasi concave}, \tag{42}$$

$$\alpha_1^* = \tfrac{1}{2}, \qquad \alpha_1^* = \tfrac{1}{8} = \alpha_3^*, \qquad \alpha_4^* = \tfrac{1}{4}.$$

However, (42) is not a Bentham–Bergson–Harsanyi additive function. If we insist on B–B–H functions and that, for *any* choice of $(\lambda_1, \ldots, \lambda_J)$, parameters invariant fractional vectors are to be optimal, then (36) implies

$$U^j(\mathbf{x}^j) \equiv a_j + b_j[H(\mathbf{x}^j)^\gamma - 1]\gamma^{-1}, \qquad \gamma \leq 1, \tag{43.1}$$

$$1 \equiv \frac{\lambda_j \, \partial U^j(\alpha_j\bar{\mathbf{x}})/\partial x_i^j}{\lambda_1 \, \partial U^1(\alpha_1\bar{\mathbf{x}}) \, \partial x_i^1} = \frac{\lambda_j b_j \alpha_j^{\gamma-1}[\partial H(\bar{\mathbf{x}})/\partial x_i]}{\lambda_1 b_1 \alpha_1^{\gamma-1}[\partial H(\bar{\mathbf{x}})/\partial x_i]} = \frac{\lambda_j b_j \gamma_j^{\gamma-1}}{\lambda_1 b_1 \gamma_1^{\gamma-1}}, \tag{43.2}$$

$$\alpha_j{}^* = (\lambda_j b_j)^{1/(1-\gamma)}\left[\sum_1^J (\lambda_k b_k)^{1/(1-\gamma)}\right]. \tag{43.3}$$

6. QUALIFICATIONS

For brevity I have assumed away all consumption externalities: envy, altruism, public goods, etc. A complete analysis would have to take account of realistic externalities.

The present analysis has concentrated exclusively on the problem of allocating a given available total vector of society's consumption goods $(\bar{x}_1, \ldots, \bar{x}_n)$ among a set of specified persons. When one must take account of production of outputs out of inputs, some of which must be provided by the persons themselves—as for example, irksome skilled labor—proper analysis must become more complicated. Indeed, the original perceptions in Bergson (1938) of that nonoptimality of equal money incomes, in the sense of equal $\sum x_i^j p_i - \sum$ factor returns, come in the context of the variable input case.

The cautious reader will take warning of the special features required for simple income-sharing to be even approximately optimal.

REFERENCES

Arrow, K. J. (1964). *Aspects of the Theory of Risk-Bearing*. Helsinki: Yrjö Jahnssonin säätio. Reproduced as Chapters 2 and 3 in *Essays in the Theory of Risk-Bearing*. Chicago: Markham, 1971.

Bergson, A. (1936). Real Income, Expenditure Proportionality, and Frisch's 'New Methods of Measuring Marginal Utility,' *Review of Economic Studies* **4**, 33–52.

Bergson, A. (1938). A Reformulation of Certain Aspects of Welfare Economics, *Quarterly Journal of Economics* **52**, 310–334.

Bergson, A. (1966). *Essays in Normative Economics*. Cambridge, Massachusetts: Belknap Press of Harvard Univ. Press.

Bergson, A. (1976). Taste Differences and Optimal Income Distribution: A Paradox Illustrated. Discussion Paper 82, Harvard Inst. of Econ. Res. Harvard Univ.

Chipman, J. S. (1974). Homothetic Preferences and Aggregation, *Journal of Economic Theory* **8**, 1, 26–38.

Chipman, J. S. (1976). The Paretian Heritage, *Revue European de Sciences Sociales et Journal Cahiers Vilfredo Pareto* **14**, No. 37, 65–171.

Diamond, P. A. (1967). Cardinal Welfare, Individualistic Ethics and Interpersonal Comparison of Utility: Comment, *Journal of Political Economy* **75**, 765–766.

Fisher, F. M. and J. Rothenberg.(1961 and 1962).How Income Ought to be Distributed: Paradox Lost [and] Paradox Enow, *Journal of Political Economy* **69** and **70**, 162–180 and 88–93.

Gorman, W. M. (1953). Community Preference Fields. *Econometrica* **21**, 63–80.

de V. Graaf, J. (1967). *Theoretical Welfare Economics*. London and New York: Cambridge Univ. Press.

Harsanyi, J. C. (1955). Cardinal Welfare, Individualistic Ethics, and Interpersonal Comparisons of Utility, *Journal of Political Economy* **63**, 309–321.

Hicks, J. R. (1939). The Foundations of Welfare Economics, *Economic Journal* **49**, 696–712.

Kaldor, N. (1939). Welfare Propositions of Economics and Interpersonal Comparisons of Utility, *Economic Journal* **49**, 549–552.

Kemp, M., and Ng Y–K (1976). On the Existence of Social Welfare Functions, Social Orderings and Social Decision Functions, *Econometrica* **43**, 59–66.

Lange, O. (1942). The Foundations of Welfare Economics, *Econometrica* **10**, 215–228.

Lerner, A. P. (1934a). The Concept of Monopoly and the Measurement of Monopoly Power, *Review of Economic Studies* **1**, 157–175.

Lerner, A. P. (1934b). Economic Theory and Socialist Economy, *Review of Economic Studies* **3**, 51–61.

Lerner, A. P. (1944). *Economics of Control*. New York: Macmillan.

Marschak, J. (1950). Rational Behavior, Uncertain Prospects, and Measurable Utility, *Econometrica* **18**, 111–141; Errata, *Econometrica* **18**, 312.

Merton, R. C. (1969). "Lifetime Portfolio Selection under Uncertainty: The Continuous-Time Case, *Review of Economics and Statistics* **51**, 247–257.

Pareto, V. (1896, 1897). *Cours d' Economie Politique*, Vol. I. Lausanne: F. Rouge, editeur, 1896; Vol. II. Lausanne: F. Rouge, librarie-editeur, 1897.

Pareto, V. (1909). *Manuel d'Economie Politique*. Paris: V. Giard et E. Briere.

Pareto, V. (1913). Il massimo di utilità per una collettività in Sociologia, *Giornale degli Economisti* **3**, 337–341.

Pfanzangl, J. (1959). A General Theory of Measurement—Applications to Utility, *Naval Research Logistics Quarterly* (Office Naval Res.) **6**, 283–294.

Pratt, J. W. (1964). Risk Aversion in the Small and in the Large, *Econometrica* **32**, 122–136.

Ramsey, F. (1931). *Foundations of Mathematics*. London: Kegan Paul.

Robbins, L. (1932). *An Essay on the Nature and Significance of Economic Science*. New York: Macmillan.

Rothblum, V. G. (1975). Multivariate Constant Risk Posture, *Journal of Economic Theory* **10**, 309–312.

Samuelson, P. A. (1947). *Foundations of Economic Analysis*. Cambridge, Massachusetts: Harvard Univ. Press.

Samuelson, P. A. (1956). Social Indifference Curves, *Quarterly Journal of Economics* **70**, 1, 1–22. Reproduced in *The Collected Scientific Papers of Paul A. Samuelson*, Vol. II, Chapter 78, pp. 1073–1094. Cambridge, Massachusetts: MIT Press, 1966.

Samuelson, P. A. (1969a). Risk-Taking with Respect to Commodities. Mimeo. Referred to by Stiglitz (1969).

Samuelson, P. A. (1969b). Lifetime Portfolio Selection by Dynamic Stochastic Programming, *Review of Economics and Statistics* **51**, 4, 239–246. Reproduced in *The Collected Scientific Papers of Paul A. Samuelson*, Vol. III, Chapter 204, pp. 883–890. Cambridge, Massachusetts: MIT Press, 1966.

Samuelson, P. A. (1974). A Curious Case Where Reallocation Cannot Achieve Optimum Welfare, in Warren L. Smith and John M. Culbertson, eds., *Public Finance and Stabilization, Essays in Honor of Richard A. Musgrave*. (New York: North Holland/American Elsevier), 145–150.

Samuelson, P. A. (1977). Reaffirming the Existence of 'Reasonable' Bergson–Samuelson Social Welfare Functions, *Economica* **44**, 81–88.

Savage, L. J. (1954). *Foundations of Statistics*. New York: Wiley.

Stiglitz, J. E. (1969). Behavior towards Risk with Many Commodities, *Econometrica* **37**, 660–667.

Strotz, R. H. (1958). "How Income Ought to Be Distributed: A Paradox in Distributive Ethics, *Journal of Political Economy* **66**, 189–205.

Thiel, H. (1954). *Linear Aggregation of Economic Relations*. Amsterdam: North-Holland Publ.

POLICY AND APPLICATIONS

Optimal taxes on foreign lending

MICHAEL CONNOLLY

UNIVERSITY OF FLORIDA
GAINESVILLE

1. INTRODUCTION

This paper stresses the one-to-one correspondence between Fisherian capital theory, involving trade over time, and the opportunity cost trade model developed by Haberler (1936) and others, involving trade at the same point in time, and draws the implications of this correspondence for the theory of optimal taxation on foreign lending. In doing so we relate two lines of thought that emphasize the kinship of capital theory and trade theory, the first being the work of Baldwin (1966), Miller (1968), and Webb (1970) which sprang from a neoclassical treatment of capital accumulation by Leontief (1958), and the second, a Fisherian approach to capital theory in an international setting by Connolly and Ross (1970).

Let us start with a few obvious remarks. Borrowing and lending are processes involving time. A lender can always be said to sacrifice the present in return for future reward and a borrower to draw upon the future to live (consume or invest) beyond current means. Thus, a borrower is one who supplies future income, a lender one who demands it. In terms of securities, or contracts for future income, the roles are reversed: a lender is a demander and a borrower a supplier. Further, for any individual or country, the supply of loans equals the value of future repayments. This is, in fact, Mill's law of

I am particularly indebted to Philip Friedman, Larry Kreicher, and Yoram Peles for helpful comments.

reciprocal demand applied to trade over time. To press the analogy, we can treat a foreign lender as an exporter of present income and as an importer of claims to future income. A borrower, on the other hand, imports present income, and exports current indebtedness. Interest rates play the role of terms of trade over time, and equilibrium entails finding those terms of trade which equate desired exports and imports. In familiar terms, interest rates serve to equate desired loans and borrowings.[1]

2. THE OPTIMUM TAX: SIMPLE CASE

It follows from this parallel that the well-known theory of optimum tariffs can be directly applied to determine the optimum tax on foreign lending. For simplicity, suppose there are only two countries *A* and *B*, a single commodity called income, and two periods, the present and the future. Further, assume perfect foresight to eliminate the element of uncertainty. In this setting, trade over time will take place between the countries in the form of borrowing, and gains will result from such exchange.[2] In Figure 1,

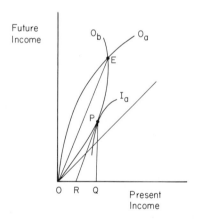

FIGURE 1

[1] In Irving Fisher's terms, the "... supply and demand we have to deal with are ... the supply and demand of future income," and the interest rate is "... that sort of price which links one point of time with another point of time in the markets of the world" (1930, pp. 32–33). Fisher made the formal analogy between capital theory and trade theory in 1907 and Samuelson (1967) has remarked that Fisher's approach to capital theory "... completely anticipates in its formal structure the post-1930 models of international trade that Haberler, Viner, Lerner, Leontief, Meade and others developed." The full implications of this correspondence were drawn in a trade setting by Mosak (1944).
[2] On the gains from trade, see Baldwin (1952).

the offer curves of countries A and B, O_a and O_b respectively, are drawn. They can be derived from the *investment opportunity* and *time preference*[3] schedules in the exact same manner as offer curves are derived from production functions and indifference curves [see Meade (1952)]. At the origin O, the slope of O_b is less than the slope of O_a, indicating less time preference so that after trade B will lend to A.

The equilibrium terms of trade between present and future income are indicated by the slope of the line drawn from the origin to point E, the equilibrium borrowing pattern. The slope of OE is greater than unity as drawn, so equilibrium rates are positive.[4] The possibility of borrowing from abroad has lowered interest rates in A, and foreign lending has raised them in B.[5]

Now suppose that the trade equilibrium at E is disturbed by the imposition of a tax by A on borrowing from B. In particular, what is the optimum tax on borrowing from abroad assuming that the foreign country does not retaliate? The answer to this question is provided in the optimum tariff literature (Johnson, 1953–1954), and briefly, it requires the imposition of an ad valorem tax on borrowing equal to the reciprocal of the elasticity of supply of present income with respect to the intertemporal terms of trade. Such a tax will bring into equality the domestic marginal rates of time preference and investment opportunity in line with the *marginal* cost of borrowing from abroad; that is, the optimal trade indifference curve I_a can be reached via a tax restricting borrowing to the point P, and this tax must equal the reciprocal of the elasticity of B's offer curve at P.[6]

This argument can be expressed in terms of interest rates, savings, and investment elasticities, and the proportion of their total loans that B makes to A. First note that the amount of borrowing from B, denoted by Z, equals total savings less investment in B, or $Z = S - I$. Consequently, in terms of elasticities with respect to the intertemporal terms of trade ($p = 1 + r$, where

---

[3] These are assumed to be convex sets, thus giving the standard offer curves in the figure.

[4] Fisher gives examples of situations in which interest rates can be zero or negative (1930, pp. 186–191), but this is ruled out here. The analysis would, however, be unchanged.

[5] This can be seen since the slope of an offer curve at the origin gives the relative price (in this case, one plus the interest rate) at autarky.

[6] To demonstrate this result, note that at the optimum trading point P the domestic intertemporal terms of trade are PQ/RQ which equal $(1 + \tau)PQ/OQ$, where τ is the ad valorem tax, and PQ/OQ the foreign relative price of present income. With $PQ/RQ = (1 + \tau)PQ/OQ$, we have $\tau = (OQ/RQ - 1) = (OQ - RQ)/RQ = OR/RQ = 1/(RQ/OR) = 1/\varepsilon_{zp}$, where ε_{zp} is the supply elasticity of present income Z with respect to the intertemporal terms of trade. Note that this can be formulated as a tax on B's demand for future income equal to $(\eta_{zp} - 1)^{-1}$, where η_{zp} is the elasticity of demand for future income because $\varepsilon_{zp} = RQ/OR = (OQ - OR)/OR = \eta_{zp} - 1$ since $OQ/OR = \eta_{zp}$. Also, note that the formula does not apply for a potentially inelastic portion of B's offer curve (e.g. $\eta_{zp} < 1$ or $\varepsilon_{zp} < 0$), because in this case the tax should be increased since more present income can be borrowed for less exports of future income. Finally, tariff revenue is assumed to be redistributed to the public.

r is the interest rate) we have $\varepsilon_{zp} = (S/Z)\varepsilon_{sp} + (I/Z)\varepsilon_{ip}$; that is, the foreign elasticity of supply of loans equals a weighted sum of the foreign savings and investment schedules. Making use of the identity $\varepsilon_{zp} = [(1 + r)/r]\varepsilon_{zr}$ (and similar ones for the savings and investment elasticities), and denoting by $\mu = Z/I$, the optimal tax on borrowing is given by[7]

$$\tau = \{[(1 + r)/r][(1 + 1/\mu)\varepsilon_{sr} + (1/\mu)\varepsilon_{ir}]\}^{-1}. \tag{1}$$

The major points suggested by this formula are, firstly, that the optimum tax is larger the greater the proportion of their loans that B residents make to A, and secondly, the optimal tax is smaller the more elastic foreign savings and investment schedules. This is a familiar result from optimum tariff theory, and a similar expression can be derived for optimum taxes imposed by B on lending to A. Both solutions ignore however retaliation, which is a major shortcoming of the theory of optimum tariffs.[8]

3. THE MANY-GOOD, MANY-PERIOD CASE

The optimum tax formula derived above applies to the simple case of trade in two goods, present and future income; moreover, it is possible to extend the classical analysis of optimum taxes and tariffs (Graaff, 1953–1954) to trade in many commodities with many different time periods.[9] To do so, allow for trade in any number of goods not only in the present, but also in the future via present contracts for future delivery.

With perfect future markets, let us represent foreign (B) prices charged *today* for commodity i delivered in the tth period by P_i^t and the corresponding level of imports of the same commodity at the same time by Z_i^t. Within this framework it is not possible to identify the borrowing or lending pattern with trade in a particular type of commodity, such as capital goods, but rather we can speak only of borrowing or lending in terms of *net* value of exports in the present time period. Furthermore, if a country is borrowing (e.g. is a *net* importer in the first period), it simultaneously must offer claims on future

---

[7] By Lerner's Symmetry Theorem (1936), a tax on exports of future income would have identical real effects as the tax on imports of present income, provided the proceeds are distributed in the same fashion.

[8] The existing game theory solutions to tariffs and retaliation are found in Johnson (1953–1954) and Scitovsky (1942), and are based upon the Cournot behavioral pattern that each country retaliates to changes in the other's tax by imposing in turn an optimum tax on the assumption that the other country will not retaliate. While Scitovsky argued that trade may come to an end and that both countries must suffer losses in welfare, Johnson has shown that following a tariff retaliation sequence, trade will not halt and one country might benefit, but only at the expense of the other.

[9] This section draws upon Connolly and Ross (1970) which takes that approach.

goods equal to the value of its debt. In other words, the Z_i^t terms equal not only future imports of each good, but also represent purchases (or sales, if negative) of securities by the home country in the present. Each security entitles the holder to the future import of one unit of the commodity in which it is denominated. Clearly then, the *net* value of imports in the present must be just matched by the *net* value of exports of such claims. In short, if there is a deficit on current account there must be an equal and opposite surplus on capital account. The balance of payments is thus in equilibrium when, with m commodities and n time periods,

$$F = \sum_{(i,t)} P_i^t Z_i^t = 0 \qquad (i = 1, m, \quad t = 1, n) \tag{2}$$

which states that the present value of the balance of trade must be zero. In Graaff's terminology, F is the *foreign trade transformation* of the home country, and can be differentiated with respect to each import item to derive the marginal rates of transformation through foreign trade:

$$-\frac{dZ_j^\tau}{dZ_i^t} = \frac{\partial F}{\partial Z_i^t} \bigg/ \frac{\partial F}{\partial Z_j^\tau} = \frac{P_i^t(1 + a_i^t)}{P_j^\tau(1 + a_j^\tau)} \qquad (t, \tau = 1, n, \quad i, j = 1, m), \tag{3}$$

where

$$a_i^t = \sum_{(\alpha,k)} \frac{\partial P_k^\alpha}{\partial Z_i^t} \frac{Z_k^\alpha}{P_i^t} \qquad (i, k = 1, m, \quad t, \alpha = 1, n).$$

It is convenient to express the a_i^t terms as

$$a_i^t = \sum_{(\alpha,k)} \eta_{it}^{k\alpha} \frac{P_k^\alpha Z_k^\alpha}{P_i^t Z_i^t} \qquad (i, k = 1, m, \quad t, \alpha = 1, n), \tag{4}$$

where $\eta_{it}^{k\alpha}$ is the percentage change in the price P_k^α divided by the percentage change in extra imports of Z_i^t. It is thus an elasticity which gives a measure of the relative impact on the price of each traded good and claim as a result of extra imports of the ith good in period t. The remaining terms serve as weights: they give the value of trade in each and every item *relative* to trade in the ith good at point t in time. Their purpose is to distinguish the degree of importance to be attached to the change in the price of each item. The a_i^t terms in equation (3) are thus the sums of the foreign quantity elasticities, each weighted by the ratio of the value of trade in that good to the value of trade in Z_i^t. They express the *marginal* cost to the home country of changes in the terms of trade induced by additional imports of i in period t. Consequently, $P_i^t(1 + a_i^t)$ is the total marginal cost *in the present* to the home country of increasing such imports, or analogously, the present marginal export revenue if Z_i^t is negative. If the home country can have no effect whatsoever on any price, all the a_i^t terms are zero. From equation (3), this absence of monopoly power means that the marginal rates of transformation through trade *equal* the foreign relative prices.

4. OPTIMUM TAXES ON EXCHANGE: GENERAL CASE

In the absence of externalities, Pareto optimality requires the equality of the domestic marginal rates of substitution in consumption, DRS, and the domestic marginal rates of transformation, DRT. In an open economy both must be brought into equality with the marginal rates of transformation through foreign trade.[10] These conditions are unaltered when exchange over time is included along with exchange at a given moment of time. On the assumption that the domestic price ratios π_i^t/π_j^τ reflect the DRS and DRT, the efficiency conditions become

$$\frac{\pi_i^t}{\pi_j^\tau} = \frac{P_i^t(1 + a_i^t)}{P_j^\tau(1 + a_j^\tau)} \qquad (t, \tau = 1, n, \quad i, j = 1, m). \tag{5}$$

Pareto optimality may then be satisfied by levying an ad valorem tax equal algebraically to a_i^t on each good i traded at time t. For commodities traded in the present, the tax is expressed as a percentage of the foreign commodity price. For trade in contracts to future commodities, the tax is expressed as a percentage of the current foreign price of the *claim* entitling the holder to future delivery of one unit of the commodity in which it is denominated. We have, in short, taxes levied simultaneously on goods and securities in the present. The taxes are payable in the present, and not necessarily when the good crosses the border. If the taxes were payable upon delivery, they would be costed up at an appropriate interest rate. This procedure defines a system of tariffs, some of which may be subsidies due to cross effects.[11] This happens when the own effects are outweighed by substitutability and complementarity relationships.

The multiperiod, many-good case gives rise to possibilities of substitutability and complementarity at the same point in time, and over time, while in the simple two-good case, substitution over time is the sole possibility. In both instances, the problem of optimum taxes on capital movements, including borrowing and lending, can be treated as a branch of optimum tariff

---

[10] See Graaff (1953–1954) for the full proof of this proposition.

[11] Since only relative prices are of importance, the efficiency conditions can be satisfied with only $m - 1$ taxes. This would amount to choosing one of the goods as a *numéraire*. To guarantee that a global maximum is reached by this system of taxation, convexity of production and consumption sets is sufficient.

analysis. Further, as in tariff theory, the optimal tax structure depends directly upon the relative monopoly power of the country in world capital and commodity markets.

5. RELATED APPROACHES

This section briefly discusses related approaches[12] to the problem of international borrowing and lending.

A. The Baldwin–Miller–Webb Model
with Leontief Capital Goods

In separate papers, Baldwin (1966), Miller (1968), and Webb (1970) extended Leontief's (1958) period-by-period treatment of the accumulation of capital to an international setting. New capital is produced from one period to the next by refraining from consumption, and for each level of the capital stock, there corresponds a particular consumption stream for each and every future consumption period. Miller stresses the one-to-one correspondence between trade and capital theory in a striking fashion by using the Meade trade indifference curve technique to show the formal identity. As pointed out by Melvin (1970), trade eventually comes to an end in the Leontief setting, but that meanwhile the standard offer curve analysis, such as depicted in Figure 1, is fully applicable as argued by Miller (1970). Consequently, so is the theory of the optimum tariff as presented here once one takes into account shifts in offer curves brought about by trade in capital goods.

B. The Jones–Kemp Solution
to the Heckscher–Ohlin Model

Very similar remarks apply to the problem of optimum tax-tariff structures in the Heckscher–Ohlin trade model. The solution for optimum taxes and tariffs in the H–O model offered by Jones (1967) and Kemp (1966) can be reached by the application of the general Graaff (1953–1954) formula for the optimum tariff structure by taking into account the technical relationships of substitutability and complementarity between traded factors of production and final products that is embodied in the factor intensity assumptions. This information can be substituted directly into the Graaff formula, as is done by Connolly and Ross, to derive the Jones–Kemp results.

---

[12] The portfolio approach to capital movements applies to situations involving risk and uncertainty not discussed here. See e.g. Grubel (1968), Levy and Sarnat (1970), and Willett and Forte (1969).

C. The Lusky Dynamic Optimization Approach

It is perhaps fitting that we close with a simple analytical example of optimum foreign borrowing provided to me by Rafael Lusky to illustrate a possible dynamic solution to the problem of the optimum foreign debt.[13] The Lusky solution highlights the dynamic nature of the choice of an ideal consumption *path over time*, given the possibility of borrowing from abroad, and at the same time, stresses the main points of the time preference framework in a context of dynamic optimization.

Briefly, the Lusky solution denotes the home country's current stock of foreign debt as D, so that new borrowings equal $\dot{D}$, and assumes a static population and a constant stream of income denoted by y. Further, let r equal the world rate of interest which is assumed to be both positive and constant over time (e.g. the country is small in the sense that the rate of interest it pays is independent of its borrowing.)[14]

The country's consumption pattern c is greater or less than its income if net imports m are positive or negative respectively:

$$c = y + m. \tag{6}$$

With only one good, net imports equal new borrowing $\dot{D}$ *less* the value of interest rebates abroad, or

$$m = \dot{D} - rD. \tag{7}$$

Finally, denote the country's internal rate of time preference by δ, which is assumed positive. The problem is to maximize the present value of utility[15]:

$$\max J = \int_0^\infty U(c)e^{-\delta t}\, dt \tag{8}$$

subject to (6) and (7), which can be expressed as

$$\dot{D} = rD + c - y \tag{9}$$

as well as

$$c(t) \geq 0 \tag{10}$$

which serves as a minimum consumption requirement.

---

[13] The previous analysis, and that of Connolly and Ross, is intrinsically static, despite the element of trade over time.

[14] Hanson (1974) has pointed out that a small country may nevertheless face an upward sloping supply curve of foreign capital if the risk of default or national expropriation rises with increased foreign indebtedness.

[15] The analysis is reported in full in an unfinished working paper by Lusky (1975).

For brevity, let us report only the solution to the *optimal path of the foreign debt*, which is[16]

$$D(t) = y/r + e^{rt} \int e^{-rt} c(p)\, dt \qquad \text{where} \quad p(t) = p_0 e^{(\delta - r)t}. \qquad (11)$$

Along the optimum consumption path, p equals the negative of the marginal utility of consumption. With diminishing marginal utility, consumption is positively related to p and consequently the consumption path depends upon the relationship between δ and r. For the case in which $\delta > r$, the optimal path over time is characterized by continuous new borrowing, a growing stock of debt, and a declining flow of consumption.[17] This is accomplished by the country initially enjoying positive imports (new borrowings exceeding interest payments) in an "immature debtor" phase, then becoming a net exporter as foreign rebates exceed new borrowings in a "mature debtor" phase.

6. SUMMARY

This paper stresses the theme of foreign lending as trade over time. The familiar optimum tariff argument is applied and consequently, it becomes clear that one need not treat taxes on capital movements as a different species than taxes on trade in goods. It is trade that is taxed, and the purpose is the same; namely, to improve the terms on which it takes place. That the terms of trade over time are called interest rates makes no difference. From this point of view, the optimum tax-tariff structure entails the familiar equalization of the domestic and foreign marginal rates of transformation through trade and foreign lending.

REFERENCES

Baldwin, R. E. (1952). The New Welfare Economics and Gains in International Trade, *Quarterly Journal of Economics* **66** (February), 91–101.
Baldwin, R. E. (1966). The Role of Capital-Goods Trade in the Theory of International Trade, *American Economic Review* **56** (September), 841–848.
Connolly, M., and Ross, S. (1970). A Fisherian Approach to Trade, Capital Movements, and Tariffs, *American Economic Review* **60** (June), 478–484.
Fisher, I. (1907). *The Rate of Interest.* New York: Macmillan.
Fisher, I. (1930). *The Theory of Interest.* New York: Macmillan.
Graaff, J. de V. (1953–1954). On Optimum Tariff Structures, *Review of Economic Studies* **17**, 47–59.
Grubel, H. (1968). Internationally Diversified Portfolios: Welfare Gains and Capital Flows, *American Economic Review* **58** (December), 1299–1314.

[16] Impose the conditions $U(0) = 0$, $U'(0) = \infty$, $U'(\infty) = 0$, $U'(c) > 0$, and $U''(c) < 0$ on the utility function.

[17] Note that p_0 is negative.

Haberler, G. (1936). *The Theory of International Trade.* London: Hodge.

Hanson, J. A. (1974). Optimal International Borrowing and Lending, *American Economic Review* **64** (September), 616–629.

Johnson, H. G. (1953–1954). Optimum Tariffs and Retaliation, *Review of Economic Studies* **21** (2), 142–153.

Jones, R. (1967). International Capital Movements and the Theory of Tariffs and Trade, *Quarterly Journal of Economics* **81** (February), 1–38.

Kemp, M. (1966). The Gain from International Trade and Investment: A Neo-Heckscher–Ohlin Approach, *American Economic Review* **56** (September), 788–809.

Leontief, W. (1958). Theoretical Note on Time-Preference, Productivity of Capital, Stagnation, and Economic Growth, *American Economic Review* **48** (March), 105–111.

Lerner, A. (1936). The Symmetry between Import and Export Taxes, *Economica* **3** (August), 306–313.

Levy, H., and Sarnat, M. (1970). International Diversification of Investment Portfolios, *American Economic Review* **60** (September), 668–675.

Lusky, R. (1975). The Optimum Foreign Debt (unpublished manuscript).

Meade, J. (1952). *A Geometry of International Trade.* London: Allen & Unwin.

Melvin, J. (1970). A General Equilibrium Theory of International Capital Flows: A Comment, *Economic Journal* **80** (September), 742–746.

Miller, N. (1968). A General Equilibrium Theory of International Capital Flows, *Economic Journal* **78** (June), 312–319.

Miller, N. (1970). A General Equilibrium Theory of International Capital Flows: A Reply, *Economic Journal* **80** (September), 747–749.

Mosak, J. (1944). *General Equilibrium Theory in International Trade.* Indiana: Cowles Commission.

Samuelson, P. A. (1967). Irving Fisher and the Theory of Capital, in *Ten Economic Studies in the Tradition of Irving Fisher* (W. Fellner *et al.*, eds.). New York: Wiley.

Scitovsky, T. (1942). A Re-Consideration of the Theory of Tariffs, *Review of Economic Studies* **9** (Summer), 89–110.

Webb, L. R. (1970). The Role of International Capital Movements in Trade and Growth: The Fisherian Approach, in *Studies in International Economics: The Monash Conference Papers* (I. A. McDougall and R. H. Snape, eds.). Melbourne: Monash Univ. Press.

Willett, T., and Forte, F. (1969). Interest Rate Policy and External Balance, *Quarterly Journal of Economics* **83** (May), 242–262.

Monopoly regulation, waiting lines, and investment in service capacity

ISRAEL LUSKI

BEN GURION UNIVERSITY
BEER SHEBA

DAVID LEVHARI

THE HEBREW UNIVERSITY
JERUSALEM

1. INTRODUCTION

In the usual textbook discussion of monopolies we assume that social regulation deals with appropriate control of the price, charged so that the profit-maximizing firm would increase its output. The aim is to induce the monopoly to produce an output closer to the social optimal output and to reduce the gap between social marginal costs and social marginal benefits.

The discussion is carried out in a framework of output and its price, and deals with the ways by which control or subsidy can induce the firm to produce the "proper" output. However, in many realistic cases the monopoly has more than one policy variable (i.e. output), and controlling only one policy variable may bring about undesired results. An example is that the quality as well as the quantity is a decision variable of the firm, and controlling

Research support from the National Science Foundation under Grant SOC-76-11583 is gratefully acknowledged.

just one variable may cause ill effects. Thus control of the price at its competitive level is no guarantee of increased welfare if there exist other unregulated policy variables of the monopoly.

The present paper analyzes within a simple queueing model a firm supplying a service to customers. The customers form a waiting line and as their turn comes receive the service supplied. Thus, besides the benefit from the service and its price, the customers have to take into account the alternative cost of waiting. The firm, on the other hand, can by an appropriate investment change its "capacity" to produce the service. It can increase the "channels" of service and thus reduce the waiting lines. It is assumed that the firm is a monopolist in supplying the specific service. The firm has two policy variables to decide: the price charged for the service and the level of investment in capacity for producing the service. It is assumed that "capacity" is measured by the expected speed of service. The higher the investment in capacity, the shorter the expected service time. With a given price for the service it is clear that by producing a service faster, the firm induces more people to ask for the service.

The direction of distortions in ordinary monopoly is well known. Thus the aim of regulation is usually to induce the firm to increase its output (reduce its price to consumers). In our case, however, the interaction of the variables—the price of the service, the speed of service, the total amount of service supplied, and the total waiting time—makes it harder to deduce the direction of the distortions. In fact, it is found that the distortions are not necessarily in the same directions in all cases. It is possible to find cases in which the price charged by the monopolist will be lower than the "social optimal price." The question of whether a monopoly provides faster or slower service than that under a social optimal arrangement also does not have a definite answer. In these cases it is not obvious how to apply the standard textbook regulation of monopoly. It will be shown in all cases considered that to achieve optimal provision of service, we need to apply a combination of subsidizing the service charge together with an appropriate tax on investment in capacity of service.

It may be somewhat surprising to find that a method of regulating only the price charged by the monopolist and making him charge the "social optimal price" is quite frequently inefficient in the sense that it reduces social welfare (as compared to a monopolist with no regulation).

2. THE MODEL

There exists a stream of potential customers arriving randomly and requesting a specific service. In view of their expectation of the benefits from the service on the one hand and the alternative time costs in waiting and obtaining service on the other hand, the potential customers have to decide whether to join the waiting line or to leave. Different customers may have different time costs, and it is assumed that the firm knows the distribution of time costs of its potential customers.

It is assumed that both the firm and the customers are risk neutral, so that they consider only expected profit and expected net benefits, ignoring possible risk aversion.

Let R be the benefit to each customer from obtaining the service. It is assumed that R is measured in dollars (R is identical for all customers). We denote by P the price charged for the service. Let C be the alternative cost of a unit of time for a specific customer, and let W be the expected waiting time (the waiting time includes both the time spent in queueing and in service). If U is the net benefit, we find

$$U = R - WC - P. \tag{1}$$

A specific customer decides to obtain service if U is positive; otherwise he just balks. Thus the customer obtains service if

$$C \leqq (R - P)/W; \tag{2}$$

R, P, and W are assumed to be the same for all customers and that only C varies among customers.

The customers arrive randomly with a Poisson distribution at the rate of λ per unit of time. The cost per unit of time C is distributed according to $F(C)$, with $f(C)$ being the density function. For given values of P and W, the proportion of customers actually obtaining service is $F[(R - P)/W]$. Therefore the number of customers obtaining service per unit of time is $F[(R - P)/W] \cdot \lambda$.

In the present model it is assumed that the customers decide whether to obtain service or to balk without actually observing the situation at a given time but rather on the basis of the expected waiting time. Due to transaction costs the customer does not abandon the waiting line after arrival even if there are numerous customers ahead of him. This is, as an example, the situation in computer services. (A customer decides whether to obtain service from a specific computing center according to its long-run performance and not according to the situation at a particular time.)

The service is supplied by a single firm with a single channel. The service time is distributed exponentially with a parameter v. The mean of service time is $1/v$.

Thus, the expected steady state waiting time (including the service) is [see Saaty (1959, p. 347)]

$$W = 1/(v - \tilde{\lambda}), \quad \text{where} \quad \tilde{\lambda} = \lambda F[(R - P)/W]. \tag{3}$$

Without loss of generality we may choose the time unit so that $\lambda = 1$.

The cost of the firm is assumed to be a funtion of its speed of service. Let $g(v)$ be the cost of supplying service with exponential distribution with a parameter v. The cost function $g(v)$ is assumed to be a nondecreasing function of v. For higher v the firm thus has to invest more resources in supplying faster service. We ignore the part of the cost associated with the actual number of customers requesting service. Therefore $\tilde{\lambda}$ does not appear as a parameter in the cost function.

The aim of the monopoly supplying the service is to maximize

$$\pi = PF\left[(R - P)/W\right] - g(v). \tag{4}$$

Denoting $(R - P)/W = \beta$, we can rewrite equation (4) as

$$\pi = PF(\beta) - g(v). \tag{4'}$$

The firm has two parameters at its disposal in its aim to maximize profits. These parameters can be either P and v or β and v. Thus for a given v, by determining P, the expected waiting time W is determined using (3). Alternatively, for a given v, by determining β using (3), we find

$$W = 1/\left[v - F(\beta)\right] \quad \text{and} \quad P = R - W\beta. \tag{3'}$$

In most of the analysis we take β and v to be the independent variables. The aim of the monopoly is then to maximize

$$\pi(\beta, v) = F(\beta)(R - W\beta) - g(v). \tag{5}$$

The first-order conditions for maximization are

$$\partial\pi/\partial\beta = f(\beta)(R - W\beta) - F(\beta)\,\partial W/\partial\beta\,\beta - F(\beta)W = 0, \tag{6}$$

$$\partial\pi/\partial v = -F(\beta)\beta\,\partial W/\partial v - g'(v) = 0. \tag{7}$$

Using $\partial W/\partial v = W^2$ and $\partial W/\partial\beta = W^2 f(\beta)$, we can rewrite (6) and (7) as

$$\partial\pi/\partial\beta = f(\beta)R - W\beta f(\beta) - F(\beta)\beta W^2 f(\beta) - F(\beta)W = 0, \tag{6'}$$

$$\partial\pi/\partial v = F(\beta)\beta W^2 - g'(v) = 0. \tag{7'}$$

Let us now assume that the service is supplied by a social agency with the aim of maximizing social welfare. The aim of the agency should then be to maximize

$$\theta(\beta, v) = RF(\beta) - F(\beta)W \int_0^\beta \frac{Cf(C)}{F(\beta)}\,dC - g(v). \tag{8}$$

$F(\beta)$ is the stream of customers requesting and receiving service. The second term on the RHS of (8) gives the expected cost of waiting for all consumers requiring service. The third term gives the direct cost of the agency for supplying service at a rate v per unit of time. The service outlay of the consumer is looked upon as a transfer payment and therefore does not enter (8).

The first-order conditions for maximization with respect to β and v are

$$\partial\theta/\partial\beta = f(\beta)R - \partial W/\partial\beta \int_0^\beta Cf(C)\,dC - W\beta f(\beta) = 0, \tag{9}$$

$$\partial\theta/\partial v = -\partial W/\partial v \int_0^\beta Cf(C)\,dC - g'(v) = 0. \tag{10}$$

Simplifying as before, we find

$$\partial\theta/\partial\beta = R - W\beta - W^2 \int_0^\beta Cf(C)\,dC = 0, \tag{9'}$$

$$\partial\theta/\partial v = W^2 \int_0^\beta Cf(C)\,dC - g'(v) = 0. \tag{10'}$$

Using (9′) and (10′), we find

$$P = R - W\beta = g'(v). \tag{11}$$

So in a social optimal setting the service price equals the marginal cost of v. Increasing v by a unit means that the firm is able to supply an expected extra unit of service and this should equal the price of a unit of service P. This is somewhat surprising, since usually with externalities the social optimal price should be equal to marginal cost plus the marginal extra external cost to society. To see the reason for this, notice that from (9′) we find that

$$P = R - W\beta = W^2 \int_0^\beta Cf(C)\,dC. \tag{12}$$

The RHS of (12) is the marginal social cost of an extra unit of λ. So the price, in fact, equals the marginal social costs. Equation (10′) on the other hand yields $g'(v) = W^2 \int_0^\beta Cf(C)\,dC$, i.e. the marginal cost of increasing v equals the marginal social benefit due to an increase in v. In our queueing framework, since $\partial W/\partial v = -\partial W/\partial\lambda$, the marginal social cost (with respect to λ) equals the marginal social benefit (of an extra v). Therefore we find that the price equals the marginal cost of v.[1]

3. COMPARISON BETWEEN MONOPOLY AND THE SOCIAL OPTIMAL CASE

Intuitively it is hard to infer whether the monopoly price is higher or lower than the social optimal price. This is also the case in comparing capacity v, expected waiting time W, and the proportion of customers obtaining service β.

---

[1] In this paper we ignore the cost associated with supplying the service. If we have an additional cost $h(F(\beta))$ associated with supplying a service to a "stream" of $F(\beta)$ customers, then the social optimal price is $P = h'[F(\beta)] + g'(v) = h'[F(\beta)] + W^2 \int_0^\beta Cf(C)\,dC$. Thus the price equals the sum of direct marginal cost and the social marginal cost, or the sum of the firm marginal costs.

In comparing monopoly with the social optimal setting, notice that on integrating by parts, we find

$$\theta(\beta, v) = \pi(\beta, v) + W \int_0^\beta F(C) \, dC. \tag{13}$$

If we draw (Figure 1) in the (β, v) plane the sets of points solving (6′) and (7′), it is not hard to see that we obtain curves with positive slopes. We assume that the relative positions of these curves are such that the second-order conditions for maximization are fulfilled.

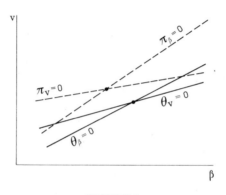

FIGURE 1

Similar considerations show that the slope and relative position [in the (β, v) plane] of the curves [equations (9′) and (10′)] hold for the social optimal maximization.

Using equation (13) we would like to show that the set of points [in the (β, v) plane] satisfying the equation $\pi_\beta = 0$ lies to the left of points satisfying $\theta_\beta = 0$. This is so, since

$$\theta_\beta = \pi_\beta + WF(\beta) + W^2 f(\beta) \int_0^\beta F(C) \, dC,$$

and at (β, v) such that $\pi_\beta = 0$, $\theta_\beta > 0$; hence by the second-order condition we have to increase β for $\theta_\beta = 0$.

Similar considerations will show us that $\pi_v = 0$ is above $\theta_v = 0$ [as $\theta_v = \pi_v - W^2 \int_0^\beta F(C) \, dC$].

Thus, as can be seen from Figure 1, the information about the relative location of $\theta_v = 0$, $\pi_v = 0$ and $\theta_\beta = 0$, $\pi_\beta = 0$ does not enable us to obtain definite results with regard to the size of β and v in both cases.

In fact, the only situation ruled out is for the monopoly β to be greater than that of the social optimal β, and at the same time v of the monopoly is smaller than that of the social optimal v. In Table I we show examples in

TABLE I

Comparisons of Social Optimum and Monopoly: P, v, β, W

$R = 10; g(v) = v^2$

C_0	γ	Social optimal P	Monopoly P	Social optimal v	Monopoly v	Social optimal β	Monopoly β	Social optimal W	Monopoly W
1	1.8	3.27	7.14	1.64	1.44	4.7	2.1	1.43	1.39
4.75	1.8	2.91	2.61	1.45	0.88	6.87	5.27	0.42	0.23
0.1	2.5	2.52	9.07	1.25	1.28	1.9	0.32	3.9	2.9
2	2	3.47	6.10	1.7	1.4	5.6	3.2	1.16	1.20
5	10	4.1	4.67	2.05	1.75	6.57	5.62	0.90	0.95
0.3	2.5	2.8	8.5	1.41	1.40	2.97	0.76	2.41	2.02

which β, v, W, and P under monopoly and the social optimal setting have various relationships. For the calculations we assumed a known simple cost function. We assumed that the cost of time distributed according to a Pareto distribution with a density function

$$f(C) = \gamma C^\gamma C^{-(\gamma+1)}, \qquad C \geq C_0 > 0. \tag{14}$$

The benefit from the service is $R = 10$ in all calculations. In the various calculations we change the parameters C_0 and γ of the Pareto distribution.

We find that no general propositions are possible. The price charged by the monopolist may be higher (in most of our examples) or lower. The investment in speed of service may be lower or higher. The expected waiting time is also ambiguous.[2] Thus in a case of two decision variables P (or β) and v, the classical results of comparing monopoly and the social optimal levels of these variables are ambiguous.[3]

4. REGULATION OF MONOPOLY

As is well known in the classical discussion of the regulation of monopoly, one of the methods to deal with the distortion created by the monopoly is to determine a maximal price at the level of the social optimal price. In the classical case this price regulation induces the monopoly to produce the social optimal output. In our case this is not so, as we also have to consider the determination of the speed of service v. In fact it is possible to prove that with the price determined at the social optimal level the monopolist v will be lower than the social optimal one. The social optimal price P^* by equation (11) satisfies $P^* = g'(v^*)$ (where v^* is the social optimal level of v). Thus the aim of a regulated monopoly is to maximize

$$\max_{v} \pi(v) = P^*F(\beta) - g(v), \tag{15}$$

where

$$\beta = (R - P^*)/W = (R - P^*)[v - F(\beta)]. \tag{16}$$

Notice that by (16) β is an implicit function of v (for a given P^*). The first-order condition for maximization is

$$\frac{\partial \pi}{\partial v} = P^*f(\beta)\frac{\partial \beta}{\partial v} - g'(v) = 0. \tag{17}$$

---

[2] In none of the examples calculated did we succeed in finding a higher β for the monopolist. Thus in all our examples the proportion of customers served by the monopolist is smaller than that under the social optimal settings. We were not able to prove this as a general theorem.

[3] In certain special cases of $f(C)$, e.g. a uniform distribution, it is possible to prove that the v of a monopoly is smaller while β is also smaller and P higher than the social optimal levels.

Using (16), we find

$$\frac{\partial \beta}{\partial v} = \frac{R - P^*}{1 + (R - P^*)f(\beta)}. \tag{18}$$

Substituting in (17), we find

$$\frac{\partial \pi}{\partial v} = \frac{P^*f(\beta)(R - P^*)}{1 + (R - P^*)f(\beta)} - g'(v) = 0 \tag{19}$$

$$\left(\frac{1}{f(\beta)(R - P^*)} + 1\right)^{-1} = \frac{g'(v)}{P^*}. \tag{20}$$

Using $P^* = g'(v^*)$, we find that $g'(v)/g'(v^*) < 1$. Assume $g''(v) > 0$; this implies $v < v^*$.[4]

In fact, in most of the examples calculated we find that this kind of price regulation reduces welfare (compared with nonregulated monopoly). As an example with $R = 10$ and $C_0 = 1$, $\gamma = 1.5$, $g(v) = v^2 - 0.5$; then the social optimum welfare is $\theta = 4.64$. With nonregulated monopoly we find $\theta = 4.03$. With regulated monopoly we find $\theta = 3.29$.

In fact, for an efficient regulation we need to regulate both the price and the speed of service of the monopoly. It turns out that we need a combination of an appropriate price subsidy and a tax on investment in v in order to achieve the social optimal level of service. The result is independent of whether the monopolist v is greater or less than that of the social optimal level of v or whether the monopolist price P is lower or higher.

Let s be the subsidy per unit of service and t the tax per unit of v (so that vt is the sum of tax collected). The aim of the monopolist is to maximize

$$\pi(\beta, v) = F(\beta)[R - W\beta + s] - g(v) - tv. \tag{21}$$

The first-order conditions are

$$\partial \pi / \partial \beta = f(\beta)[R - W\beta + s] - F(\beta)\,\partial W/\partial \beta\, \beta - F(\beta)W = 0, \tag{22}$$

$$\partial \pi / \partial v = -F(\beta)\beta\,\partial W/\partial v - g'(v) - t = 0. \tag{23}$$

These equations can be rewritten as

$$R - W\beta + s - F(\beta)\beta W^2 - [F(\beta)/f(\beta)]W = 0, \tag{24}$$

$$W^2 \beta F(\beta) - t = g'(v). \tag{25}$$

---

[4] With a linear $g(v)$, we have $g'(v)/g'(v^*) = 1$; but as can be seen from (20), in this case we obtain a boundary solution for v with $v = 0$.

Integrating by parts, we can rewrite the condition for social optimum as

$$R - W\beta - W^2 F(\beta)\beta + W^2 \int_0^\beta F(C)\,dC = 0, \tag{9''}$$

$$W^2 F(\beta)\beta - W^2 \int_0^\beta F(C)\,dC = g'(v). \tag{10''}$$

Observing (24)–(25) and (9'')–(10''), we find that by setting

$$s = \frac{F(\beta^*)W^*}{f(\beta^*)} + W^{*2} \int_0^{\beta^*} F(C)\,dC, \tag{26}$$

$$t = W^{*2} \int_0^{\beta^*} F(C)\,dC \tag{27}$$

(where β^*, W^*, and v^* denote the social optimal level of the variables), the solution of (24) and (25) is identical to the social optimal solution $[(9'')$ and $(10'')]$. Notice that $s > 0$ and $t > 0$. In fact,

$$s = \frac{F(\beta^*)W^*}{f(\beta^*)} + t. \tag{28}$$

The results are independent of the relative magnitudes of v and P (under monopoly and the social optimum).

Thus we find that in the case of multidecision variables the regulator has to find a mixed policy to induce the monopoly to produce a social optimal output.[5]

REFERENCE

Saaty, T. L. (1959). *Mathematical Methods of Operation Research*. New York: McGraw-Hill.

[5] As an example with $R = 10$, $C_0 = 1$, $\gamma = 1.5$, we find that for a social optimum, $P = 3.231$ and $\beta = 4.644$. The same is achieved by a monopoly with $s = 48.5$ and $t = 5.39$.

Identification and estimation problems in limited dependent variable models

G. S. MADDALA

UNIVERSITY OF FLORIDA
GAINESVILLE

1. INTRODUCTION

There have been, in recent years, a large number of studies using limited dependent variable models starting with the simple Tobit models to the censored regression model discussed by Nelson (1975), the simultaneous equations model considered by Heckman (1974) and its extensions by Hanoch (1975), the disequilibrium models discussed by Fair and Jaffe (1972), Maddala and Nelson (1974), and Goldfeld and Quandt (1975), and several other such models. The purpose of this paper is to bring all these models together and discuss the identification and estimation problems in a unified framework. This enhances an understanding of these models and their interrelationships.

2. THE SIMPLE PROBIT MODEL

Consider a regression model

$$Y_t^* = X_t\beta + u_t, \tag{1}$$

where u_t are $\text{IN}(0, \sigma^2)$.

Financial support from the National Science Foundation under grant SOC-76-04356 to the University of Florida is gratefully acknowledged.

Suppose Y_t^* is not observed. Instead we observe the dichotomous variable Y_t defined as

$$Y_t = 1 \qquad \text{iff} \qquad Y_t^* \geq 0 \Rightarrow u_t \geq -X_t\beta,$$
$$ = 0 \qquad \text{iff} \qquad Y_t^* < 0 \Rightarrow u_t < -X_t\beta. \qquad (2)$$

The condition $u_t \geq -X_t\beta$ can be written as $u_t/\sigma \geq -X_t(\beta/\sigma)$, and u_t/σ has a standard normal distribution.

The likelihood function for this model is

$$L = \prod_{Y_t=0} F\left(-X_t\frac{\beta}{\sigma}\right) \prod_{Y_t=1} \left[1 - F\left(-X_t\frac{\beta}{\sigma}\right)\right], \qquad (3)$$

where $F(\cdot)$ is the cumulative distribution function for the standard normal density.

Clearly, β and σ are not separately estimable in this model. It is only β/σ that is estimable. Hence, σ is often fixed at the value 1. It is also customary to use a *logit* model in this case. The logit model assumes that the residuals u_i have a sech^2 distribution (rather than the normal) given by

$$f(u) = e^u/(1 + e^u)^2 \qquad (-\infty < u < \infty). \qquad (4)$$

The cumulative distribution function for this is the logistic

$$F(Z) = e^Z/(1 + e^Z). \qquad (5)$$

If this model is used, the relations (2) yield the likelihood function

$$L = \prod_{Y_t=0} \left(\frac{e^{-X_t\beta}}{1 + e^{-X_t\beta}}\right) \prod_{Y_t=1} \left(\frac{1}{1 + e^{-X_t\beta}}\right). \qquad (6)$$

In this formulation the factor σ does not appear *explicitly*. This is because the sech^2 distribution has variance $\pi^2/3$. Both the cumulative normal and the logistic distribution have the same shape except that they deviate slightly at the tails. Hence, unless there are a lot of extreme observations, the results obtained from both the "probit" and "logit" models[1] will be the same. However, while comparing the numerical results one should take account of the normalizing value of σ. In the probit model we obtain the coefficients β/σ. In the logit model we get the estimates of β but assuming $\sigma^2 = \pi^2/3$. Hence the estimates of β obtained from the logit model have to be multiplied by $\sqrt{3}/\pi$ to be comparable to the estimates obtained from the probit model (where we normalize σ to be equal to 1).

---

[1] See Goldberger (1964, p. 250). The terminology may not be exactly appropriate because the term "probit" is used by biometricians to denote something else. Nevertheless, this is the accepted terminology which we shall maintain.

All this discussion is assuming that the threshold value in (2) is zero. If we have different known threshold values c_t, then equation (2) reads

$$
\begin{aligned}
Y_t &= 1 \qquad \text{iff} \quad Y_t^* \geq c_t \quad \text{or} \quad u_t \geq c_t - X_t\beta, \\
&= 0 \qquad \text{iff} \quad Y_t^* < c_t \quad \text{or} \quad u_t < c_t - X_t\beta.
\end{aligned}
\tag{7}
$$

In this case the likelihood function (3) is

$$
L = \prod_{Y_t = 0} F\left(\frac{c_t - X_t\beta}{\sigma}\right) \prod_{Y_t = 1} \left[1 - F\left(\frac{c_t - X_t\beta}{\sigma}\right)\right].
\tag{8}
$$

Now $1/\sigma$ and β/σ are estimable (as coefficients of c_t and $-X_t$ respectively). Hence we get estimates of both σ and β. Thus, both the parameters are identified.

An interesting example of the application of the variable threshold is a study on implicit discount rates by Gilman (1976). Using data on employees who have or have not joined the TIAA–CREF program, he tried to estimate the implicit personal discount rates. For each individual, c_t is the rate of return offered by the plan and Y_t^* is the implicit discount rate. If $Y_t^* < c_t$, the individual joins TIAA–CREF; otherwise he does not. The model is

$$
Y_t^* = X_t\beta + u_t,
$$

where X_t are individual characteristics such as age, sex, race, and education. Y_t^* are not observed and in fact in this problem it is the predicted values of Y_t^* for different characteristics X_t which are our main concern. What we observe is the dummy variable—whether or not the individual has participated in TIAA–CREF.

In actual practice there are fast computer routines available to maximize the likelihood functions (3) or (8) by iterative procedures, and it has been found that the iterations converge rapidly, because the likelihood function for this simple probit model is globally concave.

3. THE TOBIT MODEL

An immediate extension of the model considered in the previous section is the following model first discussed by Tobin (1958).

The observed Y_t is defined by

$$
\begin{aligned}
Y_t &= Y_t^* \qquad \text{if} \quad Y_t^* > 0, \\
&= 0 \qquad\quad \text{otherwise.}
\end{aligned}
\tag{9}
$$

The threshold value in (9) can be a known constant c_t instead of 0. This model was called the Tobit (Tobin's probit) model by Goldberger (1964,

p. 253). The likelihood function for this model is

$$L = \prod_{Y_t > 0} (1/\sigma)f(X_t\beta/\sigma) \prod_{Y_t = 0} F(-X_t\beta/\sigma), \tag{10}$$

where $f(\cdot)$ is the standard normal density function. Now the availability of some observations on Y_t^* enables us to estimate both β and σ even if the threshold value is 0. The Tobit model has been widely applied. But in almost all economic applications, a more meaningful model is one in which the threshold itself is a random variable. These models are considered in greater detail in Section 5.

Amemiya (1973) proved the consistency of the ML estimates in the Tobit model and suggested initial consistent estimates to start the iterations for the ML estimation. He criticized the initial estimates suggested by Tobin saying that they are inconsistent. Recently, Olsen (1976) has demonstrated that if the parameters β and σ are reparametrized to β/σ and $1/\sigma$, the resulting likelihood function is globally concave and thus, even if the initial estimates are not consistent, one converges to the (unique) global maximum of the likelihood function. Thus, there is no advantage in using Amemiya's consistent estimates as opposed to Tobin's inconsistent estimates as initial values in the iterative process. However, one important argument for having initial consistent estimates is that one can use them in a one-step iteration of the ML equations in Newton's method. The resulting estimator is a linearized ML estimator which, in general, has the asymptotic distribution as the ML estimator.

Amemiya's procedure for obtaining initial consistent estimates is as follows: Consider the model given by equations (1) and (9) and the *nonzero* observations Y_t:

$$E(Y_t|Y_t > 0) = X_t\beta + E(u_t|u_t > -X_t\beta) = X_t\beta + \sigma(f_t/F_t), \tag{11}$$

where

$$f_t = f(X_t\beta/\sigma) \qquad \text{and} \qquad F_t = F(X_t\beta/\sigma). \tag{12}$$

Also, $E(Y_t^2|Y_t > 0) = X_t\beta E(Y_t) + \sigma^2$ which we can write as

$$Y_t^2 = X_t Y_t\beta + \sigma^2 + \eta_t \qquad \text{where} \quad E(\eta_t) = 0. \tag{13}$$

This equation, however, cannot be estimated by ordinary least squares since $\text{cov}(\eta_t, X_t Y_t) \neq 0$. What Amemiya suggests is to regress Y_t on X_t, X_t^2, etc., get $\hat{Y}_t$, and use $X_t\hat{Y}_t$ as instrumental variables to estimate equation (13).

An alternative procedure first used by Heckman (1975a,b) is the following: Since the likelihood function for the probit model is well-behaved, we define a dummy variable

$$I_t = 1 \qquad \text{if} \quad Y_t^* > 0,$$
$$= 0 \qquad \text{otherwise.}$$

Then, using the probit model, we get consistent estimates of β/σ. Using these, we get estimated values $\hat{f}_t$ and $\hat{F}_t$ of f_t and F_t respectively. Now we get consistent estimates of β and σ, using equation (11), by regressing Y_t on X_t and $\hat{f}_t/\hat{F}_t$.

Instead of using only the nonzero observations on Y_t, we can use all the observations (zero and nonzero). In this case [see Lee (1976)],

$$E(Y_t) = F_t X_t \beta + \sigma f_t, \tag{11'}$$

so that, after getting a consistent estimate of β/σ from the probit model and constructing $\hat{f}_t$ and $\hat{F}_t$, we now use (11') and regress Y_t on $\hat{F}_t X_t$ and $\hat{f}_t$ to get consistent estimates of β and σ.

4. SIMPLE EXTENSIONS OF THE TOBIT MODEL

There have been some straightforward extensions of the simple Tobit model. One of them—the two-decision model—is similar in spirit to the "twin linear probability model" discussed by Goldberger (1964, p. 252). Take for example the demand for automobiles. First, a probit model is fitted to the data based on the information—purchase or no-purchase. Next, a usual linear regression model is estimated from the data for the individuals that made the purchase. If Y is the amount of purchase,

$$P(Y > 0) = F(X\beta_1/\sigma_1) \quad \text{and} \quad E(Y|Y > 0) = Z\beta_2. \tag{14}$$

X and Z may be the same or different variables. Such two-decision models were considered by Cragg (1971). The major limitation of these two-decision models is that the decision of whether or not to buy and how much to buy are usually interrelated—not independent.

Some other extensions of the simple Tobit model are the "friction model" discussed by Rosett (1959) and the "two-limit probit model" discussed by Rosett and Nelson (1975). The "friction" model is one in which the dependent variable responds only to large changes in the explanatory variables. The model can be written as

$$Y_t^* = X_t \beta + u_t \quad \text{where} \quad u_t \sim IN(0, \sigma^2).$$

The observed variable Y_t is

$$\begin{aligned}
Y_t &= Y_t^* - \alpha_1 && \text{if} \quad Y_t^* < \alpha_1, \\
&= 0 && \text{if} \quad \alpha_1 < Y_t^* < \alpha_2, \\
&= Y_t^* - \alpha_2 && \text{if} \quad Y_t^* > \alpha_2.
\end{aligned} \tag{15}$$

The likelihood function is

$$L = \prod_1 \frac{1}{\sigma} f\left(\frac{Y_t + \alpha_1 - X_t\beta}{\sigma}\right) \prod_2 \left[F\left(\frac{\alpha_2 - X_t\beta}{\sigma}\right) - F\left(\frac{\alpha_1 - X_t\beta}{\sigma}\right)\right]$$

$$\times \prod_3 \frac{1}{\sigma} f\left(\frac{Y_t + \alpha_2 - X_t\beta}{\sigma}\right). \tag{16}$$

The model provides for a different intercept in the two sets of continuous observations. One can easily change the slope coefficient as well as error variances in the two continuous regimes by making suitable changes in (15) and defining two underlying functions Y_1^* and Y_2^*. This will result in minor changes in the likelihood function (16). This model is useful in analyzing dividend policies, changes in wage offers by firms, and similar examples in which firms do not respond in a continuous fashion but respond by jumps after a certain cumulative effort.

The "two-limit probit" model of Rosett and Nelson (1975) is the following[2]:

$$Y_t^* = X_t\beta + u_t,$$

$$Y_t = L_{1t} \quad \text{if} \quad Y_t^* < L_{1t},$$
$$= Y_t^* \quad \text{if} \quad L_{1t} \leq Y_t^* \leq L_{2t},$$
$$= L_{2t} \quad \text{if} \quad Y_t^* > L_{2t}.$$

The likelihood function for this model is

$$L = \prod_1 F\left(\frac{L_{1t} - X_t\beta}{\sigma}\right) \prod_2 \frac{1}{\sigma} f\left(\frac{Y_t - X_t\beta}{\sigma}\right) \prod_3 \left[1 - F\left(\frac{L_{2t} - X_t\beta}{\sigma}\right)\right].$$

An example of a problem to which this model has been applied is the demand for health insurance by people on medicare. A certain minimum coverage (the lower threshold) is provided to all participants. They may purchase supplemental insurance only up to some maximum that falls short of full coverage.

None of these models pose any special identification problems or problems with numerical computations. Identification problems arise when we start making the thresholds stochastic. For instance, Dagenais (1969) tries to introduce stochastic elements into the friction model considered by Rosett. Thus, in equations (15) we can make α_1 and α_2 stochastic by writing

$$\alpha_1^* = \alpha_1 + V_{1t}, \qquad \alpha_2^* = \alpha_2 + V_{2t},$$

where V_{1t}, V_{2t} have a bivariate normal distribution with variances σ_1^2, σ_2^2 respectively and correlation coefficient ζ. It is easy to verify that these parameters are not identified without some restrictions. Not realizing this,

---

[2] This model was also discussed by Johnson (1972).

Dagenais (1975) discusses the computational problems he encountered in the maximization of the likelihood function and finally says he fixed $\zeta = 0$ and $\sigma_1{}^2 = \sigma_2{}^2$. The notation of Dagenais (1969, 1975) is rather awkward and messy, and since the problem he considered can be analyzed more elegantly by alternative stochastic threshold models considered by Nelson (1975) and Lee (1976), we will discuss this formulation rather than the stochastic version of the friction model.

5. STOCHASTIC THRESHOLD MODELS

Consider again the problem of demand for automobiles. If y is expenditure and X the set of explanatory variables, a naive Tobit model[3] would be to define

$$y = \beta'X + \varepsilon \quad \text{if} \quad y > 0,$$
$$= 0 \quad \text{otherwise.}$$

The problem with this formulation is that the threshold zero does not make sense. The prices at which cars can be purchased run in thousands of dollars for new cars and hundreds of dollars for used cars. Further, the threshold will be different for different individuals. The Cragg two-decision model given by (14) does not solve this problem either. An alternative and more meaningful formulation is the following: Let y_1 denote the expenditures the family can afford to make and y_2 the value of the minimum acceptable car to the family (the threshold value). The actual expenditure y will then be defined as

$$y = y_1 \quad \text{iff} \quad y_1 \geq y_2,$$
$$= 0 \quad \text{otherwise.} \tag{17}$$

Note that y_2 is never observed. Both y_1 and y_2 will be functions of some explanatory variables so that we can write

$$y_1 = \beta_1'X_1 + \varepsilon_1, \qquad y_2 = \beta_2'X_2 + \varepsilon_2, \tag{18}$$

where $\varepsilon_1, \varepsilon_2$ have a bivariate normal distribution with variances $\sigma_1{}^2, \sigma_2{}^2$ and covariance σ_{12}. This is the model considered by Nelson (1975, 1976). Some other examples of applications for this model given by Nelson are bank-borrowing behavior and wage and labor supply equations. In the case of bank borrowing, one hears of the "needs versus reluctance" hypothesis which argues that banks are reluctant to frequent the discount window too

---

[3] Such naive Tobit models though not very meaningful are common in the literature. See for instance its application in the demand for housing by Poirier (1974). For a more meaningful formulation of the same problem see Trost (1976).

often for fear of adverse sanctions from the Federal Reserve.[4] One can define y_2 as the threshold level below which banks will not use the discount window. y_1 is the desired borrowings. The structure of this model is somewhat different from that given in equation (17) because we observe y_1 all the time. We do not observe y_2 but we know for each observation whether $y_1 > y_2$ (the bank borrows in the Federal funds market) or whether $y_1 \leq y_2$ (the bank borrows from the discount window).

The labor supply model is similar in structure to the durable goods model. Let y_1 be the market wage and y_2 the reservation wage for the individual. If $y_1 \geq y_2$, we observe that the individual is in the labor force and the observed wage is y_1. Otherwise the individual is not in the labor force and we do not observe y_1. In either case y_2 is not observed.

Unlike the models in the previous sections, these models pose some identification problems. Specifically, in the model given by equations (17) and (18) we can show that we have to impose either the condition $\sigma_{12} = 0$ or the condition that there is at least one explanatory variable in X_1 that does not occur in X_2. We can prove this result by considering the relevant reduced forms and examining what functions of the parameters are estimable.[5]

Since many of these models fall in the category of switching regression models with two regimes, we will first consider the identification and estimation problems in such models. Consider the model

$$y_t = \beta_1' X_{1t} + \varepsilon_{1t} \qquad \text{iff} \quad \alpha' Z_t \geq \varepsilon_t, \qquad (19)$$

$$y_t = \beta_2' X_{2t} + \varepsilon_{2t} \qquad \text{iff} \quad \alpha' Z_t < \varepsilon_t. \qquad (20)$$

The model is like a switching regression model considered by Goldfeld and Quandt (1973), but since ε_t is correlated with ε_{1t} and ε_{2t} we can call it a switching regression model with endogenous switching, as suggested by Maddala and Nelson (1975). We shall assume that ε_{1t}, ε_{2t}, and ε_t have a trivariate normal distribution with mean vector zero and covariance matrix Σ, which can be singular:

$$\Sigma = \begin{bmatrix} \sigma_1^2 & \sigma_{12} & \sigma_{1\varepsilon} \\ & \sigma_2^2 & \sigma_{2\varepsilon} \\ & & 1 \end{bmatrix}. \qquad (21)$$

The likelihood function for this model is

$$L(\beta_1, \beta_2, \gamma, \sigma_1^2, \sigma_2^2, \sigma_{1\varepsilon}, \sigma_{2\varepsilon})$$

$$= \prod \left[\int_{-\infty}^{\alpha' Z_t} g(y_t - \beta_1' X_{1t}, \varepsilon_t) \, d\varepsilon_t \right]^{I_t} \left[\int_{\alpha' Z_t}^{\infty} f(y_t - \beta_2' Z_{2t}, \varepsilon_t) \, d\varepsilon_t \right]^{1 - I_t}, \qquad (22)$$

---

[4] See e.g. Polakoff and Sibler (1967).
[5] For an alternative derivation of the identifiability conditions, see Nelson (1976).

where

$$I_t = 1 \qquad \text{if} \quad \gamma'Z_t \geq \varepsilon_t,$$
$$\quad = 0 \qquad \text{otherwise,} \tag{23}$$

and g and f are the bivariate normal density functions of ε_{1t}, ε_t and ε_{2t}, ε_t respectively. Note that σ_{12} does not occur at all in this expression and thus σ_{12} is not estimable. Only $\sigma_{1\varepsilon}$ and $\sigma_{2\varepsilon}$ are estimable. In the special case $\varepsilon_t = (\varepsilon_{1t} - \varepsilon_{2t})/\sigma$, where $\sigma^2 = \text{var}(\varepsilon_{1t} - \varepsilon_{2t})$, it can be easily verified that from the consistent estimates of σ_1^2, σ_2^2, $\sigma_{1\varepsilon}$, and $\sigma_{2\varepsilon}$, we can get a consistent estimate of σ_{12}. This is the case with the model considered in equations (17) and (18).

The maximization of the likelihood function (22) can be cumbersome in practice. Lee (1976) discusses a simple two-stage estimation method for this model as follows: Define the dichotomous variable I_t as in equation (23). Then using the probit method we can get consistent estimates of γ which will be used in further analysis:

Define

$$u_{1t} = f(\gamma'Z_t)/F(\gamma'Z_t) \qquad \text{and} \qquad u_{2t} = f(\gamma'Z_t)/(1 - F(\gamma'Z_t)), \tag{24}$$

where $f(\cdot)$ and $F(\cdot)$ are the density function and the distribution function of the standard normal. Then we have the relations[6]

$$E(\varepsilon_{1t}|I_t = 1) = -\sigma_{1\varepsilon}u_{1t},$$
$$E(\varepsilon_{1t}^2|I_t = 1) = \sigma_1^2 - \sigma_{1\varepsilon}^2(\gamma'Z_t)u_{1t}, \tag{25}$$
$$E(\varepsilon_{2t}|I_t = 0) = \sigma_{2\varepsilon}u_{2t},$$
$$E(\varepsilon_{2t}^2|I_t = 0) = \sigma_2^2 + \sigma_{2\varepsilon}^2(\gamma'Z_t)u_{2t}. \tag{26}$$

Hence

$$E(y_t|I_t = 1) = \beta_1'X_{1t} - \sigma_{1\varepsilon}u_{1t}, \tag{27}$$
$$E(y_t|I_t = 0) = \beta_2'X_{2t} + \sigma_{2\varepsilon}u_{2t}. \tag{28}$$

These equations can be written as

$$y_t = \beta_1'X_{1t} - \sigma_{1\varepsilon}u_{1t} + \eta_{1t} \qquad \text{for} \quad I_t = 1, \tag{29}$$
$$y_t = \beta_2'X_{2t} + \sigma_{2\varepsilon}u_{2t} + \eta_{2t} \qquad \text{for} \quad I_t = 0, \tag{30}$$

where $E(\eta_{1t}|I_t = 1) = E(\eta_{2t}|I_t = 0) = 0$,

$$\text{var}(\eta_{1t}|I_t = 1) = \sigma_1^2 - \sigma_{1\varepsilon}^2u_{1t}(\gamma'Z_t + u_{1t}), \tag{31}$$
$$\text{var}(\eta_{2t}|I_t = 0) = \sigma_2^2 + \sigma_{2\varepsilon}^2u_{2t}(\gamma'Z_t - u_{2t}). \tag{32}$$

---

[6] These are well-known formulas for moments of the truncated normal. See e.g. Johnson and Kotz (1972, pp. 112–113).

The estimation procedure is the following. Using data as I_t, obtain a consistent estimate $\hat{\gamma}$ of γ using the probit method. Then construct $\hat{u}_{1t}$, $\hat{u}_{2t}$ by substituting $\hat{\gamma}$ for γ in (24). Next estimate (29) and (30) by ordinary least squares by regressing y_t on X_{1t} and $\hat{u}_{1t}$ for the subset of observations for which $I_t = 1$ and y_t on X_{2t} and $\hat{u}_{2t}$ for the subset of observations for which $I_t = 0$ to obtain consistent estimates $\hat{\beta}_1$, $\hat{\beta}_2$ of β_1 and β_2. Next compute

$$\hat{\varepsilon}_{1t} = y_t - \hat{\beta}_1' X_{1t} \qquad \text{for the set} \quad I_t = 1, \tag{33}$$

$$\hat{\varepsilon}_{2t} = y_t - \hat{\beta}_2' X_{2t} \qquad \text{for the set} \quad I_t = 0, \tag{34}$$

and regress $\hat{\varepsilon}_{1t}^2$ on $(\hat{\gamma}'Z_t)\hat{u}_{1t}$ and $\hat{\varepsilon}_{2t}^2$ on $(\hat{\gamma}'Z_t)\hat{u}_{2t}$ to get consistent estimates of $\sigma_1{}^2$, $\sigma_{1\varepsilon}$, and $\sigma_2{}^2$, $\sigma_{2\varepsilon}$ respectively [see equations (25) and (26)].

Thus, we get consistent estimates of all the parameters (except σ_{12} which is not estimable). These estimates can be used either as final estimates or as starting values for a one-step Newton iteration in the computation of maximum likelihood estimates. They can also be used in the computation of weighted least squares estimates from (29) and (30). Note that the residuals in equations (29) and (30) do not have constant variances. Their variances are given by (31) and (32) which can be estimated from the previously mentioned initial consistent estimates. Using these estimated variances, one can use a weighted least squares procedure to get more efficient estimates of the parameters in (29) and (30).

One can also combine equations (29) and (30) and write the unconditional expectation of y_t as

$$E(y_t) = E(y_t|I_t = 1) \ P(I_t = 1) + E(y_t|I_t = 0) \ P(I_t = 0)$$
$$= \beta_1' X_{1t} F_t + \beta_2' X_{2t}(1 - F_t) + (\sigma_{2\varepsilon} - \sigma_{1\varepsilon})f_t, \tag{35}$$

where $f_t = f(\gamma'Z_t)$ and $F_t = F(\gamma'Z_t)$. Thus, regressing y_t or $X_{1t}F_t$, $X_{2t}(1 - F_t)$, and f_t, we get consistent estimates of β_1, β_2, and $(\sigma_{2\varepsilon} - \sigma_{1\varepsilon})$. Then using (33), (34), (25), and (26) we get consistent estimates of $\sigma_1{}^2$, $\sigma_2{}^2$, $\sigma_{1\varepsilon}$, and $\sigma_{2\varepsilon}$. If we write

$$y_t = E(y_t) + W_t, \tag{36}$$

where $E(y_t)$ is given by (35), then $E(W_t) = 0$ and var(W_t) can be evaluated once we have consistent estimates of all the parameters. Hence, again one can estimate the parameters in (35) by a weighted least squares method.

Consider now the model given by equations (17) and (18). We have

$$\gamma'Z_t = \frac{\beta_1' X_{1t} - \beta_2' X_{2t}}{\sigma} \qquad \text{and} \qquad \varepsilon_t = \frac{\varepsilon_{2t} - \varepsilon_{1t}}{\sigma},$$

where $\sigma^2 = \sigma_1{}^2 + \sigma_2{}^2 - 2\sigma_{12}$. Thus, from the probit regression model (based on the dichotomous variable I_t), we get consistent estimates of β_{1j}/σ and

β_{2j}/σ for the elements of β_1 and β_2 corresponding to nonoverlapping variables in X_1 and X_2, and $(\beta_{1k} - \beta_{2k})/\sigma$ corresponding to the common variables in X_1 and X_2. Next from equation (29) we can get consistent estimates of β_1 and $\sigma_{1\varepsilon} = (\sigma_{12} - \sigma_1^2)/\sigma$. Since we now have estimates of all the elements of β_1, if there is at least one variable in X_1 not included in X_2, then, from the estimate of β_{1j}/σ corresponding to this variable, we now get a consistent estimate of σ and hence consistent estimates of all the elements of β_2. Next we use equations (33) and (25) as before to get a consistent estimate of σ_1^2, and given estimates of σ, σ_1^2, and $\sigma_{1\varepsilon}$, we can now get an estimate of σ_{12}. Finally, from an estimate of σ^2, we can get an estimate of σ_2^2. Thus, all parameters are estimable.

Alternatively, if $\sigma_{12} = 0$, we have $\sigma^2 = \sigma_1^2 + \sigma_2^2$ and $\sigma_{1\varepsilon} = -\sigma_1^2/\sigma$. From the estimates of $(\beta_1 - \beta_2)/\sigma$ obtained from the probit regression, β_1 and σ_1^2/σ from equation (29), and σ_1^2 from equations (33) and (25), we can get estimates of all the parameters. Finally, the likelihood function for this model is

$$L(\beta_1, \beta_2, \sigma_1^2, \sigma_2^2, \sigma_{12}) = \prod_t \left[\int_{-\infty}^{g_{2t}} f(g_{1t}, \varepsilon_{2t}) \, d\varepsilon_{2t} \right]^{I_t} [(1 - F_t)]^{1 - I_t}, \quad (37)$$

where

$$g_{1t} = y_t - \beta_1' X_{1t}, \qquad g_{2t} = y_t - \beta_2' X_{2t}, \qquad F_t = F[(\beta_1' X_{1t} - \beta_2' X_{2t})/\sigma].$$

In his empirical work Nelson (1976) obtained the maximum likelihood estimates by maximizing the likelihood function (37). He had to impose the condition $\sigma_{12} = 0$ since all the variables in X_1 were also included in X_2 in his model.

A more general formulation of the model given by equations (19) and (20) is the following model where the endogenous variables y_1 and y_2 occur in the choice function. This is the model considered by Westin (1975), for which Lee (1976) derived both the identifiability conditions as well as two-stage estimation methods:

$$\begin{aligned} y_{1t} = X_{1t}\beta_1 + \varepsilon_{1t} & \quad \text{iff} \quad Z_t\gamma + y_{1t}\zeta_1 + y_{2t}\zeta_2 \geq v_t, \\ y_{2t} = X_{2t}\beta_2 + \varepsilon_{2t} & \quad \text{iff} \quad Z_t\gamma + y_{1t}\zeta_1 + y_{2t}\zeta_2 < v_t. \end{aligned} \qquad (38)$$

We assume all the error terms are serially independent, normally distributed with zero mean and convariance matrix Σ,

$$\Sigma = \text{cov} \begin{bmatrix} \varepsilon_{1t} \\ \varepsilon_{2t} \\ v_t \end{bmatrix} = \begin{bmatrix} \sigma_1^2 & \sigma_{12} & \sigma_{1v} \\ \sigma_{21} & \sigma_2^2 & \sigma_{2v} \\ \sigma_{1v} & \sigma_{2v} & \sigma_v^2 \end{bmatrix}.$$

This model can be written as

$$y_{1t} = X_{1t}\beta_1 + \varepsilon_{1t} \quad \text{iff} \quad Z_t\frac{\gamma}{\sigma^*} \quad X_{1t}\frac{\zeta_1\beta_1}{\sigma^*} + X_{2t}\frac{\zeta_2\beta_2}{\sigma^*} \geq \varepsilon_t,$$

$$y_{2t} = X_{2t}\beta_2 + \varepsilon_{2t} \quad \text{iff} \quad Z_t\frac{\gamma}{\sigma^*} + X_{1t}\frac{\zeta_1\beta_1}{\sigma^*} + X_{2t}\frac{\zeta_2\beta_2}{\sigma^*} < \varepsilon_t,$$

$$(39)$$

where

$$\varepsilon_t = (1/\sigma^*)(v_t - \zeta_1\varepsilon_{1t} - \zeta_2\varepsilon_{2t}) \quad \text{and} \quad \sigma^{*2} = E(v_t - \zeta_1\varepsilon_{1t} - \zeta_2\varepsilon_{2t}). \quad (40)$$

As before, one can define a dichotomous variable I_t, apply the probit method to get estimates of the parameters of the criterion function, and then get consistent estimates of β_1 and β_2 from equations of the form (29) and (30). Thus, if y_1 and y_2 are observed, β_1, β_2, σ_1^2, and σ_2^2 are always estimable. The problem is with the estimation of the parameters in the criterion function in (39). On first sight it appears that γ/σ^*, ζ_1/σ^*, and ζ_2/σ^* are estimable. However, even these parameters cannot be identified easily without further restrictions. It is clear that if the vector of exogenous variables Z_t contains all the exogenous variables in X_{1t} and X_{2t}, the parameters γ/σ^*, ζ_1/σ^*, ζ_2/σ^* cannot be identified. It can readily be verified that a necessary condition for the identification of these parameters is that there is at least one variable in each of X_{1t} and X_{2t} that does not occur in Z_t. In the special case in which there are too many variables missing in Z_t, we get multiple estimates for these parameters (a case of overidentification). To solve this problem Lee (1976) suggests the following *two-stage probit method*. This procedure is simply to modify the decision function to

$$I^* = z_t(\gamma/\sigma^*) + (X_{1t}\hat{\beta}_1)(\zeta_1/\sigma^*) + (X_{2t}\hat{\beta}_2)(\zeta_2/\sigma^*) - \tilde{\varepsilon},$$

where $\tilde{\varepsilon}$ can be shown to be asymptotically standard normal and then apply the usual Probit analysis to estimate the parameters γ/σ^*, ζ_1/σ^*, and ζ_2/σ^*.

Finally it remains to consider the identification of the parameters of the residuals. From the reduced form estimates, the parameters $\sigma_1^2 = \text{var}(\varepsilon_{1t})$, $\sigma_2^2 = \text{var}(\varepsilon_{2t})$, $\sigma_{1\varepsilon} = \text{cov}(\varepsilon_{1t}\varepsilon)$, and $\sigma_{2\varepsilon} = \text{cov}(\varepsilon_{2t}\varepsilon)$ are identifiable. Also we have the condition $\text{var}(\varepsilon_t) = 1$;

$$\sigma_{1\varepsilon} = \frac{\sigma_{1v}}{\sigma^*} - \left(\frac{\zeta_1}{\sigma^*}\right)\sigma_1^2 - \left(\frac{\zeta_2}{\sigma^*}\right)\sigma_{12}, \qquad \sigma_{2\varepsilon} = \frac{\sigma_{2v}}{\sigma^*} - \left(\frac{\zeta_1}{\sigma^*}\right)\sigma_{12} - \left(\frac{\zeta_2}{\sigma^*}\right)\sigma_2^2$$

and

$$1 = \left(\frac{\sigma_v}{\sigma^*}\right)^2 + \left(\frac{\zeta_1}{\sigma^*}\right)^2\sigma_1^2 + \left(\frac{\zeta_2}{\sigma^*}\right)^2\sigma_2^2 - 2\left(\frac{\zeta_1}{\sigma^*}\right)\left(\frac{\sigma_{1v}}{\sigma^*}\right)$$

$$- 2\left(\frac{\zeta_2}{\sigma^*}\right)\left(\frac{\sigma_{2v}}{\sigma^*}\right) + 2\left(\frac{\zeta_1}{\sigma^*}\right)\left(\frac{\zeta_2}{\sigma^*}\right)\sigma_{12}.$$

From these three equations, we cannot identify four unknown parameters $\sigma_{12}, \sigma_{1v}/\sigma^*, \sigma_{2v}/\sigma^*, \sigma_v/\sigma^*$ without extra restrictions.

Under the additional assumption that $\sigma_{12} = 0$, the parameters σ_{1v}/σ^*, σ_{2v}/σ^*, and σ_v/σ^* will be identifiable and hence they can be estimated consistently. Alternatively, if v_t is independent of ε_{1t} and ε_{2t}, the other two unknown parameters σ_{12} and σ_v/σ^* will be identifiable and estimable whenever $\zeta_1 \neq 0$ or $\zeta_2 \neq 0$. If $\zeta_1 = 0$ and $\zeta_2 = 0$, the system will be exactly the switching equations model and σ_{12} will not be identifiable. Extensions of this model to the case where each of the two regimes can be described by a simultaneous equation system are given by Lee (1976).

6. SIMULTANEOUS EQUATIONS MODELS

Broadly speaking, there are two classes of simultaneous equations models that have been discussed in the literature. One is the class of models in which some variables are continuous and the others qualitative. The other is the class of models which are extensions of the Tobit model to simultaneous equations systems. The first category of models can be further classified into two types: the usual type of simultaneous equations models and recursive-type models (see Maddala and Lee, 1976). Consider the simultaneous equations model

$$By_t + \Gamma X_t = u_t,$$

where the endogenous variables y_t can be partitioned into two sets y_{1t}^* and y_{2t}. The variables y_{2t} are observed but y_{1t}^* are not. Instead we observe y_{1t}, each element of which is 1 or 0 depending on whether the corresponding element of y_{1t}^* is $\geq$ or < 0 respectively. Consider the reduced form for the system,

$$y_t = \Pi X_t + v_t, \qquad \text{where} \quad \Pi = -B^{-1}\Gamma \quad \text{and} \quad v_t = B^{-1}u_t.$$

The covariance matrix of v_t is $\Omega = B^{-1}\Sigma B'^{-1}$, where Σ is the covariance matrix of u_t. Note that the rows of Π corresponding to y_{1t}^* are estimable only up to a proportionality factor. Define

$$\Lambda = \begin{bmatrix} D & 0 \\ 0 & I \end{bmatrix},$$

where D is a diagonal matrix with elements $1/\lambda_i$ and λ_i is variance of the reduced form residual corresponding to the ith element of y_{1t}^*. Thus $\Lambda\Pi$ and $\Lambda\Omega\Lambda$ are the reduced form parameters that can be estimated in this model. To see what structural parameters are estimable we can write the condition $B\Pi + \Gamma = 0$ as

$$(B\Lambda^{-1})(\Lambda\Pi) + \Gamma = 0. \tag{41}$$

Since Λ is a diagonal matrix, the usual rank conditions for Π are applicable to $\Lambda\Pi$. However, the normalization rule $\beta_{ii} = 1$ does not help in the identification for the first set of equations because the diagonal elements have a multiplicative factor λ_i, where λ_i are unknown. Hence to have all diagonal elements unity we have to write (41) as

$$(\Lambda B\Lambda^{-1})(\Lambda\Pi) + \Lambda\Gamma = 0.$$

Under the usual rank conditions, $\Lambda B\Lambda^{-1}$ and $\Lambda\Gamma$ are estimable. Also, the condition

$$\Sigma = B\Omega B'$$

can be written as

$$\Lambda\Sigma\Lambda = (\Lambda B\Lambda^{-1})(\Lambda\Omega\Lambda)(\Lambda B\Lambda^{-1})'.$$

Thus, from the estimable reduced form parameters $\Lambda\Pi$ and $\Lambda\Omega\Lambda$ we see that in this model, under the usual rank conditions, we can get estimates of $\Lambda B\Lambda^{-1}$, $\Lambda\Gamma$, and $\Lambda\Sigma\Lambda$ only.

To illustrate what this means, consider the simple two-equation model

$$y_1^* = \beta_{12}y_2 + \gamma_1 x_1 + u_1, \qquad y_2 = \beta_{21}y_1^* + \gamma_2 x_2 + u_2. \qquad (42)$$

y_1^* is not observed. Instead we observe y_1 defined by

$$y_1 = 1 \qquad \text{iff} \quad y_1^* > 0,$$
$$= 0 \qquad \text{otherwise.} \qquad (43)$$

Let the variance of the reduced form residual for y_1^* be λ^2, and the covariance matrix of the residuals u_1 and u_2 be

$$\Sigma = \begin{bmatrix} \sigma_1^2 & \sigma_{12} \\ & \sigma_2^2 \end{bmatrix}.$$

Then the parameters that are estimable are

$$\beta_{12}/\lambda, \quad \lambda\beta_{21}, \quad \gamma_1/\lambda, \quad \gamma_2, \quad \sigma_1/\lambda, \quad \sigma_{12}/\lambda, \quad \text{and} \quad \sigma_2^2.$$

If we have known variable thresholds rather than zero thresholds as in (43), then the identification conditions are the same as in the usual simultaneous equation models. Under the usual rank conditions all the parameters are estimable.

The model considered till now and illustrated by (42) is characterized by the fact that the unobserved continuous variable y_1^* occurs in both the equations but the observed dichotomous variable y_1 does not. If this is not so, only models with a triangular B matrix are valid. Maddala and Lee (1976) consider the following models.

Model 1

$$y_1^* = X\gamma_1 + \varepsilon_1, \qquad y_2^* = X\gamma_2 + \beta y_1 + \varepsilon_2. \tag{44}$$

y_1^* and y_2^* are not observed. Instead we observe

$$\begin{aligned} y_1 &= 1 \quad \text{iff} \quad y_1^* > 0, \qquad y_2 = 1 \quad \text{iff} \quad y_2^* > 0, \\ &= 0 \quad \text{otherwise}, \qquad\qquad\quad = 0 \quad \text{otherwise.} \end{aligned}$$

Model 2

$$y_1^* = X\gamma_1 + \varepsilon_1, \qquad y_2 = X\gamma_2 + \beta y_1 + \varepsilon_2. \tag{45}$$

y_2 is continuous. y_1^* is not observed. We observe only y_1 where

$$\begin{aligned} y_1 &= 1 \quad \text{iff} \quad y_1^* > 0, \\ &= 0 \quad \text{otherwise.} \end{aligned}$$

The estimation of these models does not pose any special problems. One has to apply the usual rank conditions, and the parameters in any probit-type equation are estimable only up to a proportionality factor. On the other hand, models of the following kind are not valid since they lead to logical inconsistencies[7]:

$$y_1^* = X_1\gamma_1 + \beta_1 y_2 + u_1, \qquad y_2 = X_2\gamma_2 + \beta_2 y_1 + u_2. \tag{46}$$

This model leads to logical inconsistency because it results in an equation of the form

$$y_1^* = X\gamma + \delta y_1 + u,$$

where the unobservable variable y_1^* is related to the dichotomous variable y_1 through another relation of the form

$$\begin{aligned} y_1 &= 1 \quad \text{iff} \quad y_1^* > 0, \\ &= 0 \quad \text{otherwise.} \end{aligned}$$

Similarly, models of the form

$$y_1^* = X_1\gamma_1 + \beta_1 y_2 + u_1, \qquad y_2^* = X_2\gamma_2 + \beta_2 y_1 + u_2 \tag{47}$$

and

$$y_1^* = X_1\gamma_1 + \beta_1 y_2 + u_1, \qquad y_2^* = X_2\gamma_2 + \beta_2 y_1^* + u_2 \tag{48}$$

are also inconsistent. The models given by (46)–(48) have the common feature that the reduced forms are not defined.

Another class of simultaneous equation models is the extension of the Tobit model by Amemiya (1974). To illustrate it consider the two-equation

---

[7] Such logical inconsistencies have also been discussed by Heckman (1975b).

model

$$y_{1t} = \gamma_1 y_{2t} + \beta_1' x_{1t} + U_{1t} \qquad \text{if} \quad y_{1t} > 0 \quad \text{and} \quad = 0 \quad \text{otherwise,}$$
$$y_{2t} = \gamma_2 y_{1t} + \beta_2' x_{2t} + U_{2t} \qquad \text{if} \quad y_{2t} > 0 \quad \text{and} \quad = 0 \quad \text{otherwise.} \qquad (49)$$

Amemiya shows that this model is logically consistent iff $\gamma_1 \gamma_2 < 1$. Divide the observations into four sets:

$$\begin{aligned}
S_1: & \quad y_{1t} > 0, & y_{2t} > 0, \\
S_2: & \quad y_{1t} > 0, & y_{2t} = 0, \\
S_3: & \quad y_{1t} = 0, & y_{2t} > 0, \\
S_4: & \quad y_{1t} = 0, & y_{2t} = 0.
\end{aligned}$$

Amemiya uses only the observations in S_1 and suggests an indirect least squares type procedure which gives multiple solutions in the case of over-identified models. There are three comments that can be made on the procedure that Amemiya suggests. Firstly, it is easy to modify the procedure to get a two-stage least squares type method so that we do not have the problem of multiple solutions in the case of overidentified models. Secondly, there may be many situations where S_1 contains a small number of observations. In such cases it is desirable to use all the observations rather than just the subset S_1. Thirdly, there may be cases where looking at the other subsets S_2, S_3, and S_4 can aid the identification of the parameters of the structural model. We will elaborate on these three points.

The procedure that Amemiya suggests is to evaluate the first and second moments of y_{1t} and y_{2t} in S_1 (this is similar to the procedure he suggests for the simple Tobit model). Firstly, the reduced form equations can be written as

$$y_{1t} = \alpha_1' x_t + V_{1t}, \qquad y_{2t} = \alpha_2' x_t + V_{2t}. \qquad (50)$$

Then, using the moments of a truncated multinormal distribution and noting that (V_1, V_2) have a bivariate normal distribution with variances σ_1^2, σ_2^2 and covariance σ_{12}, he obtains

$$E(V_{1t}|S_1) = (1/P)\sigma_1^2 f_1 F_2 + (1/P)\sigma_{12} f_2 F_1,$$
$$E(V_{2t}|S_1) = (1/P)\sigma_2^2 f_2 F_1 + (1/P)\sigma_{12} f_1 F_2, \qquad (51)$$

where

$$\sigma_1^{*2} = \sigma_1^2 - (\sigma_{12}^2/\sigma_2^2), \qquad \sigma_2^{*2} = \sigma_2^2 - (\sigma_{12}^2/\sigma_1^2),$$

and f_1 is the density of $N(0, \sigma_1^2)$ evaluated at $\alpha_1' x_t$, f_2 the density of $N(0, \sigma_2^2)$ evaluated at $\alpha_2' x_t$, F_1 the distribution of $N(0, \sigma_1^{*2})$ evaluated at $\alpha_1' x_t - (\sigma_{12}/\sigma_2^2)\alpha_2' x_t$, F_2 the distribution of $N(0, \sigma_2^{*2})$ evaluated at $\alpha_2' x_t - (\sigma_{12}/\sigma_2^2) \cdot \alpha_1' x_t$, and $P = \text{Prob}(V_{1t} > -\alpha_1' x_t, V_{2t} > -\alpha_2' x_t)$. Equations (50) can be written as

$$y_{1t} = \alpha_1'x_t + (1/P)\sigma_1^2 f_1 F_2 + (1/P)\sigma_{12}f_2 F_1 + W_{1t},$$
$$y_{2t} = \alpha_2'x_t + (1/P)\sigma_2^2 f_2 F_1 + (1/P)\sigma_{12}f_1 F_2 + W_{2t},$$

(52)

where $E(W_{1t}) = E(W_{2t}) = 0$.

Equations (52) which are similar to equation (11) can be estimated by OLS provided we get estimates of P, f_1, f_2, F_1, and F_2. These can be obtained from initial consistent estimates of the relevant parameters. Amemiya suggests obtaining these by using an instrumental variable method applied to the equations

$$y_{1t}^2 = \sigma_1^{*2} + (\sigma_{12}/\sigma_2^2)y_{1t}y_{2t} + (\sigma_2^2\alpha_1' - \sigma_{12}\alpha_2')x_t y_{1t} + \eta_{1t},$$
$$y_{2t}^2 = \sigma_2^{*2} + (\sigma_{12}/\sigma_1^2)y_{1t}y_{2t} + (-\sigma_{12}\alpha_1' + \sigma_1^2\alpha_2')x_t y_{2t} + \eta_{2t}.$$

(53)

These equations are similar to equation (13). After obtaining initial consistent estimates of the reduced form parameters from (53), Amemiya suggests obtaining estimates of P, f_1, f_2, F_1, and F_2 and estimating (52) by OLS. However, instead of estimating the unrestricted reduced form (52) at the second stage (from which we do not get unique estimates of the structural parameters if the equation is overidentified), we can use a 2SLS-type method. Since, by the definition of the reduced forms, we have

$$\alpha_1'x_t = \gamma_1(\alpha_2'x_t) + \beta_1'x_{1t} \quad \text{and} \quad \alpha_2'x_t = \gamma_2(\alpha_1'x_t) + \beta_2'x_{2t}, \quad (54)$$

Lee (1976) suggests substituting these expressions in equations (52) and using OLS. In essence we use $\hat{\alpha}_2'x_t, x_{1t}, \hat{f}_1\hat{F}_2/\hat{P}$, and $\hat{f}_2\hat{F}_1/\hat{P}$ as regressors in the equation for y_{1t} with similar expressions for y_{2t}.

There may be cases in which the subset S_1 consists of a very few observations compared with the total. In such cases it is desirable to modify Amemiya's procedure so as to use all the observations. Though theoretically it is very difficult to prove that such estimators are (asymptotically) more efficient than those based on the data in S_1 only, from the practical point of view it is not desirable to throw away the observations corresponding to the sets S_2 and S_3. The modification is simple though the algebraic detail is messy. The first step in the procedure is as before. As for the second step, letting P_1, P_2, P_3, and P_4 denote the probabilities that the observation belongs to sets S_1, S_2, S_3, and S_4 respectively, we can write equations (52) as

$$E(y_{1t}) = P_1[\gamma_1(\alpha_2'x_t) + \beta_1'x_{1t}] + P_2(\beta_1'x_{1t}) + P_1 E(V_1|S_1) + P_2 E(V_1|S_2),$$
$$E(y_{2t}) = P_1[\gamma_2(\alpha_1'x_t) + \beta_2'x_{2t}] + P_3(\beta_2'x_{2t}) + P_1 E(V_2|S_1) + P_3 E(V_2|S_3).$$

We already have expressions for $P_1, E(V_1|S_1)$, and $E(V_2|S_1)$. However, the others can be shown to depend on the structural parameters. Thus, one has to obtain estimates of the structural parameters initially using the data in S_1 before these equations can be used. Thus, the identification problems in this model can be studied by concentrating on the identification problems in S_1.

There are, however, cases in which the identification of the model has to be discussed by considering all the subsets. Lee (1976) gives an example of a two-equation model where this is so.[8] Consider

$$y_{1t} = \gamma_1 y_{2t} + \delta_1' X_t + \varepsilon_{1t}, \qquad y_{2t} = \gamma_2 y_{1t}^* + \delta_2' X_t + \varepsilon_{2t}, \qquad (55)$$

where

$$y_{1t}^* = \begin{cases} y_{1t} & \text{when} \quad y_{1t} > 0, \\ 0 & \text{otherwise.} \end{cases}$$

Denote $S_1 = \{t | y_{1t} > 0\}$ and $S_2 = \{t | y_{1t} \le 0\}$. Then we have the following two sets of reduced forms:

$$y_{1t} = \frac{1}{1 - \gamma_1\gamma_2}(\delta_1' + \gamma_1\delta_2')X_t + \frac{1}{1 - \gamma_1\gamma_2}(\varepsilon_{1t} + \gamma_1\varepsilon_{2t}),$$

$$\hspace{6cm} \forall t \in S_1, \quad (56)$$

$$y_{2t} = \frac{1}{1 - \gamma_1\gamma_2}(\delta_2' + \gamma_2\delta_1')X_t + \frac{1}{1 - \gamma_1\gamma_2}(\gamma_2\varepsilon_{1t} + \varepsilon_{2t}),$$

and

$$y_{1t} = (\delta_1' + \gamma_1\delta_2')X_t + (\varepsilon_{1t} + \gamma_1\varepsilon_{2t}), \qquad y_{2t} = \delta_2' X_t + \varepsilon_{2t}, \qquad \forall t \in S_2. \quad (57)$$

From the observations in S_1, the parameters

$$\pi_1' = \frac{1}{1 - \gamma_1\gamma_2}(\delta_1' + \gamma_1\delta_2'), \qquad \pi_2' = \frac{1}{1 - \gamma_1\gamma_2}(\delta_2' + \gamma_2\delta_1')$$

can be estimated by instrumental variable methods. The question is whether equations (57) give any more information that will help identification of the structural parameters. [In the case of the model given by (49), the answer is negative.]

Define $\varepsilon_t = (1/\sigma^*)(\varepsilon_{1t} + \gamma_1\varepsilon_{2t})$ with $\sigma^{*2} = \text{var}(\varepsilon_{1t} + \gamma_1\varepsilon_{2t})$. Then

$$E(\varepsilon_{2t}|y_{1t} < 0) = -\sigma_{2\varepsilon} f\left(-\frac{\delta_1' + \gamma_1\delta_2'}{\sigma^*}X_t\right) \Big/ F\left(-\frac{\delta_1' + \gamma_1\delta_2'}{\sigma^*}X_t\right),$$

where $\sigma_{2\varepsilon} = \text{cov}(\varepsilon_{2t}, \varepsilon_t)$. Thus, if we can get a consistent estimate of $(\delta_1' + \gamma_1\delta_2')/\sigma^*)$, we can use the second equation in (57) to get consistent estimates of δ_2 and $\sigma_{2\varepsilon}$. Fortunately, a probit estimation based on

$$I_t = 1 \qquad \text{if} \quad y_{1t} > 0,$$
$$= 0 \qquad \text{otherwise.}$$

---

[8] The discussion of this particular two-equation model was motivated by an unpublished paper by Sickles and Schmidt which arrived at different conclusions.

yields such a consistent estimate in this model. Thus in addition to $\pi_1{}'$ and $\pi_2{}'$ we get estimates of $\delta_2{}'$. With δ_2 identified, it can be readily verified that γ_2 is identified. However, it is not possible to identify γ_1 and δ_1 without imposing the usual zero restrictions on the equation for y_1. The second equation is identified without the imposition of the usual zero restrictions.

In this example we have a two-equation model with a single truncated variable. The model considered by Heckman (1974) is a two-equation model where both variables are truncated but by a single criterion. In his model the identifiability conditions are as in the usual simultaneous equations model. The model consists of the shadow-wage function

$$S = \gamma_0 + \gamma_1 H + \gamma_2 Z + U_1 \tag{58}$$

and the market wage function

$$W = \beta_0 + \beta_1 X + U_2; \tag{59}$$

X and Z are exogenous variables and hours worked H adjusts so that $S = W$. Hence

$$H = \frac{\beta_0 + \beta_1 X - \gamma_0 - \gamma_2 Z}{\gamma_1} + \frac{U_2 - U_1}{\gamma_1}. \tag{60}$$

If $H > 0$, the person is in the labor force and we observe H and W. If $H \le 0$, the person is not in the labor force. Write $S = W = y_1$ and $H = y_2$. Then the model is

$$\left.\begin{array}{l} y_1 = \gamma_0 + \gamma_1 y_2 + \gamma_2 Z + U_1 \\ y_1 = \beta_0 + \beta_1 X + U_2 \end{array}\right\} \text{if} \quad y_2 > 0 \tag{61}$$
$$y_1 = y_2 = 0 \qquad\qquad \text{otherwise.}$$

The identifiability conditions are $\text{cov}(U_1, U_2) = 0$ or there is at least one variable in X that is missing in Z. Because of the special structure, it is possible to estimate this model by methods simpler than those for Amemiya's model. If y_2 occurs also in the second equation, i.e., hours worked H appears in the market wage equation, then this will not be the case.

7. CONCLUSIONS

The paper discusses in a unified framework the identification and two-stage estimation of a large variety of limited dependent variable models. More details and further discussion can be found in the references cited, in particular the theses by Lee (1976) and Nelson (1975).

The two-stage estimation methods give consistent estimates, but their asymptotic properties are as yet unknown. Further work needs to be done on this aspect. In many problems the ML estimation methods are cumbersome and one has no practical alternative to the two-stage methods. It would be interesting to see how these methods perform as compared to the ML procedures in the case of those models where the latter can be computed. Trost and Lee (1976) made such a comparison in a special case and found rather remarkable differences in the results. Further work needs to be done along these lines.

REFERENCES

Amemiya, T. (1973). Regression Analysis When the Dependent Variable is Truncated Normal, *Econometrica* **41**, No. 6, 997–1016.
Amemiya, T. (1974). Multivariate Regression and Simultaneous Equation Models When the Dependent Variables Are Truncated Normal, *Econometrica* **42**, No. 6, 999–1012.
Cragg, J. G. (1971). Some Statistical Models for Limited Dependent Variables with Application to the Demand for Durable Goods, *Econometrica* **39**, No. 5, 829–844.
Dagenais, M. G. (1969). A Threshold Regression Model, *Econometrica* **37**, No. 1, 193–203.
Dagenais, M. G. (1975). Application of a Threshold Regression Model to Household Purchases of Automobiles, *The Review of Economics and Statistics* **72**, No. 3, 275–285.
Fair, R. C., and Jaffee, D. M. (1972). Methods of Estimation for Models in Disequilibrium, *Econometrica* **40**, No. 3, 497–514.
Gilman, H. (1976). Estimation of Implicit Discount Rates, Center for Naval Anal. (October).
Goldberger, A. S. (1964). *Econometric Theory*. New York: Wiley.
Goldfeld, S. M., and Quandt, R. E. (1973). The Estimation of Structural Shifts by Switching Regressions, *Annals of Economic and Social Measurement* **2**, No. 4, 475–485.
Goldfeld, S. M., and Quandt, R. E. (1975). Estimation in a Disequilibrium Model and the Value of Information, *Journal of Econometrics* **3**, No. 4, 325–348.
Hanoch, G. (1975). Theory and Estimation of a Complete Labor Supply Model, Rand discussion paper (September).
Heckman, J. (1974). Shadow Prices, Market Wages and Labor Supply, *Econometrica* **42**, No. 4, 679–694.
Heckman, J. (1975a). Shadow Prices, Market Wages and Labor Supply Revisited: Some Computational and Conceptual Simplifications and Revised Estimates. (June) (manuscript).
Heckman, J. (1975b). Simultaneous Equations Models with Both Continuous and Discrete Endogenous Variables with and without Structural Shift in the Equations (August) (manuscript).
Heckman, J. (1976). Dummy Endogenous Variables, *Econometrica* (to be published).
Johnson, T. (1972). Qualitative and Limited Dependent Variables in Economic Relationships, *Econometrica* **40**, No. 3, 455–462.
Johnson, N. L., and Kotz, S. (1972). *Distribution in Statistics: Continuous Multivariate Distributions.* New York: Wiley.
Lee, L.-F. (1975). Estimation of Some Limited Dependent Variable Models by Two-Stage Methods, Discussion paper, Univ. of Rochester (September).
Lee, L.-F. (1976). Estimation of Limited Dependent Variable Models by Two Stage Methods, Unpublished doctoral dissertation, Univ. of Rochester.
Maddala, G. S., and Lee, L.-F. (1976). Recursive Models with Qualitative Endogenous variables, *Annals of Economic and Social Measurement* **5**, No. 4, 525–545.

Maddala, G. S., and Nelson, F. D. (1974). Maximum Likelihood Methods for Models of Markets in Disequilibrium, *Econometrica* **42**, No. 6, 1013–1030.

Maddala, G. S., and Nelson, F. D. (1975). Switching Regression Models with Exogenous and Endogenous Switching, *Proceedings of the Business and Economics Statistics Section* 423–426. Amer. Statist. Assoc.

Nelson, F. D. (1975). Estimation of Economic Relationships with Censored, Truncated and Limited Dependent Variables, Unpublished doctoral dissertation, Univ. of Rochester.

Nelson, F. D. (1976). Censored Regression Models with Unobserved, Stochastic, Censoring Thresholds, Social Science Working Paper No. 115 (March) California Inst. of Technol.

Olsen, R. J. (1976). Note on the Uniqueness of the Maximum Likelihood Estimator for the Tobit Model, Manuscript, Yale Univ. (April).

Polakoff, M. E., and Sibler, W. L. (1967). Reluctance and Member Bank Borrowing: Additional Evidence, *Journal of Finance* **22**, No. 1, 88–92.

Poirier, D. J. (1974). The Determinants of Home Buying in the New Jersey Graduated Work Incentive Experiment, Working Paper, Univ. of Illinois, Urbana (December).

Rosett, R. N. (1959). A Statistical Model of Friction in Economics, *Econometrica* **27**, No. 2.

Rosett, R. N., and Nelson, F. D. (1975). Estimation of the Two-Limit Probit Regression Model, *Econometrica* **43**, No. 1, 141–146.

Tobin, J. (1958). Estimation of Relationships for Limited Dependent Variables, *Econometrica* **26**, No. 1, 24–26.

Trost, R. P. (1976). Demand for Housing: A Model Based on Inter-related Choices between Owning and Renting, Discussion paper, Univ. of Florida (September).

Trost, R. P., and Lee, L.-F. (1976). On the Maximum Likelihood Estimation of a Limited Dependent Variables Model with Binary Choices: The Housing Expenditure Model Re-visited, Discussion paper No. 76-77-11, Univ. of Florida (October).

Westin, R. B. (1975). Statistical Models for Inter-related Discrete and Continuous Choices, Paper presented at the Econometric Society World Congress, Toronto (August).

An extended linear permanent expenditure system (ELPES)

PHILIP MUSGROVE

THE BROOKINGS INSTITUTION

1. INTRODUCTION

Estimating Engel curves from household budget data presents something of a dilemna. If expenditures are related to observed, current income, the analysis will be biased by the presence of transitory variation in both income and spending. Savings relations may be particularly distorted, making it difficult to understand current behavior in terms of a longer horizon. The solution to this problem would appear to be to relate spending to permanent income, except that the latter cannot be observed, but must be estimated with errors whose size is often unknown. A further difficulty is that the permanent income hypothesis (Friedman, 1957) includes a number of assumptions which are at least open to question, so that accepting the hypothesis for the sake of analysis may create biases as objectionable as those due to transitory flows.

It is desirable, therefore, to analyze consumer behavior according to a model which is based on permanent income, but which permits some of the assumptions of that hypothesis to be tested instead of simply accepted, and which also offers an indication of how well permanent income can be estimated. Conceptually, three kinds of "error" can be distinguished in a relation between spending and income—two transitory components, plus the error of estimation of the permanent components—and these should be separated when estimating such a relation. To the extent that the permanent-income hypothesis is a statement about the behavior of some of these errors, a technique which distinguishes among them can be used to test the hypothesis.

In what follows we present a model of this sort, by modifying the extended linear expenditure system (ELES) of Lluch (1973), which in turn is an extension of the linear expenditure system (LES) developed by Klein and Rubin (1947–1948), Samuelson (1947–1948), Geary (1950–1951), and Stone (1954). The modified system is based on permanent income, but can be estimated entirely from observable variables at one point in time.

In the ELES, the consumer is assumed to have an additive utility function

$$u(t) = \sum_i^n \beta_i \log(q_i(t) - \gamma_i) \tag{1}$$

over n commodities, with $\sum_i^n \beta_i = 1$. Consumption of good i in period t is $q_i(t)$, and for utility to be defined this must exceed the subsistence or minimum level of consumption γ_i. The stream of future utility is discounted at the subjective rate δ, so that the consumer's objective is to maximize

$$U = \int_0^\infty e^{-\delta t} u(t)\, dt, \tag{2}$$

subject to the constraint that the present value of future expenditure, discounted at the interest rate ρ, cannot exceed initial wealth. The latter consists of nonhuman wealth W which earns interest at the rate ρ, plus the present value of the stream of future labor income $L(t)$. The constraint is then

$$\int_0^\infty e^{-\rho t} \sum_i^n p_i(t) q_i(t)\, dt \le W + \int_0^\infty e^{-\rho t} L(t)\, dt, \tag{3}$$

where $p_i(t)$ is the price of good i at time t. Equality holds if the consumer derives no utility from bequests.

Maximizing (2) subject to (3) leads to the system of expenditure functions

$$v_i = p_i q_i = p_i \gamma_i + \mu \beta_i \left(y^* - \sum_j^n p_j \gamma_j \right), \tag{4}$$

where v_i is spending on good i. y^* is permanent income, and μ is the marginal propensity to consume, once subsistence needs $\sum_j^n p_j \gamma_j$ are met. The MPC is the ratio of the discount rate and the interest rate,

$$\mu = \delta/\rho, \tag{5}$$

so that saving arises because consumers are less impatient than capital markets (Lluch et al., 1976, Sections 2.1.1 and 2.1.4). The difficulty is that y^* is unobservable, so that the ELES is usually estimated using in its place observed income y, which includes both labor and nonlabor receipts. This substitution is justified only if it is further assumed that prices p_i and the interest rate ρ are not expected to change, and that the present value of expected changes in labor income is zero. If the consumer can have this degree of certainty about the future, his behavior is described only by current total income, current (stable) prices, and subsistence needs,

$$v_i = p_i \gamma_i + \mu \beta_i \left(y - \sum_{j}^{n} p_j \gamma_j \right). \tag{6}$$

The assumptions necessary to derive (6) are not particularly plausible: it is especially unlikely that a consuming unit will expect no change in the present value of its labor income, no matter when it begins its consumption plan. This assumption must be modified as soon as the plan is of finite length, and the approximation of an infinite stream becomes less useful as the consumer ages. Moreover, the expenditure functions (6) can be derived without any reference to a multiperiod plan, if it is simply assumed that current saving enters the utility function (1) in the same way as expenditures, but with a zero subsistence or threshold level.[1] This approach was independently developed by Betancourt (1973) and Howe (1974, 1975).

Rather than make the assumptions necessary to base the expenditure system on current spending and income, we assume that the utility function is defined in terms of permanent consumption levels, so that the system is defined for permanent (unobservable) income and spending,

$$v_i^* = p_i \gamma_i^* + \mu^* \beta_i^* \left(y^* - \sum_{j}^{n} p_j \gamma_j^* \right), \tag{7}$$

where an * refers to a permanent variable or parameter.[2]

Aggregation of (7) over the n expenditure categories yields the total consumption function

$$v^* = \sum_{j}^{n} v_j^* = \sum_{j} p_j \gamma_j^* + \mu^* \left(y^* - \sum_{j} p_j \gamma_j^* \right) = (1 - \mu^*) \sum_{j} p_j \gamma_j^* + \mu^* y^*. \tag{8}$$

This function embodies Friedman's assumption of a constant marginal propensity to consume, independent of the level of permanent income, but it differs from his hypothesis in recognizing a level of spending below which the consuming unit cannot continue to exist.[3] Estimates of the terms $p_i \gamma_i^*$

---

[1] That is, $U = \sum_i^{n-1} \beta_i \log(q_i - \gamma_i) + \beta_n \log s$, where s is $y - v$ or saving. $\sum_i^{n-1} \beta_i = \mu < 1$, and β_n, the marginal income share saved, is $1 - \mu$.

[2] This differs from the usual ELES notation, where $\gamma_i^* = p_i \gamma_i$ and $\beta_i^* = \mu \beta_i$, independently of the income concept used. We designate these parameters by $^0\gamma_i$ and $^0\beta_i$, respectively.

[3] Friedman explicitly assumes that any reduction in current consumption can be compensated by a sufficiently large increase in future consumption. This is possible in (1) only if $q_i(t) > \gamma_i$ for all $i = 1, \ldots, n$ and all $t \geq 0$. For a graphic analysis treating $(\gamma_1, \ldots, \gamma_n)$ as the origin of a Friedman consumption function, see Musgrove (1974, pp. 12–14) or Lluch et al. (1976, Figure 2.1).

therefore furnish a test of the assumption that the marginal and average propensities to consume permanent income are equal. The system (7) is also consistent with the assumptions of the permanent-income hypothesis, that the MPC depends on the interest rate and on the proportions of human and nonhuman wealth. These assumptions are embodied in expressions (3) and (5), which hold for the permanent income ELES (4) and not only for the current income version (6).

A complete formulation of the extended linear permanent expenditure system (ELPES) is given in Section 3, and the estimation of its parameters and their standard errors is discussed in Sections 4 and 5. Before proceeding, however, it may be useful to review some of the previous theoretical and empirical modifications to the parent system (ELES).

2. PERMANENT-INCOME APPROACHES

Given that transitory variation is likely to be large in household budgets, it is not surprising that while numerous empirical estimates of the ELES in cross section give reasonable values of the marginal budget shares β_i, the values of the MPC are sometimes implausible. Any bias in the estimate of μ will also affect the estimates of the subsistence quantities γ_i and thereby bias the price responses derived from the system.[4] As the authors of the most extensive set of estimates of the ELES observe,

> The main theoretical weakness of our model appears to lie in its fairly simple treatment of the allocation of consumption over time. Certainly the empirical results were poorest when they related to the consumption–saving choice: the model proved inadequate to explain demand and savings behaviour of those household groups with negative mean saving; [and] estimates of the marginal propensity to consume were particularly low in several cross-section studies (Lluch et al., 1976, Chapter 10).

There have been several recent theoretical extensions to the model, but none has directly attacked this problem. Betancourt (1973), Klijn (1974), and Mattei (1973) have introduced finite horizons; Betancourt (1973) and Powell (1974) have allowed for discrete time periods; and variation over time has been treated for δ and ρ by Klijn and for γ_i by Lluch (1974). It is also possible

---

[4] If prices are observed (and differ among observations), then μ, β_i, and γ_i can be estimated and are exactly identified by observed y and v_i. If price variation is not observed, as may be the case in cross-section information, it is still possible to identify μ, β_i, and subsistence expenditures $^0\gamma_i = p_i\gamma_i$, and these suffice to describe price responses. The (uncompensated) own-price elasticity n_{ii} is $(1 - \mu\beta_i)(p_i\gamma_i/v_i) - 1$, and the cross elasticity with respect to the price of good j, η_{ij}, is $-\mu\beta_i(p_j\gamma_j/v_i)$. It suffices to estimate $^0\beta_i = \mu\beta_i$ and $^0\gamma_i = p_i\gamma_i$ to estimate all price elasticities.

to estimate δ and ρ separately (Powell, 1973) instead of only their ratio μ, or to take ρ as an observable variable and estimate δ.

In recent empirical work there have been at least three attempts to replace y by a better estimate of y^*, but none of these has been entirely satisfactory. Lluch et al., (1976, Section 4.5) used three different definitions of y^* in estimates based on annual national accounts data for Taiwan. The simplest and most successful of these models makes permanent income a geometric-distributed lag function of current and past income, so that (4) is replaced by

$$v_i(t) = p_i(t)\gamma_i + \mu\beta_i\left(y(t) - \sum_j p_j(t)\gamma_j\right)$$
$$- \lambda\left[p_i(t-1)\gamma_i + \mu\beta_i\left(y(t) - \sum_j p_j(t-1)\gamma_j\right)\right] + \lambda v_i(t-1), \quad (9)$$

where λ is an adjustment parameter, and current and past prices are observed. This formulation gives estimates of μ, β_i, and γ_i very slightly different from those obtained using only current income and prices, and λ does not appear to differ significantly from zero. This is not surprising, since one year's income may approximate y^* very well for aggregate data even if it is a poor approximation for individual consumers.[5]

Howe (1974, pp. 188–213) in estimating the ELES for Colombian households, replaced y by estimated normal income

$$\hat{y}_N = (X'X)^{-1}X'y, \quad (10)$$

where X includes such variables as age, education, occupation, and social class. Both linear and logarithmic specifications were tested. The use of $\hat{y}_N$ gave better estimates of μ, lower values of β_i for food and higher marginal budget shares for other categories, and systematically much higher estimates of all the subsistence expenditures $^0\gamma_i$. Because these exceeded observed expenditures v_i more often than when y was used, the normal-income version was judged unsatisfactory.

Finally, Betancourt (1973) in analyzing Chilean household data used in place of y an estimator

$$y^* = (1 - \lambda)y_j^P + \lambda(y/\bar{y}_j)y_j^P, \quad (11)$$

where y is current income, $\bar{y}_j$ is mean income in the reference group j to which the household is assigned, λ a parameter to be estimated, and y_j^P an estimate of permanent income for an average household in the reference group, for whom $\lambda = 0$. y_j^P is estimated from the mean incomes of households older than the household considered, and incorporates assumptions about price

[5] See the discussion of aggregation in Friedman (1957, pp. 18–19), and compare the analysis of family budget data (Chapter IV) with that of time-series data (Chapter V).

changes, the interest rate, and the secular rate of growth of income.[6] The object of this formulation is to allow for nonstationary expectations under inflationary conditions, and to distinguish permanent from transitory price responses [which is not possible with the formulation (9) of Lluch *et al.*]. Nonetheless the current-income formulation gives values of the ELES parameters which are often more reasonable and are estimated with smaller errors.[7]

None of these approaches has entirely eliminated the problem of transitory income and expenditure variation, which can be quite severe with short-period budget data. (It is undoubtedly less important for estimation with time series aggregates.) The severity of this problem appears notably when the ELES is based on current income y, but in order to create more homogeneous groups, households are first stratified by a proxy for permanent-income level. Howe and Musgrove (1976, Section 7.3.1) find, in estimates for six strata in each of four Latin American cities, that the lowest values of μ correspond to groups for which transitory variation can be expected to be high, or to cities where exogenous estimates show large transitory variances.

3. FORMULATION OF THE ELPES

The reduced form corresponding to the ELPES, expression (7), is

$$v_i^* = \alpha_i^* + {}^0\beta_i^* y^* \tag{12}$$

with $\alpha_i^* = {}^0\gamma_i^* - {}^0\beta_i^* \sum_j^n {}^0\gamma_j^*$. The parameters μ^*, β_i^* and ${}^0\gamma_i^*$ can be recovered from estimates of α_i^* and ${}^0\beta_i^*$, provided $\sum_j^n {}^0\beta_j^* \neq 1$, by the transformations

$$\mu^* = \sum_j^n {}^0\beta_j^*, \qquad \beta_i^* = {}^0\beta_i^*/\mu^*$$

$$\sum_j^n {}^0\gamma_j^* = (1 - \mu^*)^{-1} \sum_j^n \alpha_j^*$$

$${}^0\gamma_i^* = \alpha_i^* + {}^0\beta_i^* \sum_j^n {}^0\gamma_i^* = \alpha_i^* + {}^0\beta_i^*(1 - \mu^*)^{-1} \sum_j^n \alpha_j^*. \tag{13}$$

---

[6] Estimation of y_j^P from current incomes of comparable but older households follows the procedure suggested by Watts (1960).

[7] Betancourt finds the current income version superior in part because the permanent version yields many positive own-price elasticities. Howe and Musgrove (1976, Section 7.4.4) argue, however, that some positive responses—particularly for durable and semidurable goods—may reflect consumer reaction to *acceleration* of inflation. Such responses cannot really be permanent, but they could show up in a permanent-income model because the latter assumes expectations of a constant rate of inflation, whereas actual inflation may be highly variable. For further discussion of inflation and expectations see the "Discussion" by Klevorick (1973) and Betancourt's "Reply."

In order to estimate α_i^* and $^0\beta_i^*$, y^* must be replaced by observable variables. We assume that v_i and y each consist of a permanent and a transitory component, that the two components are uncorrelated with each other, and that the transitory components have zero expected values.[8]

$$v_i = v_i^* + v_i^{**}, \qquad\qquad y = y^* + y^{**},$$
$$v_i^{*\prime}v_i^{**} = 0, \qquad\qquad y^{*\prime}y^{**} = 0, \qquad\qquad (14)$$
$$E(v_i^{**}) = 0, \qquad\qquad E(y^{**}) = 0.$$

No assumption is made about the correlation of transitory components across equations; that is, the transitory part of spending in any category may be correlated (positively or negatively) with transitory income, or with any other transitory expenditure. It is then possible to test one of the most questionable assumptions of the permanent-income hypothesis, namely that transitory consumption is unrelated to transitory income.

One further substantive assumption is required; that is, that y^* is a linear function of m observable variables represented by the matrix X,

$$y^* = X\phi^* + \varepsilon, \qquad\qquad (15)$$

where the error ε has zero expected value and is uncorrelated with all the variables in X and also with all the transitory components. Substituting (15) and (14) into (12) yields the reduced form of the ELPES,

$$v_i = \alpha_i^* + {}^0\beta_i^*X\phi^* + {}^0\beta_i^*\varepsilon + v_i^{**} = \alpha_i^* + {}^0\beta_i^*X\phi^* + e_i^*,$$
$$y = X\phi^* + \varepsilon + y^{**} = X\phi^* + e_y^*. \qquad\qquad (16)$$

We can generalize one step further, following Betancourt (1973), Howe (1974), and Howe and Musgrove (1976), by supposing that the subsistence expenditures $^0\gamma_i^*$ are not the same for all observations (households) but are linear functions of a subset H of r of the variables included in X.[9] Then from (12),

$$\alpha_i^* = H\theta_i^*, \qquad\qquad (17)$$

and substitution of (17) into (16) leads to the form whose parameters are to be estimated,

$$v_i = H\theta_i^* + {}^0\beta_i^*X\phi^* + e_i^*, \qquad y = X\phi^* + e_y^*, \qquad\qquad (18)$$

---

[8] As in the permanent-income hypothesis, the last assumption is not essential in theory and may not be plausible, but is adopted for estimation, because otherwise the system is under-identified. Prior information on the size of $E(v_i^{**})$ or $E(y^{**})$ can of course be used to lift this restriction.

[9] Howe and Musgrove make the $^0\gamma_i^*$ differ between large and small families, Betancourt makes them a function of household size (with allowance for economies of scale), and Howe makes them depend on both size and composition (number of adults, of adolescents, and of children). The same approach could be used in estimation from time series, if the variables causing $^0\gamma_i^*$ to change from one period to another, as in Lluch (1974, 1977), also affect y^*.

where e_i^* and e_y^* are compound errors including a transitory component and the estimation error ε. This distinction between the two kinds of "error," whose variances are to be estimated separately, differentiates this approach from the normal-income procedure of Howe (1974) or the permanent-income estimator of Betancourt (1973), expressions (10) and (11). The other distinguishing feature of the ELPES is that the parameters of the income equation in (18) are estimated using information from the expenditure equations: the system is estimated simultaneously rather than by first estimating y^* and then making v_i a function of $\hat{y}^*$.

The matrix H may consist entirely of variables not in X, but it is more interesting to let it be a subset of X: then the direct effect on v_i of a variable in H can be distinguished from the indirect effect exercised through y^*. Not all variables can be allowed to have both direct and indirect influence, however, since $r < m$ is required for identification.

Aggregation of (18) over categories leads to the total expenditure function

$$v = H\theta^* + \mu^* X\phi^* + \mu^*\varepsilon + v^{**} = H\theta^* + \mu^* X\phi^* + e_v^*, \qquad (19)$$

where $\theta^* = \sum_j^n \theta_j^*$. Since v^* is an exact function of y^*, the parameters $^0\gamma_i^*$ and β_i^* are the same whether the system is estimated from permanent income or from permanent expenditure. This is not true of LES and ELES in current variables, because observed v is not an exact function of observed y (Lluch et al., 1976, Section 2.2.1).

The system (18) includes $(n + 1)^2$ variances and covariances of the compound errors e_i^*, e_y^*, which can be estimated by OLS regression of v_i on X and y on X. There are, however, $(n + 1)^2 + 1$ variances and covariances of interest in (16), assuming ε to be uncorrelated with v_i^{**} and y^{**}:

$$\begin{aligned}
\text{var}(e_i^*) &= (^0\beta_i^*)^2 \, \text{var}(\varepsilon) + \text{var}(v_i^{**}), \\
\text{var}(e_y^*) &= \text{var}(\varepsilon) + \text{var}(y^{**}), \\
\text{covar}(e_i^*, e_j^*) &= {}^0\beta_i^* \, {}^0\beta_j^* \, \text{var}(\varepsilon) + \text{covar}(v_i^{**}, v_j^{**}), \\
\text{covar}(e_i^*, e_y^*) &= {}^0\beta_i^* \, \text{var}(\varepsilon) + \text{covar}(v_i^{**}, y^{**}).
\end{aligned} \qquad (20)$$

The RHS of (20) can be identified, provided the $^0\beta_i^*$ are estimated and provided that one other relation is known involving $\text{var}(\varepsilon)$ or one or more of the transitory variances and covariances. The additional relation is obtained by extending Friedman's (1957, p. 31) discussion of the association of measured consumption and measured income, but without his assumption that the transitory components v^{**} and y^{**} are uncorrelated. Then

$$\begin{aligned}
\text{covar}(v, y) &= \text{covar}(v^*, y^*) + \text{covar}(v^{**}, y^{**}) \\
&= \text{covar}(H\theta^*, X\phi^*) + \mu^* \, \text{var}(X\phi^*) + \mu^* \, \text{var}(\varepsilon) \\
&\quad + \sum_j^n \text{covar}(v_j^{**}, y^{**}),
\end{aligned} \qquad (21)$$

where the first three terms decompose $\text{covar}(v^*, y^*)$ according to (15) and (19), and the last term is $\text{covar}(v^{**}, y^{**})$. Then it is only necessary to know the covariance of observed expenditure and income, and to estimate the $m + nr + n$ elements of ϕ^*, θ_i^*, and $^0\beta_i^*$, to estimate the ELPES and recover all the variances and covariances of interest. This approach makes it possible to test Friedman's assumption of uncorrelated transitory components, not only for v^{**} and y^{**}, but for each v_i^{**} separately with y^{**} and with every other category of transitory expenditure. Estimation of $\text{var}(\varepsilon)$ also makes it possible to say how accurately y^* is estimated, using the static $R^2(y^*)$,

$$\frac{(\hat{y}^*)}{(y^*)} = \frac{\text{var}(y) - \text{var}(y^{**}) - \text{var}(\varepsilon)}{\text{var}(y) - \text{var}(y^{**})}. \tag{22}$$

From (16), a similar statistic can be computed for each consumption category,

$$R^2(v_i^*) = \frac{\text{var}(\hat{v}_i^*)}{\text{var}(v_i^*)} = \frac{\text{var}(v_i) - \text{var}(v_i^{**}) - {}^0\beta_i^* \, \text{var}(\varepsilon)}{\text{var}(v_i) - \text{var}(v_i^{**})}. \tag{23}$$

These statistics do not test any of the assumptions of the permanent-income hypothesis, but they provide some judgment as to whether the entire estimation procedure was successful. They can also be used to choose among different specifications of the determinants of y^* (the matrix X).

4. ESTIMATION OF PARAMETERS

It remains to estimate the parameters of (18). This is accomplished using a procedure suggested by Zellner (1970) and extended by Goldberger (1972) and Musgrove (1974).[10] We ignore for a moment the matrix H and consider the parameters $^0\beta_i^*$ and ϕ^*. Let Π be the matrix of their true values

$$\Pi = (\phi^*, \, {}^0\beta_1^*\phi^*, \, \ldots, \, {}^0\beta_n^*\phi^*), \tag{24}$$

and let Y be the matrix $(y, v_1, \ldots, v_n)$, so that the reduced form can be expressed as

$$Y = X\Pi + E^*, \tag{25}$$

---

[10] Zellner made the following assumptions: $n = 1$ [so that (18) consists of only two equations]; $\text{covar}(v^{**}, y^{**}) = 0$ (so that the only covariance between v and y is permanent); and $H\theta^* = 0$ (or, v^* is a function only of y^*). Goldberger extended the two-equation model to allow either $\text{var}(\varepsilon) > 0$ or, equivalently, $\text{covar}(v^{**}, y^{**}) > 0$. In the extension of the model to $n > 1$, four cases are distinguished according as $\text{var}(\varepsilon)$ is zero or not, and the transitory components are correlated or not. The ELPES corresponds to Goldberger's Case 3, which is not fully identified without the additional information provided by (20). Musgrove (1974) included the assumption $H\theta^* \neq 0$, and first estimated the (two-equation) model empirically.

where $E^* = (e_y{}^*, e_1{}^*, \ldots, e_n{}^*)$. The OLS estimator of Π is P, obtained by regressing each of the observable variables on X,

$$P = (X'X)^{-1}X'Y. \tag{26}$$

We define[11]

$$A = (Y - X\Pi)'(Y - X\Pi), \qquad S = (Y - XP)'(X - XP), \tag{27}$$

and

$$\Omega = E \begin{bmatrix} \varepsilon'\varepsilon & {}^0\beta_1{}^*\varepsilon'\varepsilon + v_1^{**\prime}y^{**} & \cdots & {}^0\beta_n{}^*\varepsilon'\varepsilon + v_n^{**\prime}y^{**} \\ \cdot & ({}^0\beta_1{}^*)^2\varepsilon'\varepsilon + v_1^{**\prime}v_1^{**} & \cdots & {}^0\beta_1{}^*\beta_n{}^*\varepsilon'\varepsilon + v_1^{**\prime}v_n^{**} \\ \vdots & \vdots & & \vdots \\ & & \cdots & ({}^0\beta_n{}^*)^2\varepsilon'\varepsilon + v_n^{**\prime}v_n^{**} \end{bmatrix}.$$

Assuming that the errors are normally distributed, the log-likelihood function for the reduced form can be written

$$L(\Pi, \Omega) = \log \det(\Omega^{-1}) - \operatorname{tr}(\Omega^{-1}A). \tag{28}$$

Ω is unknown, but maximizing (28) with respect to Ω leads to the solution

$$\hat{\Omega} = A \tag{29}$$

which is to be maximized with respect to ${}^0\beta_i{}^*$ and ϕ^*. Inserting this back into (28) gives

$$L(\Pi, \hat{\Omega}) = -\log \det(A). \tag{30}$$

Maximizing this is equivalent to choosing the parameters to minimize

$$Q = \det(S^{-1}A) \tag{31}$$

since $\det(S^{-1}A) = \det(S^{-1})\det(A)$, and $\det(S^{-1})$ is a positive constant. However, the same choice of parameters minimizes both the product and the sum of the characteristic roots of $S^{-1}A$, as is shown by Goldberger and Olkin (1971). Therefore, minimizing (31) is the same as minimizing

$$G = \operatorname{tr}(S^{-1}A) \tag{32}$$

which is the second term in the likelihood expression (28), with S being the OLS estimate of Ω. Then maximum-likelihood estimates of ${}^0\beta_i{}^*$ and ϕ^* can be obtained, without iteration, by differentiating (32) with respect to each parameter in turn.

The inclusion of $H\theta_i{}^* \neq 0$, which is necessary to estimate the ELPES intercepts $\alpha_i{}^*$, leads to the following complication of the model. X can be

---

[11] We follow Goldberger's notation in part (Y, X, Π, P, Ω) but not throughout. Thus the matrix A is his W, and E^* is his V.

partioned into $(H:Z)$, where Z consists of the $m - r$ variables not presumed to affect v^* directly. If ϕ^* is partitioned conformably, (18) becomes

$$y = H\phi_H{}^* + Z\phi_Z{}^* + e_y{}^*, \qquad v_i = H(\theta_i{}^* + {}^0\beta_i{}^*\phi_H{}^*) + {}^0\beta_i{}^*Z\phi_Z{}^* + e_i{}^*. \tag{33}$$

In order to identify the elements of the compound coefficient $\theta_i{}^* + {}^0\beta_i{}^*\phi_H{}^*$, any correlation between H and Z must be removed. This is accomplished by OLS regression of y, v_i, and Z on H, leading to the transformed variables

$$\tilde{y} = [I - H(H'H)^{-1}H']y = y - H\psi_y,$$
$$\tilde{v}_i = [I - H(H'H)^{-1}H']v_i = v_i - H\psi_i, \tag{34}$$
$$\tilde{Z} = [I - H(H'H)^{-1}H']Z = Z - H\psi_Z,$$

from which, since $\tilde{H} = 0$, $\tilde{X} = (0:\tilde{Z})$. This means that $m - r + n + 1$ OLS equations must be estimated in addition to the $n + 1$ regressions on X used to estimate S, in expression (27). It is clear from these transformations why $r < m$ is required: if $r = m$, $H = X$ and the elements of $\theta_i{}^* + {}^0\beta_i{}^*\phi_H{}^*$ cannot be identified. The transformed variables are substituted into the criterion G to be minimized, and the $\theta_i{}^*$ are replaced by functions of the ${}^0\beta_i{}^*$ and ϕ^* obtained by differentiating G. Repeated differentiation and substitution leads to a criterion entirely in terms of the transformed variables $\tilde{y}$, $\tilde{v}_i$, and $\tilde{Z}$, and then to a polynomial in the last coefficient to be estimated.

One further property of this procedure should be noted; that is, the parameters $\theta_i{}^*$ and $\phi_H{}^*$ can be expressed as linear combinations of the parameters ψ in (34). This means they can be estimated from OLS regression on H, with the dependent variables being functions of y, v_i, and ${}^0\beta_i{}^*$ (in the case of $\theta_i{}^*$) or of y, Z and $\theta_Z{}^*$ (in the case of $\phi_H{}^*$). The vector $\phi_Z{}^*$ can also be estimated by OLS regression on the transformed matrix $\tilde{Z}$, the dependent variable being a linear combination of $\tilde{y}$ and $\tilde{v}_i$ whose coefficients are functions of the ${}^0\beta_i{}^*$.[12]

5. STANDARD ERRORS

The use of OLS regression gives estimates of the standard errors of ${}^0\beta_i{}^*$, $\theta_i{}^*$, and ϕ^*, but these are likely to be biased downward because they are estimated sequentially rather than simultaneously.[13] The asymptotically correct standard errors of all the parameters are given by the inverse of the

[12] The complete sequence of OLS regression and substitution back into G is presented for the two-equation case by Musgrove (1974, Part III, Section 3). The estimating criterion is reduced to a quartic in μ^*.

[13] That is, estimates of ${}^0\beta_i{}^*$ are used in the regression for $\phi_Z{}^*$ and estimates of $\phi_Z{}^*$ are then used to estimate $\phi_H{}^*$. The estimates of ${}^0\beta_i{}^*$ also enter the regressions for $\theta_i{}^*$. This is not the same as first estimating y^* and then regressing each v_i on $\hat{y}^*$.

matrix of second partial derivatives of G, evaluated at the point estimates:

$$\mathrm{var}(^0\beta_i{}^*, \theta_i{}^*, \phi^*) = [\partial^2 G / \partial(^0\beta_i{}^*, \theta_i{}^*, \phi^*)' \, \partial(^0\beta_i{}^*, \theta_i{}^*, \phi^*)]^{-1}. \tag{35}$$

Alternatively, the significance of any parameter can be measured by an appropriate F-test. Let G_v be the value of (32) obtained by minimizing without any restriction on the parameters, and let $G_v{}^R$ be the value obtained under a restriction on one or more parameters. If f parameters are restricted, the statistic

$$\frac{(T - m - nr - n)}{f} \frac{(G_v{}^R - G_v)}{G_v} \tag{36}$$

is distributed as $F(f, T - m - nr - n)$, where T is the number of observations. When $f = 1$, a single parameter ξ is restricted to the value ξ^R (which may conveniently be zero). The standard error is then given by

$$\sigma(\xi) = |\xi^R - \xi| / \sqrt{F}. \tag{37}$$

The advantage of this approach is that tests of a small number of parameters may suffice to estimate how severe is the bias in the OLS estimates of the standard errors.[14]

Once $^0\beta_i{}^*$, $\theta_i{}^*$, and ϕ^* are estimated, the transformations (13) and (17) yield the ELPES parameters $^0\gamma_i{}^*$, $\beta_i{}^*$, and μ^*. The standard errors of the latter are then found from the variance–covariance matrices of order n for α^* and $^0\beta^*$, which have been derived from the OLS regressions [adjusted by tests of the form (36)] or from (35). Denote these by $\Sigma_{\alpha^*, \alpha^*}$, $\Sigma_{\alpha^*, \,^0\beta^*}$, and $\Sigma_{^0\beta^*, \,^0\beta^*}$; then (Lluch et al., 1976, Section 2.2.4)

$$\Sigma_{\beta^*, \beta^*} = (\mu^*)^{-2}(I - \beta^* \iota')\Sigma_{^0\beta^*, \,^0\beta^*}(I - \iota'\beta^*),$$

$$\Sigma_{^0\gamma^*, \,^0\gamma^*} = (N \, \iota'^0\gamma^* N)\Sigma_{\alpha^*, \,^0\beta^*} \begin{pmatrix} N \\ \iota'^0\gamma^* N \end{pmatrix},$$

where

$$N = [I + (1 - \mu^*)^{-1} \,^0\beta^* \, \iota'], \text{ and } \mathrm{var}(\mu^*) = \iota'\Sigma_{^0\beta^*, \,^0\beta^*}\iota, \tag{38}$$

ι being the unit vector. Because we have assumed $\mathrm{var}(\varepsilon) \neq 0$, it is not possible to ignore covariances across equations when estimating the standard errors of the ELPES parameters, as can be done in the current-income ELES.

---

[14] If an element of $\phi_z{}^*$ is restricted, H is unchanged, and Z and $\tilde{Z}$ are reduced by one variable. The hypothesis that an element of $\theta_i{}^* = 0$ for one i but not for all, is equally simple to treat; if the element $\theta_{ir}^* = 0$ for some r and all i, however, the variable H_r is in effect removed from H and shifted to Z, so that calculation of $G_v{}^R$ is more difficult. The hypothesis that an element of $\phi_H{}^* = 0$—but the corresponding element of $\theta_i{}^* \neq 0$—removes the variable from the matrix X, so that H is no longer a subset of X.

6. CONCLUDING REMARKS

The extended linear permanent expenditure system described in Section 3 and estimated by the procedure of Sections 4 and 5 appears to retain the advantages of the ELES for empirical analysis of consumption behavior, while eliminating the unrealistic use of observed income y to explain expenditures. The ELPES is compatible with the interpretation (5) of the marginal propensity to consume as the ratio of a discount rate and an interest rate, but if perfect capital markets are not assumed, the system can also be based on the assumption that saving yields utility directly. The dependence of consumption on interest rates (or other indicators of opportunities to borrow and lend) can also be estimated by including such variables among the determinants of y^* (the variables Z) or of the propensity to consume (the variables H). Similarly, the ELPES can be regarded as a life-cycle model, if the life-cycle stage is included in H.[15] There are thus a number of ways to explain saving, and to relate it to observable variables, in the model.

The ELPES can be given a dynamic formulation, by including past levels of consumption (or other lagged variables) among the variables X. However, the system cannot be used to estimate permanent income and consumption as functions of current and past incomes; that is, y cannot be included in X, because the estimation procedure begins with the OLS regression of y (and v_i) on X. This restriction limits the usefulness of the ELPES for time series application, leaving it more suitable for analysis of household budgets.[16] More generally, the choice of variables X is restricted by the requirement that the correlation of v_i and y, given X, have the same sign as the unconstrained correlation (Goldberger, 1972, Section 3). Except for this limitation, and the exclusion of v_i and y, almost any observable variables can be used. In particular, X can include variables regarded as determinants of labor income or of human wealth (age, education, occupation, sex, etc.) and measures of the amount(s) or rate(s) of return of nonhuman wealth.[17] If this

[15] This approach is taken by Musgrove (1974): life-cycle stage is included in H, and its effects are separated from the effect of age on permanent income. The approach taken by Howe (1974), in which $^0\gamma_i^*$ depends on household size and composition, can also be regarded as approximating a life-cycle model, except that adults are not distinguished by age or work status.

[16] Although $y(t)$ cannot be included in $X(t)$, $y(t-1)$ can be used; the ELPES could therefore be estimated for time series in which the interval t is quite short (one month, for example), so that $v_i(t)$ need not be assumed to depend on $y(t)$. Household panel data might be analyzed in this way.

[17] The system (18) could be further disaggregated, by supposing that the variables in X explain the permanent income not of the entire household but of each of several members separately: $y_l^* = X_l\phi^* + \varepsilon_l$ for each member l, with $y^* = \sum_l y_l^*$. Then $X = \sum_l X_l$ refers not to the age, education, or other characteristics of one member (usually the household head) but to the frequency of particular characteristics in the household. A more complicated extension of the model is to suppose that ϕ^* also differs among members, so that $y_l^* = X_l\phi_l^* + \varepsilon_l$, $v_i^* = H\theta_i^* + {}^0\beta_i^*(\sum_l X_l\phi_l^*)$.

distinction is made, the average saving propensity can depend on the composition or on the level of wealth. The marginal propensity, however, does not depend on any of the X variables. Differences in μ^* or in $^0\beta_i^*$ among groups of consumers can be found only by estimating the system separately for homogeneous groups. Of course, the variables in X must all be plausible determinants of permanent income, and they must *not* include obviously transitory elements. The reduced form (33) can be given quite a different interpretation, if Z is a set of variables determining permanent income and H is a set of transitory receipts identified a priori. Then ϕ_H^* is a test of the accuracy of this identification (of whether the household regards these receipts as transitory income), and $\theta_i^* + {}^0\beta_i^*\phi_H^*$ becomes $^0\beta_i^{**}\phi_H^*$, where $^0\beta_i^{**}$ is the marginal propensity to spend transitory income on category i. This model, developed by Attfield (1976), does not include a subsistence expenditure level or allow for differences in the permanent APC among families.

The estimation of the ELPES is unquestionably more complicated than the estimation of the ELES: several more stages of regression are required, while there is no reduction in the number of transformations needed to obtain the structural parameters and their standard errors. Nonetheless, this added computation may be justified on two grounds. The first is that better estimates can be obtained for the parameters of the linear demand system. This is particularly important, because such systems are attractive partly for their ability to yield estimates of price elasticities, and those elasticities are functions of the parameters (the subsistence quantities γ_i or expenditures $^0\gamma_i$) most likely to be biased in the current income model and in most models which have tried to improve the income variable. Better descriptions of saving behavior should also result.

The second justification is the opportunity afforded to test two assumptions of the permanent income hypothesis: the equality of average and marginal propensities to consume, and the lack of correlation among transitory components. These tests are possible, moreover, in the context of a complete demand system, and without the need to identify a priori any transitory or permanent component. Finally, this procedure yields estimates of how various observable variables contribute to permanent income and—for at least some of them—allows this contribution to be distinguished from effects on propensities to consume.

REFERENCES

Attfield, C. L. F. (1976). Estimation of the Structural Parameters in a Permanent Income Model, *Economica* **43** (August), 247–254.

Betancourt, R. R. (1973). The Analysis of Patterns of Consumption in Underdeveloped Countries, paper presented to the *ECIEL Conference on Consumption, Prices and Economic*

Development, Hamburg, West Germany, October 1973. A revised version forms Chapter 8 of Lluch *et al.* (1977).

Betancourt, R. R., "Reply" to the "Discussion" by A. Klevorick.

Friedman, M. (1957). *A Theory of the Consumption Function.* Princeton, New Jersey: Princeton Univ. Press for NBER.

Geary, R. C., (1950–1951). A Note on "A Constant Utility Index of the Cost of Living," *Review of Economic Studies* **18**, 65–66.

Goldberger, A. S. (1972). Maximum-Likelihood Estimation of Regressions Containing Unobservable Independent Variables, *International Economic Review* **13** (February), 1–15.

Goldberger, A. S., and Olkin, I. (1971). A Minimum-Distance Interpretation of Limited-Information Estimation, *Econometrica* **39** (May), 635–640.

Howe, H. J. (1974). Estimation of the Linear and Quadratic Expenditure Systems: A Cross-Section Case for Colombia, Ph.D. dissertation, Univ. of Pennsylvania.

Howe, H. J. (1975). Development of the Extended Linear Expenditure System from Simple Saving Assumptions, *European Economic Review* **6** (July), 305–310.

Howe, H. J., and Musgrove, P. (1976). Analysis of ECIEL Household Budget Data for Bogota, Caracas, Guayaquil and Lima, in Lluch *et al.* (1977).

Klevorick, A. K. (1973). "Discussion" of Betancourt (1973).

Klein, L. R., and Rubin, H. (1947–1948). A Constant-Utility Index of the Cost of Living, *Review of Economic Studies* **15**, 84–87.

Klijn, N. (1974). The Specification of the Extended Linear Expenditure System: Some Alternatives, Department of Economics, Australian Nat. Univ. (August) pp. 14 (mimeo).

Lluch, C. (1973). The Extended Linear Expenditure System, *European Economic Review* **4** (April), 21–32.

Lluch, C. (1974). Expenditure, Savings and Habit Formation, *International Economic Review* **15** (October), 786–797.

Lluch, C., Powell, A. and Williams, R. (1977). *Patterns in Household Demand and Saving* (New York and Oxford: Oxford Univ. Press).

Mattei, A. (1973). An Intertemporal Model of Consumer Behavior, Inst. for Economic Research, Swiss Federal Inst. of Technol. (mimeo).

Musgrove, P. (1974). Determination and Distribution of Permanent Household Income in Urban South America, Ph.D. dissertation, Mass. Inst. of Technol.

Powell, A. (1973). Estimation of Lluch's Extended Linear Expenditure System from Cross-Sectional Data, *Australian Journal of Statistics* **15** (August), 111–117.

Powell, A. (1974). *Empirical Analytics of Demand Systems.* Lexington, Massachusetts: Heath.

Samuelson, P. A. (1947–1948). Some Implications of "Linearity," *Review of Economic Studies* **15**, 88–90.

Stone, R. S. (1954). Linear Expenditure Systems and Demand Analysis: An Application to the Pattern of British Demand, *Economic Journal* **64** (September), 511–527.

Watts, H. W. (1960). An Objective Permanent Income Concept for the Household, Cowles Foundation Discussion Paper 99 (November).

Zellner, A. (1970). Estimation of Regression Relationships Containing Unobservable Independent Variables, *International Economic Review* **11** (October), 441–454.

A
B 7
C 8
D 9
E 0
F 1
G 2
H 3
I 4
J 5